Secret Memoirs of the Court of Petersburg [By C.F.P. Masson]. Tr. [From Mémoires Secrets Sur La Russie].

Charles François P. Masson

Nabu Public Domain Reprints:

You are holding a reproduction of an original work published before 1923 that is in the public domain in the United States of America, and possibly other countries. You may freely copy and distribute this work as no entity (individual or corporate) has a copyright on the body of the work. This book may contain prior copyright references, and library stamps (as most of these works were scanned from library copies). These have been scanned and retained as part of the historical artifact.

This book may have occasional imperfections such as missing or blurred pages, poor pictures, errant marks, etc. that were either part of the original artifact, or were introduced by the scanning process. We believe this work is culturally important, and despite the imperfections, have elected to bring it back into print as part of our continuing commitment to the preservation of printed works worldwide. We appreciate your understanding of the imperfections in the preservation process, and hope you enjoy this valuable book.

SECRET MEMOIRS

OF THE

COURT OF PETERSBURG:

PARTICULARLY TOWARDS THE END OF THE

REIGN OF CATHARINE II.

AND THE COMMENCEMENT OF THAT OF

PAUL I.

SERVING AS

A SUPPLEMENT

TO

THE LIFE OF CATHARINE II.

TRANSLATED FROM THE FRENCH.

𝕾𝖊𝖈𝖔𝖓𝖉 𝕰𝖉𝖎𝖙𝖎𝖔𝖓.

LONDON:
PRINTED BY C. WHITTINGHAM,
Dean Street, Fetter Lane,
FOR T. N. LONGMAN AND O. REES, PATERNOSTER-ROW.

1801.

ADVERTISEMENT.

THE Publishers of the following Translation have been induced, by a sense of decency and propriety, to suppress or soften a few anecdotes contained in the original, the grossness of which would undoubtedly outrage the public and private feelings of Englishmen. In all other respects, the grand design and the true colouring and shade of this interesting picture of the court of St. Petersburg have been faithfully retained. The lovers of biography will, it is hoped, now receive an unqualified gratification from the perusal of the following sheets; in which, not only the portraits of the principal personages are drawn by the hand of a master, but the delineations of the various characters connected with the historical period of which they treat, will be found marked by a superior degree of accuracy and judgment. The writer was well acquainted with the court, living in the residence, and near the person of the empress, during the last ten years of her reign. In this work are developed much of the private biography of a princess whose public character cannot perhaps be too much exalted: who, in spite of her failings as a woman, was, as a great and benign sovereign, revered and beloved by the millions whom she governed by her gentle sceptre, the achievements of whose reign excited the astonishment and rendered her the arbitress of Europe, and whose memory will claim the admiration, and in numerous instances the gratitude, of posterity.

CONTENTS.

CHAPTER I.

THE KING OF SWEDEN'S VISIT TO PETERSBURG.

PAGE.

Anecdotes respecting the marriage projected between him and the grand-duchess Alexandra—Portrait of the king, and of the young princess—Remarks on the failure of this match—German princesses sent for to Russia—Marriage of the grand-dukes, account of their brides, and pomp of the court at that period 1

CHAP. II.

CATHARINE II.

Particulars of the sickness and death of Catharine—Her portrait—Her character—Observations on her court, courtiers, and ministers—Influence of the french revolution on her mind—Question examined, how far she was the patron of letters—Her literary works—Manners and monuments of her reign 40

CHAP. III.

OF THE FAVOURITES.

Their office made a distinct place at court—The Empress's generosity in this point—Installation of Zubof—List of the twelve who enjoyed in succession the title of favourite—Little Hermitage—Little Society 94

CHAP. IV.

ACCESSION OF PAUL.

Conduct and projects of Catharine with regard to her son—He is proclaimed—His first steps as Emperor—Funeral honours paid to his father and mother—Rigorous proceedings towards the guards—The wacht-parade—Graces and disgraces—His occupations—Proscription of round hats and russian harness—Re-establishment of etiquette—Its ridiculous or cruel consequences—Alterations in the army, and in the civil department—Peasants—Soldatomania—Office of punishment—Finances—A valet-de-chambre becomes favourite 120

CHAP. V.

HAS PAUL REASON TO FEAR THE FATE OF PETER III?

Parallel between Paul and his father—Portrait of the present empress—The grand-duke Alexander—The grand-duke Constantine—Zubof—Nicholas Soltikof—Markof—Arkarof—Repnin—Suvarof and Valerian Zubof—Traits of the character of Paul, and his principal courtiers or ministers—His portrait—Anecdotes of his conduct when grand-duke 172

CHAP. VI.

WHAT REVOLUTIONS MAY BE EXPECTED TO TAKE PLACE IN RUSSIA.

Attitude and strength of the sovereign power in that country—Two ukases of Paul favourable to a revolution—Debasement of the people—Other local obstacles—The sovereign power becoming more absolute—The nobility offended—These alone can change the government—How, and why—Probability of a dismemberment of that vast territory, and of a change in the manners of the people and form of government 240

CHAP. VII.

NATIONAL CHARACTER.

Of the nobleman, the courtier, the peasant, the artificer, and the soldier of Russia 264

CHAP. VIII.

RELIGION.

The Greek Church—Priests—Festivals—Fasts—Images 291

CHAP. IX.

ON FEMALE GOVERNMENT.

Its influence on the women of Russia.—Their character—immodesty—manners—baths—talents—charms—Princess Dashkof 305

CHAP. X.

EDUCATION.

Anecdotes of the education of the grand-dukes—their governors and preceptors—Education of the Russians in general—Of the utshiteli, or tutors, their influence—Of the young Russians—Proceedings of the present emperor unfriendly to civilisation—The Gazettes—Radischef—Fable of the owl and the glow-worm 330

CHAP. XI.

SUPPLEMENT.

French and Swiss in Russia—Persecutions they undergo—Proscription of some—Oath required of them—Billet of absolution—Additional traits of the present emperor—Reflexions 361

DESCRIPTION OF THE TAURIDAN PALACE, *and of the entertainment which prince Potemkin gave there to Catharine II.* 384

Additional Note concerning Korsakof 390

SECRET MEMOIRS,

&c. &c. &c.

CHAP. I.

THE KING OF SWEDEN'S VISIT TO PETERSBURG.

Anecdotes respecting the marriage projected between him and the grand-duchess Alexandra—Portrait of the king, and of the young princess—Remarks on the failure of this match—German princesses sent for to Russia—Marriage of the grand-dukes, account of their brides, and pomp of the court at that period.

THE peace of Varela having reconciled Catharine and Gustavus, their conduct and attention towards each other formed a singular contrast with the hatred, animosity, and invectives in which they had so profusely indulged during the war. The officers of the two nations were equally eager to display the esteem with which they had mutually inspired each other; for, the kozakeries of * Denisof excepted, that

---

* A kozak general, who distinguished himself by his barbarity and his ravages in the war in Finland. It is the same, or his nephew, who commanded the corps of Don Kozaks that marched into Germany. He is an ignorant man, but an intrepid soldier and a desperate gamester.

war had been carried on in a manner very different from what was usual with the Russians: in the Swedes they found enemies, whose urbanity was equal to their valour; and the well-educated Russian, while he piques himself on the possession of these qualities, esteems them in others.

Count Stackelberg, so famous for his embassy, or rather his reign in Poland, was sent into Sweden; and Catharine, who could not live in peace with her neighbours but in proportion as they were submissive or devoted to her, was seeking new means of re-establishing her interest in that country, which the talents and resolution of Gustavus had destroyed. To marry one of the young grand-duchesses to the prince-royal now became her favourite project; and it is even said that this matrimonial alliance was a secret article in the treaty of peace. This at least is certain, that the grand-duchess Alexandra was educated and grew up in the expectation of being one day queen of Sweden; while every person about her confirmed her in the idea, and entertained her with the charms and the premature accomplishments of the young Gustavus. Even the empress herself would often jocularly discourse with her on the subject. One day opening a port-folio containing portraits of several unmarried princes, she pressed her to point out which of them she should like best for a husband. The child, blushing, pointed to the portrait of him of whom she had heard so many fine things, and who was already the lover of her rising imagination. The good old lady, not considering that her grand-daughter could read, and knew the prince of Sweden by his name at the bottom of the picture, persuaded herself that sympathy had decided in his favour, and pursued her scheme with additional pleasure.

It is equally certain, that several persons about the young Gustavus endeavoured to inspire his heart with similar sentiments; but I know not whether the king his father, absolute and despotic as he was, would have given his consent to the match, as being suitable to the young lovers, though ther everse to the two countries. Be this as it may, the violent and sudden death of Gustavus frustrated the schemes of Catharine; which were nothing less than to send him at the head of his Swedes into France, there to act the same part as Gustavus Adolphus and Charles XII. had done in Germany and Poland, in hopes that he would there meet with a similar fate: while she prepared for herself that of regent over the minority of an orphan king in Sweden; whom, together with his kingdom, she would have taken under her maternal care.

But the duke of Sudermania, having seized the reins of government during the minority of his nephew, set himself directly to oppose the russian system. Not so gallant a cavalier as his brother, he did not feel himself disposed to sacrifice his country for the ladies; but hastened to repay the hatred which Catharine had conceived for him during the war, when the noise of his cannon had reached the inmost recesses of the palace of the tzars. This naval war, in which however he had little reason to boast of his success, had irritated him against the Russians: and he was not ignorant of the raillery and invective which were liberally bestowed on him at the court of Petersburg, or that plays were even acted at the Hermitage, in which he was held up as an object of ridicule.

The vilest corruption, the basest and most cowardly intrigues, had been employed against him. Europe even saw, with renovated horror, her, who pretended to be an image of God adored on the throne, exciting revolt in a kingdom, buying traitors, and hiring assassins. To remove the regent, to substitute a council of her creatures in his stead, and harness Sweden side by side with Poland to her car, were the objects at which she aimed, and which she sought to attain by all the means she could devise. Stackelberg, whose wit and urbanity had captivated the king*,

---

* Of all the ministers employed by Catharine, count Stackelberg has the most wit and the most pride; and this

and who, to use his own words, found in that prince *a true and worthy knight of his immortal sovereign,* applied for his recall. His pride could not stoop to act so insignificant a part with the regent of a young king, after having himself been so long regent of an old king of Poland.

Count Römanzof, brother of him who was so well known and esteemed in Germany, succeeded him; but, notwithstanding his ingenuity, his instructions were too treacherous and too compli-

---

he displayed particularly in Poland. Baron Thugut being sent to that country by the emperor, when he was to have his audience of Poniatofski, was introduced into a saloon, where, seeing a man gravely seated, and surrounded by polish lords respectfully standing before him, he took him for the king, and began his complimentary speech. It was Stackelberg, who was in no hurry to set him right. Thugut, informed of his mistake, was vexed and ashamed. In the evening, being at cards with the king and Stackelberg, he played a card, saying, " The king of clubs."—" You are wrong," said the king, " it is the knave." The austrian ambassador, pretending to have been mistaken, answered, slapping his forehead, " Ah, sire, pardon me; this is the second time to-" day I have taken a knave for a king." Stackelberg, ready as he was at repartee, could only bite his lips. When he returned from Sweden, he loitered away his time in the antichambers of Zubof; but he was always one in Catharine's little parties, and was thus reduced to amuse, after having served her. His greatest humiliation no doubt was that of being named by Paul lord of the bed chamber in waiting to the very king of Poland who had frequently danced attendance in his anti-chamber at Warsaw. In this sarcastic appointment the emperor shewed something ingenious and noble that does him honour.

cated for him to acquire similar respect in Sweden. The plots and intrigues of which the regent complained, soon made it necessary for him to be recalled. Who has not felt indignation at the impudence with which Armfeldt was set on, protected, and defended by Russia, in spite of the obvious proofs of his outrages, and the most forcible protestations against his proceedings? At the very time when all the kings in Europe seemed to make common cause in hunting down and prosecuting in concert every man who was barely suspected of rebellion, a regent of Sweden in vain demanded, from court to court, a man who had conspired against his life and the government of his country, which he would have sold and delivered to a foreign potentate. From court to court his demands were evaded in an insulting manner; and Armfeldt at length retired to Russia to set him at defiance, being allowed to appear at court, receiving a pension, and living there even during the visit of the king and the regent*.

I shall not trace this plot, which so long harassed the court of Sweden, through all its ramifications, or name all the agents who were still employed to carry it on; but Catharine by no means relinquished her design of ruling there, of

* In 1798 he was at Carlsbad, worn out with infirmities, and despised by all that knew him.

acting the part of protectress to the young king, and of exhibiting the regent as a tyrant who abused the minority of his nephew, or as a jacobin who intended to imitate the duke of Orleans. She even sent the king an invitation to come and put himself under her protection, or at least to pay her a visit; and nothing was left untried to get him to Petersburg without his uncle. It is surprising that the regent was not driven to extremities. Among the papers of the accomplices of Armfeldt were found several which would have made Catharine appear despicable in the eyes of all Europe; but whether from fear, from weakness, or from moderation, he forebore to make them public.

He was on the point, however, of entering into an alliance with France, which to him seemed the most effectual step towards securing the independence of Sweden against the atrocious policy, the unbounded ambition, and the unprincipled administration of a powerful neighbour; concluding, that whatever connections might be formed between Sweden and Russia, by the interference of private passions or temporary interests, they would ever prove injurious to the former.

To strike at the root of Catharine's hopes, the regent took another step, which was still more sensibly felt. He demanded in marriage for his young pupil one of the princesses of Mecklenburg, who was solemnly betrothed to him; and announced the match in form to all the courts of Europe. Count Schverin, who had already been in Russia, where his personal figure had gained him many friends among the ladies, was dispatched to Petersburg with this commission; but at Vyborg he found an order from the empress, which forbad him to make his appearance at court. This was certainly strange conduct, shewing rather the pique of an irritated woman than the discretion of a sovereign. What.. because the king of Sweden had espoused another princess instead of her grand-daughter, she refused to receive the notification conformably to established custom! A forsaken mistress, who paid no regard to decorum, and was destitute of true pride, could have done no more. The respect she owed herself, her sex, and above all her amiable grand-daughter, should at least have saved her from the humiliation of thus publishing her chagrin. On this occasion she ceased to act the part of the *great Catharine* *.

To account for this step, no less insulting than indelicate, she directed her chargé d'affaires, or rather d'intrigues, at Stockholm, to deliver to the regent that note which has been read with asto-

* The Russians have aggrandized even her name; they say, in their language, *Yekatarina*, which can only be translated *Arch-Catharine*.

nishment in some of the public papers, where she not only makes the duke of Sudermania's maintaining the connexion between Sweden and France a crime, of *treason to her imperial majesty,* but even seems to insinuate, that he was privy to the assassination of the king his brother, the avenging whereof she claims to herself. The vexation of Catharine, and folly of her ministers, proceeded still further. Every thing announced, that the king of Sweden was to be treated like Sganarelle*, by obliging him at the cannon's mouth to break his engagement to the princess of Mecklenburg, and marry the grand-duchess Alexandra †. The amiable qualities of this princess would have justified a young king in fighting to obtain her hand rather than to escape it. A report was also spread, that the king was already enamoured of her; that his uncle had done violence to his inclinations; and that he wished for nothing more than to defer his mar-

* In *L'Amour Medicin* of Moliere.

† Some planks were laid at that time with great noise and preparation on the ice of the Neva, though strong enough then to bear castles, to facilitate, as was said, the passage of the artillery to be sent into Finland. The ministers and generals talked publicly of the approaching war; a proof, that it was all a deception: but whether baron Steding were a dupe to it or not, I do not pretend to say. Prince George Dolgoruky, a general too honest and too little of a courtier to be employed by the favourites, was even sent to the frontiers by way of scarecrow.

riage with the princess of Mecklenburg till he became of age, that he might then declare in favour of the other lady who aspired to his hand.

There is no doubt, that several Swedes, gained over by the promises of Catharine, and by the hopes they had formed from the munificence of that ostentatious princess, endeavoured to inspire the young king with such resolutions, and to excite in his heart the same passion as had been raised in that of the amiable Alexandra. A regular correspondence was even kept up between Schverin, Steinbach, and some persons who had access to the grand-duchesses; and several of the letters were shewn to the empress through the medium of madame Liewen, chief governess to the princesses.

After such violent proceedings against the regent, who would have expected to see him bend and submit? This, however, he did: at least he suffered himself to be either frightened or bribed[*]. M. Budberg, who had just made

---

[*] A Genevan, named Christin, formerly the right hand and secretary to Calonne, being at Stockholm, introduced himself to the regent by means of a fable, which he composed in his praise. As he had been at Petersburg, he talked to him a great deal of Catharine, of the young princesses, of the esteem in which he was held at that court, and of the advantage of an alliance with Russia, by marrying the king to the grand-duchess. Being persuaded from the duke's answers, that

the tour of Germany to find a wife for the grand-duke Constantine, having brought with him the princess of Cobourg and her three daughters, was deemed capable of surmounting the difficulties experienced in obtaining a husband for the young grand-duchess. At first he repaired to Mecklenburg, to negotiate a renunciation; and was then sent to Stockholm as an ambassador. Threats, promises, and money at length prevailed: Catharine obtained the delay of the king's marriage till he should be of age; and the regent, willing, no doubt, to shew that his pupil was free in his choice and in his conduct, at length consented to his journey to Petersburg, whither he was so kindly invited. The affair of the marriage, which was the true motive of this invitation, was touched on but slightly, sentimentally.—*If, as it has been said, the two children have a mutual affection already; should they, on seeing each other, still prove agreeable, means may be thought of for rendering them happy.* Such was the language of the empress. If she could get the king to her court, Catharine thought she should have the game in her own hands. Reckoning on the

he was not very averse to a reconciliation with Catharine, he sent information of it to madame Huss, Markof's mistress; and upon these grounds the negotiations which had been broken off were renewed. Christin returned to Petersburg, to reap the rewards of his address; but the death of the empress deprived him of the recompence he expected.

charms of the princess, and the kindnesses which she herself should lavish on the king, the regent, and their suite, she doubted not but the young Gustavus, after having seen her whom he had ventured to refuse for reasons of state, would give both the kingdom and the glory of Charles XII. to possess such a bride.

On the 25th of August 1796, he arrived at Petersburg with his uncle and a numerous suite, and alighted at the house of baron Steding, his ambassador. All the city was anxious to see the young monarch. The empress, who was at her Tauridan palace*, came to that of the Hermitage to receive him, and give him entertainments. At their first interview she appeared enchanted, and *almost in love with him herself*†. He would have kissed her hand; but she would not allow it, saying, "No, I cannot forget that "the count Haga is a king."—"If your majesty," answered he, "will not give me permission as

---

* The empress had purchased the principal palace of Potemkin, the Tauridan; and in honour to the memory of this celebrated favourite, whom she regretted, she gave it his surname, where she resided in the spring and autumn. It is at Petersburg, a short league (a mile and two thirds) from the winter palace, and like it situated on the banks of the Neva. It was in this superb edifice that Potemkin gave his sovereign that magnificent and so much celebrated entertainment in 1791.

† These were her very words.

"empress, at least allow me as a lady, to whom
"I owe so much respect and admiration."

The interview with the young princess was still more interesting. Both were extremely embarrassed; and the eyes of all the court being turned towards them, their confusion increased. No doubt each found the other worthy of the sentiments with which they had been inspired from infancy; and there is reason to believe, that, if motives of state on the part of the king of Sweden, or the whims of the present emperor, prevent not the match from being brought to a conclusion, the most charming of princesses will be likewise the most unhappy.

No one, however, has more claims to happiness than Alexandra Pavlovna. At fourteen she was already tall and womanly: her figure was noble and majestic, softened by all the graces of her sex and age: her features were regular, and her complexion fair as alabaster: innocence, candour, and serenity, stamped their divine impressions on her brow; and light flaxen hair, which seemed always arranged by fairy hands, fell in ringlets on her well-turned neck. Her heart, her talents, and her intellect, were in unison with her exterior appearance. Miss Willamof, her private governess, had cultivated the noblest and purest sentiments in her mind. Exquisite sensibility, judgment, and understanding, distinguished her infancy, and excited the admiration of all who came near her.

It would have been difficult to find, I will not say a king, but a young man, more interesting, better educated, and of so great promise as the king of Sweden. He was seventeen years of age, tall and finely shaped, with an air of dignity, intelligence, and mildness: yet there was something of grandeur and stateliness about him, that attracted respect, notwithstanding his age; and he had all the graces of youth, without the awkwardness that usually attends it. His manners were simple, though courteous and polite. Whatever he said was spoken with reflection. To serious things he paid an attention not expected from youth: he displayed knowledge, that announced a very careful education: and a certain gravity, that bespoke his rank, never forsook him. All the pomp of the russian empire, which was sedulously exhibited to his view, seemed in nowise to dazzle him. In that brilliant and numerous court, he soon appeared more at ease than the grand-dukes themselves, who had not the art of entertaining any body; so that both court and city soon drew comparisons between them very flattering to the young stranger. The empress herself could not conceal the pain she felt at the disparity between him and the second of her grand-children, whose brutal and rude boyish tricks offended her to such a degree, that she put him under arrest once or twice during the stay of the king of Sweden*.

All the great men of the empire were eager to participate in the joy of Catharine, who selected such as should give entertainments to her young guest, and fixed the days. Counts Stroganof, Ostermann, Besborodko, and Samoilof, distinguished themselves by the sums they expended, and the magnificence they displayed. The courtiers sought to surpass each other in the richness of their dress, and the generals in the military spectacles which they exerted themselves in exhibiting to the king. The old general Melissino particularly distinguished himself by the manœuvres and artificial fireworks executed and played off under his direction. Gustavus was in a state of continual enchantment; yet he wisely em-

* On several occasions, when the king appeared in public with the grand-dukes, foreigners were shocked, and the honest Russians humbled, at the courtly demeanour of the former, contrasted with the rustic behaviour of the latter. At a review of the corps of cadets of the artillery, where the young Gustavus appeared attentive to every thing most worthy of notice, conversing with the generals around him, and with the grand-duke Alexander, who was appointed to do the honours of the empire, the grand-duke Constantine was running and bawling behind the soldiers, imitating them in a burlesque manner, threatening them, and even beating them. It is certain, that the king of Sweden left Petersburg as well acquainted with the city, as with those who were one day to reign there.

ployed his mornings in traversing the city on foot with the regent, and seeing every thing that could be interesting or instructive: every where putting such questions, or giving such answers, as shewed the understanding he possessed, and the education he had received.

The regent, who appeared to enjoy the fruits of his own work in the approbation bestowed on his pupil, is a very little man. His manners are easy and polished; he has an air of acuteness and observation; his eyes are sparkling and full of fire; every thing he says displays the man of understanding, and excites reflection in those who hear him.

It may readily be supposed, that during this succession of entertainments, the two lovers had frequent opportunities of seeing each other, conversing and dancing together they became familiar, and appeared mutually enchanted. The aged Catharine assumed an appearance of youth, and again indulged in those scenes of joy and pleasure which she had long since renounced. The approaching marriage was no longer a secret; it was the common topic of conversation. The empress already addressed the young king and her grand-daughter as betrothed lovers, and encouraged them to mutual affection. One day she made them give the *first kiss of love* in her presence: the first, no doubt, that the virgin lips of the young princess ever received; and which may have left a pleasing and cherished impression, that will long render her unhappy.

In the meantime steps were taking to bring this desired match to a conclusion. The only difficulty which presented itself, was that of religion. Catharine had felt the pulse of her court on this subject; and even consulted the archbishop, to know, whether her grand-daughter might abjure the orthodox faith. Instead of answering as she flattered herself he would have done, he merely replied: " Your majesty is all powerful." The metropolitan of Russia, not finding himself supported by the opinions of his clergy, whom he expected would be more tractable, was then desirous of appearing more russian than the Russians themselves; and, to flatter the national pride, rather than from respect to the greek church, resolved to make a queen of Sweden of the greek religion. In proportion as this appeared new and humiliating to the swedish nation in the eyes of the metropolitan, the more flattering was it to his vanity, and that of his ministers: besides, the popes, chaplains, and others, whom it would place about the young queen, would be trusty persons, and well calculated to keep the princess in the interests of Russia. The king was enamoured, dazzled: the regent appeared to be completely gained over: could it then be supposed that they would reject this arrangement, after such decisive steps had been taken? In the private conversations that had passed, this delicate subject had been but slightly touched upon: it was scarcely expected that Catharine would have any scruples; and the king had hinted, that, from respect to the russian nation and the prejudices of the people, the princess should not be obliged to abjure the greek religion in form. The empress, persuaded that there was no room for retreat, left to her favourite ministers Zubof and Markof the care of drawing up the contract conformably to her views. On the other hand, the swedish ambassador demanded the princess in marriage, at an audience which was given him for the purpose of making the demand in form; and the day and hour on which the parties were to be publicly betrothed, were fixed.

This day, which was the 21st of September, exposed the happy and imperious Catharine to the greatest chagrin and humiliation she had ever experienced. The whole court received orders to assemble in full dress in the apartment of the throne. The young princess, habited as a bride, and attended by her sisters, the grand-dukes and their wives, and all the ladies and gentlemen, with the grand-duke, father to the princess, and the grand-duchess, who came from Gatshina to be present at the ceremony of betrothing their daughter, were assembled by seven o'clock in the evening. The empress herself arrived in all her pomp. No one was wanting but the young bridegroom, whose tardiness at first excited astonishment. The repeated exits and entrances of prince Zubof, and the impatience discovered by the empress, soon excited the curiosity and whisperings of the ladies. " What is the " matter? is the king taken ill? He is not very " gallant, however.—How could he dare thus to " make the sovereign wait, in the apartment of " her very throne, and with all her court assem-" bled!" The king, however, expected like the spouse of the eleven thousand virgins, did not appear.

The following was the occasion of this strange delay. The king was to have been at court at seven in the evening. At six, the minister Markof brought him the contract and the articles of alliance, which he had just drawn up with Zubof. Gustavus having read them over, appeared greatly astonished at finding them to contain particulars on which he had not agreed with the empress; and asked, whether it were from her that they were brought him to sign *?

* These articles were, that the princess should have her private chapel and clergy in the royal palace, besides certain engagements into which the Swedes were to enter against France, which have been kept very secret.

Markof answering in the affirmative, the king replied, that he could not possibly comply. He observed, that he would lay no restraint on the conscience of the princess; that she might profess her own religion in private, but he could not allow her either a chapel or priests in the palace: on the contrary, in public, and in all outward ceremonies, she must profess the religion of the country. The reader may conceive the surprise and embarrassment of the insipid Markof: he was obliged to take up his papers, and make report to Zubof, that the king refused his signature. He soon after returned in the greatest agitation, to say, that the empress was already in the apartment of the throne, surrounded by all her court; that it was no longer possible to speak to her; that she waited for the king; and that he flattered himself he would not bring the affair to an open rupture, which would be an unheard of insult to his sovereign, to the young princess, and to the whole empire. Besborodko, and several others, arrived in succession, exhorting, urging, praying the king to yield. All the Swedes who were called in were disposed to submit. The regent contented himself with saying, that it depended entirely on the king; drew him aside, and took a turn round the room with him, appearing himself to press him, while speaking to him in a low voice. The king answered aloud, " No,

" no, I will not; I cannot; I will never sign
" them!" He withstood all the remonstrances,
all the importunities of the russian ministers; and
at length, vexed at the pertinacity with which
they beset him, he retired to his chamber, and
fastened the door, after giving again a clear and
peremptory refusal to sign anything inconsistent
with the laws of his country. The russian ministers remained stupified at the audacity of a boy,
who dared thus to resist their sovereign, and consulted how to break the catastrophe to her.

If the firmness displayed by the young Gustavus on this occasion were *his own*; if the solicitations which his counsellors appeared to make,
were not feigned, he has given his nation a proof
of the greatest firmness of character, which cannot
be too highly admired in a young prince of seventeen, whom, it might be expected, love alone
would have been sufficient to subdue. It is to
be presumed, however, for the honour of the regent, that the entreaties which he appeared to
use with his nephew were insincere; and that he
wished only to charge the obstinacy of the king
with a resistance which would probably have
drawn upon himself the immediate vengeance of
Catharine. Most of the Swedes who attended
Gustavus were actually bribed or seduced: being
young courtiers, their expectations were highly
raised on the wedding gifts, and they were much

mortified at the disappointment. Steding, the ambassador, had a difficult part to act: but M. Flemming publicly declared his sentiments, by saying, that he would never advise the king to act contrary to the laws of his realm.

These debates between the ministers of the empress and the king continued till near ten o'clock. Catharine and her court were still waiting: but at last it was necessary to inform her, that the affair was broken off. Prince Zubof went cautiously up to her, and whispered something in her ear: she rose, attempted to speak, but her tongue faltered; was like to faint; and even had a slight fit, the precursor of that which carried her off a few weeks after. The empress withdrew, and the court was dismissed, under pretence of a sudden indisposition of the king. However, the true reasons soon came out. Some were offended at the audacity of a petty king of Sweden: others blamed the imprudence of the wise Catharine, who had so lightly exposed herself to such a scene; but the presumption of Zubof and Markof, who had attempted to impose on the Swedes by their artifice, in procuring a matrimonial contract to be signed without being read, was particularly censured.

The most interesting victim to this foolish stratagem was the amiable Alexandra. She had scarcely strength to enter her apartment; and there, no longer able to restrain her tears, she gave herself up, before her governesses and maids of honour, to a grief that affected all about her, and rendered her really ill. The next day but one after this unexpected explanation being the birth-day of the grand-duchess Anna Feodorovna*, the etiquette of the court prescribed a ball; but nobody was inclined to dance. The king went to it however, and the empress also made her appearance for a moment, but did not speak to him. Zubof even visibly behaved with sullenness to the young monarch. Embarrassment was legible on every countenance. Alexandra, being ill, was not present. The king danced with the other princesses, conversed a moment with the grand-duke Alexander, and retired early, saluting every person with still greater politeness than usual. This was the last time of his appearance at court.

These public days of pomp and festivity were suddenly changed into those of retirement and irksomeness: and never did a king spend any so melancholy and unpleasant at a foreign court. Every one was ill, or pretended to be so. The interest that Alexandra had inspired, and Gustavus merited, softened every heart in their favour.

* The wife of the grand-duke Constantine, daughter of the prince of Saxe Coburg.

She was pitied, as the victim of vanity and folly; he, for being obliged to make a sacrifice that must have cost him so dear*. Execrations were openly bestowed on Zubof and Markof; whilst the conduct of the empress, who gave herself up to the most poignant chagrin, appeared inexplicable. It is said, that her favourites felt themselves so humiliated that they took the liberty of suggesting violent measures with the young prince, who was in her power. She went and shut herself up a whole day, almost alone, in her tauridan palace, under pretence of celebrating the foundation of her chapel, but in fact to conceal from the eyes of her court the uneasiness of her mind, and to consult with her clergy and favourites on the embarrassing situation in which she fancied herself placed.

Endeavours were made to bring the affair a little in train again. The king saw her still in private, and the ministers held several conferences. Gustavus at length eluded the business, by declaring, that as he could not grant what the empress desired according to the laws of Sweden, he would

---

* He has since married the young princess Frederica of Baden, sister of the grand-duchess Elizabeth. Notwithstanding the charms of his young bride, it is supposed that he is not happy with her; and it is to be feared that Alexandra, who, it is said, is to be married to an arch-duke of Austria, will not be more so.

refer the matter to the estates of the kingdom that would be assembled at his coming of age; and if the estates consented to have a queen of the greek religion, he would then send for the princess. The russian despotism hearing with indignation a king hold such language, attempted in vain to excite him to set the estates at defiance, and offered him the forces necessary to punish them in case they should *revolt*. The king, however, would assent to no other terms.

Such was the result of this journey, of which the public papers scarcely ventured to speak. The king quitted Petersburg the very day on which the anniversary of the birth of the grandduke Paul * was celebrated, one week after the breach; leaving with the empress much ill-humour and resentment; and much grief and affection in the heart of the young princess, who became sick and melancholy from it, and a general regret and esteem. Notwithstanding this unforeseen catastrophe, in order to avoid scandalous reports, presents were made on both sides; and the Russians were so much the more surprised at the splendor and taste displayed in those of the king of Sweden, as they had affected always to speak of him by the epithet of *the poor little boy*.

* The present emperor: it is the 20th of September, old style, or the 1st of October, new style.

If, throughout this transaction, so little has been said of the grand-duke Paul, it is because he had no more to do in what concerned his children than in the affairs of government. He was at his seat of Gatshina, and was seen at Petersburg only once or twice during the whole time of the king's stay, which was about six weeks. The grand-duchess, his wife, on the contrary, made that irksome and fatiguing journey three or four times a week, to be present at the entertainments given, and assert, in appearance at least, the rights and duties of a mother. This worthy princess said, " If all my daughters " cost me so much pains to provide them hus- " bands, I shall die on the road." Once, for form's sake, the king was at Gatshina and at Pavlofsky. Paul and the regent seemed by no means congenial to each other; and on this occasion he appeared for the first time to be of his mother's opinion, and even to surpass her in his scruples and devotion to the orthodox greek religion. It is not improbable, however, but the whims of Paul may throw as many obstacles in the way of his daughter's happiness, as the vanity of Catharine, and the unskilfulness of her ministers*: the dress of the Swedes, their short

* Some time after his accession to the throne, Paul, going into the apartment of his daughters, began to joke with one of their maids of honour on the subject of her approaching

coats, cloaks, ribands, and round hats, are sufficient to beget in him an incurable aversion.

This frustrated comedy of the Forced-marriage completely overwhelmed with ridicule the russian ministers; and it must have been very humiliating to the old empress to have suffered such wretched means to have been employed. Does it not appear much beneath the russian empire to show itself so embarrassed about the settlement of its amiable princesses, and to play off so many great and little tricks to provide them husbands? It is true, that the unbounded ambition of Catharine seems to have made it a point to render their marriage difficult: like mademoiselle Montpensier formerly, she has killed their husbands with cannon-balls. A king of Poland, a duke of Courland, or even a hospodar of Moldavia: these were the husbands she might have left them.

marriage. "As to my daughter Alexandra," added he, "she cannot be married, for her lover has not yet learned to write." The fact was, he had just received a letter from the king of Sweden, whose secretary had omitted in the address some of the emperor's titles; among others, the perfectly new one, duke of Courland, &c. That none in future might be guilty of this criminal neglect, Paul issued a particular ukase, in which he prescribed at full length the manner in which he chose to be styled; and, as if the vast russian empire stood in need of spanish amplifications to make it appear great and powerful, he took the titles of all the ancient principalities: those, by which it is his pleasure to be addressed even in a petition, are sufficient to fill a good page.

Let the destiny reserved for the grand-duchesses, however, be what it may, they will undoubtedly be happier than the german princesses married in Russia, most of whom have experienced the most wretched fate. The horrid lot of Sophia of Brunswick, the wife of the miserable tzarevitch Alexius, is well known. That of the regent Anne, the unfortunate mother of the no less deplorable Ivan III. was still more melancholy. Did not the grand-duchess Natalia Alexievna, the former wife of Paul, come to a miserable end? Who does not lament the vexations experienced by Mary of Wurtemberg, the present empress? and who does not pity the young princess of Saxe Coburg for falling to the lot of the grand duke Constantine? Even the great Catharine herself, I hope, will not be urged as an exception: for though surrounded with all the splendor of her court, yet the violent death of her husband secretly preyed on her mind. The only exception that can be made to this series of unfortunate brides, is Elizabeth of Baden-Durlach, whose character, and particularly that of her husband, the grand-duke Alexander, seem to promise her a more happy life *.

* Even this exception seems now to have ceased: as, in consequence of the king of Sweden's intermarriage with her sister, a restraint, if not a total prohibition, is put upon her correspondence with her family.

Young and affecting victims, whom Germany seems to send by way of tribute to Russia, as formerly Greece sent her daughters to be devoured by the minotaur, how often do ye bedew in secret with your tears the gilded apartments in which ye dwell! How often are your thoughts cast with regret on the loved abodes where you spent your infant years! Would not those you might have passed in the arms of a husband in your own country, in a climate favoured by heaven, amid a people more polished and more happy, at a court less pompous and less corrupt, have been far preferable? Those chains you wear are but the more heavy for being of gold: the pomp that surrounds you, the riches with which you are decked, are not yours, for you enjoy them not. If love embellish not by his illusions the abode of wearisomeness and constraint in which you dwell, it will soon become to you a gloomy prison. Your lot unquestionably merits the compassion of those who envy it: as the title, so brilliant and so contended for, of grand-duchess of all the Russias, has hitherto been a title to be excluded from happiness.

What may not be said of the want of pride in those german princes who send their daughters to Russia, to undergo the almost equal hazard of being chosen or rejected? She that is approved is unhappy, and they who are sent back are insulted; for the dowry given them, and the riband with which they are decorated, are but proofs that they have been offered, examined, and rejected. The mother of these princesses usually accompanies her daughters on this distant journey, thus to dispose of one of them by exposing them all to a degrading choice. The times are certainly much changed. When the tyrant Ivan Vasilievitch (Basilides), as cruel and less capricious than Paul, desirous of forming an alliance with the princes of Europe, sent to Augustus Sigismond, king of Poland, to demand his sister in marriage, his ambassador was dismissed with a grey mare dressed like a woman. This coarse piece of raillery was worthy of the age, and, no doubt, of the idea then entertained of a *veliki-kniaz*, or grand prince of Russia. Now, at the first beck of a russian autocrate, the german princes hasten to send their amiable daughters, with their mothers, that the *veliki-kniaz* may choose such as they like, and send back the rest covered with a confusion, which neither their ribands, nor jewels, nor rubles, can conceal. The autocrates behave at present to the german princesses exactly as they used formerly to the daughters of their slaves whom they convened to their palace for the purpose of selecting the handsomest. How, let me repeat it, can the princes of Germany submit to this dastardly tribute, pay so little respect to decorum, and so wound the delicacy of their children!

Of all the victims thus led into * Russia, the two young princesses of Baden-Durlach appeared to be the handsomest and most interesting. Their mother, by birth princess of Darmstadt, had already been sent thither in her youth with her sisters, one of whom had the misfortune to become the first wife of Paul. This princess, an amiable woman, and the worthy mother of a charming family, would not appear again with her daughters on a stage on which she herself had been exposed, but entrusted them to the care of the countess Schuvalof, widow of the author of the Epistle to Ninon, who was charged with the negotiation, together with one Strekalof, who behaved like a kozak sent to Georgia to carry off maidens for the seraglio of the sultan.

These princesses, after a long and toilsome

* Catharine has sent for eleven german princesses to provide wives for her sons or grandsons: three princesses of Darmstadt, brought by their mother; three princesses of Wurtemburg, but these came no farther than Prussia, Frederic the *unique* insisting that the grand-duke should be gallant enough to meet them half way; two princesses of Baden; and three princesses of Coburg, conducted also by their mother. The young king of Sweden has made three journies out of his kingdom to choose himself a wife, while three princesses have been sent from the farther part of Germany for a junior grand-duke of Russia!

journey, arrived at night, towards the end of autumn 1792, and in terrible weather, which seemed materially to affect them. They were made to alight at the palace in which Potemkin had resided, where they were received by the empress, accompanied by madame Branicka, her favourite. At first the young princesses took the latter for the empress; but the countess Schuvalof having undeceived them, they threw themselves at her majesty's feet, and with tears kissed her robe and her hand, till she raised them up and embraced them: they were then left to sup in full liberty.

The next day Catharine came to see them, while they were yet at their toilette, and presented them the riband of the order of St. Catharine, jewels, and stuffs; then shewing them their wardrobe, looking at it, she said, " My young " friends, when I arrived in Russia I was not so " rich as you *."

The young grand-dukes were introduced to them the same day. The eldest, who already suspected the motive of their arrival, had a pensive and embarrassed air, and said nothing. Catharine told them, that knowing the mother of

* Catharine often said, toward the end of her life, " I ar-
" rived in Russia poor, but I shall not die in debt to the em-
" pire, since I shall leave her Taurida and Poland as a join-
" ture."

these princesses, and their country being taken by the French*, she had sent for them to have them educated at her court. On their return from the palace, the two young princes talked much about them, and Alexander said, that he thought the eldest very pretty†. "O, not in the least," cried the younger, "neither of them; they should "be sent to Riga to the princes of Courland: "they are only fit for them ‡."

What Alexander had said, however, was reported to his grandmother, who was delighted to find that the lady she designed for him, and with whom she herself seemed enchanted, appeared handsome in his eyes. Catharine pretended that she resembled Louisa of Baden when she arrived in Russia; and ordered the picture taken of her at that time to be brought, that she might compare it with the princess: when, as may be supposed, every one present declared that two drops

---

* It was at the time of Custine's expedition into Germany.

† She was in reality charming: the grand-duchess Alexandra is the only beauty in the court of Russia that can be compared with her. Her sister was but a child, being only thirteen, but she had something still more striking and sprightly.

‡ These princes were educated there at that time, as being one day to succeed their uncle in the throne. The elder was intended for the second grand-duchess Helena Pavlovna. But the scene is much changed with them: they are now subalterns in the army, and the elder has even been banished to a garrison of invalids.

of water could not be more alike. From that moment she became singularly attached to Louisa, redoubled her tenderness towards Alexander, and engaged with more pleasure in the scheme of leaving the throne to them as her immediate successors.

The young strangers made their first appearance at court on the day when the deputies of Poland were admitted to thank Catharine for the honour she had done the republic by keeping three-fourths of it for herself*. The princesses were as much dazzled with the magnificence that surrounded them, as others were with their opening charms; but the elder met with an accident, which led the superstitious Russians

---

* At this period, part of the kingdom or republic of Poland was left. The deputies, however, were received only as those of a subject province: they stood uncovered, the empress sitting; and she saluted them only by a slight motion of the head, after they had prostrated themselves before her. Count Branicki, husband of the empress's favourite, was the orator of this humliating embassy, who resolved, however, to deliver his harangue in the polish language. Among much other nonsense, he said: " The great Catharine deigned to " speak a word, and give the signal; and despotism, ready " to seize on the throne of Poland, fell like an idol." This *word* of Catharine was a pamphlet composed by Altesti, in which all the nobles of Poland were treated as jacobins, and the king as the partizan of a faction: this *signal* was the sending of two armies into the country, who burnt and destroyed whatever they could not pillage, and the *idol of despotism* was the constitution of the 3d of May!

to say that she would be unfortunate in their country. As she approached the throne of Catharine, she struck her foot against the corner of one of the steps, and fell flat on the ground before the throne. May the sad presage never be realised!

While the young sister spent her days sorrowfully in tears for her absence from her country and relations, which all the pomp of the court could not obliterate from her mind, and was at length sent away loaded with presents, which afforded her less pleasure than the expectation of soon beholding again the banks of the Rhine *,

* Besides several diamonds which she received, a pension was given her, which was to be exchanged for a marriage portion. As she is become a queen of Sweden, I know not whether she has received her russian dower. Among the presents made her was a riband of the order of St. Andrew for her father: this was the first order in Russia, and Catharine did not even know the number of its knights; as it appeared that the prince of Baden was one of them already. The empress, however, would not allow the riband to be sent back, but permitted the prince to bestow it on his son, then a child. It frequently happened that officers were presented with the insignia of orders, which had been given to them before: one of these, having solicited some other recompence in vain, wore his two similar crosses at once. Catharine, it must be added, so magnificent on some occasions, displayed a ridiculous parsimony in bestowing on the governess of the princesses of Baden, who had educated them, and conducted them into Russia, a paltry pension of two hundred rubles (20*l.*), at which even the court of Carlsruhe was offended. Similar acts of meanness frequently disgraced the

the princess Louisa appeared to smile at the destiny that awaited her. An unknown comforter had entered her heart, and dried her tears. The sight of the young prince, who was to be her husband, and who equalled herself in beauty of person and gentleness of mind, had inspired her with love. She submitted gracefully to everything required of her, learned the russian language, was instructed in the greek religion; and was soon in a capacity of making public profession of her new faith, and receiving on her arms and bare delicate feet the unctions administered by a bishop, who proclaimed her grandduchess under the name of Elizabeth Alexievna. Catharine chose rather to give her her own surname than leaveher that of her father, as is customary *.

liberalities of Catharine. She never gave willingly, except to those who had already too much: she liked better to gratify than to recompense. Towards the end of her life she grew niggardly, in particular towards the imperial family, who were sometimes in want of necessaries, while the favourite and his creatures wallowed in profusion.

* The patronymic names of the Russians have something antique and respectable. A Russian might call the empress, even when speaking to her, *Ekaterina Alexievna*, Catharine daughter of Alexius. The princess of Baden, therefore, should have called herself *Elizabetha Carlovna*, as she was the daughter of prince Charles. The Greeks had the same custom; and we, elegantly translating the russian termina-

In the month of May following, the ceremony of betrothing was performed with extraordinary pomp and entertainments. Russia had just finished three wars, almost equally triumphant. A multitude of generals and other officers, covered with the laurels they had gathered in battle, added to the number of the court. A great many Swedes, admirers of Catharine; almost all the polish magnats who had submitted or were devoted to her; tartarian khans; envoys from Great Bukharia; turkish pashas; greek and moldavian deputies; sophis of Persia; with french emigrants, demanding at once protection and vengeance *; increased at this juncture the crowd of courtiers attending the proud autocratrix of the north. No court ever exhibited so brilliant and variegated a spectacle. These were the last resplendent days that Catharine enjoyed. She dined on a throne raised in the midst of different

tions by the greek, might say Ivan Basilides, Alexander Nicolaïdes, &c. in like manner as Alcides, Seleucides, Heraclides.

* One day the young Richelieu, a persian envoy, some kalmuk deputies, and an old russian ideot, whom Catharine created a knight, at the recommendation of Nicholas Soltikof, for having prayed for her, were presented to the empress at the same time. Richelieu kissed her hand with all the ease of a Frenchman; the Persian, with the ceremonies of the orientals; the Kalmuks, prostrating themselves on the ground; and the old Russian, kneeling down, and raising his eyes to heaven.

tables. Crowned and covered with gold and diamonds, her eye carelessly wandered over the immense assembly, composed of persons of all nations, whom she seemed to behold at her feet. Surrounded by her numerous and brilliant family, a poet would have taken her for Juno seated amidst the gods*.

The arrival of the princess of Saxe-Coburg with her three daughters, one of whom became the wife of the grand-duke Constantine, was less striking. The Russians even indulged in witty remarks on these princesses, and on the antiquity and bad taste of their dress. They were not presented till their wardrobe had been renewed. Constantine did not like either of them: he said

---

* This in fact took place, particularly in the following strophe of the epithalamium:

<blockquote>
Ni la reine de Thèbe au milieu de ses filles,
Ni Louis de ses fils assemblant les familles,
Ne formèrent jamais un cercle si pompeux.
Trois générations vout fleurir devant elle,
Et c'est elle toujours qui charmera nos yeux :
Fière, d'être leur mère, & non d'être immortelle,
Telle est Junon parmi les dieux.
</blockquote>

<blockquote>
The Theban queen amid her daughters fair,
   The sons of Lewis, an illustrious race,
   Ne'er form'd a circle proudly born to grace
The wond'ring world with majesty so rare!
</blockquote>

<blockquote>
Three glorious sprigs shall deck the reverend tree,
   Whose stem immortal parentage shall claim,
And still the peerless origin shall be
   Like Juno, first in splendor as in fame
</blockquote>

they had a german air; fo russian was his taste. It was found necessary to inflame his imagination to induce him to make a choice; and this fell on the youngest, a little brunette, who displayed marks of wit, which excited interest in her behalf, and who was deserving of more happiness than the temper of her husband promised; of which we shall have occasion to speak more hereafter.

CHAP. II.

CATHARINE II.

Particulars of the sickness and death of Catharine—Her portrait—Her character—Observations on her court, courtiers, and ministers—Influence of the french revolution on her mind—Question examined, how far she was the patron of letters—Her literary works—Manners and monuments of her reign.

THE visit of the king of Sweden to Petersburg, the entertainments to which it gave rise, and the mortifying circumstances in which it terminated, hastened, no doubt, the death of Catharine. For six weeks she had given herself up to one continued round of amusements and fatigue: for to her, the going up and down the stairs of the palace, the business of dressing, and appearing in public, had long been a wearisome task; and the more so, as she was still desirous of looking young and healthful, and was always averse to the use of a sedan. Aware of the first of these difficulties, feveral of her courtiers, upon occasion of the balls and entertainments that were given by them in honour of the king, transformed for her eafe the stairs of their houses into gentle afcents, which were richly carpeted. A gallantry of this kind cost Besborodko no less a sum than three thousand rubles (300*l*.), which he expended to render his house commodious for her reception *.

Towards the close of her life, Catharine had so increased in size, as to be an object almost of deformity. Her legs, which were always swollen and often ulcerated, had entirely lost their shape, and she could no longer boast that handsome foot which had formerly been so much admired. The noted pirate Lambro Canziani, whom admiral Ribas, through the favour of Zubof, had introduced to the empress, and who acted in quality of buffoon, after having previously served her as corsair in the Archipelago, was desirous also of prescribing as her physician. He accordingly persuaded her that he had an infallible remedy for her legs; and he himself was even at the pains of fetching water from the sea for the purpose of a cold bath, to be used once a day for her

* Let not the russian highnesses and excellencies, who may happen to read my book, be scandalized at seeing themselves here called by their simple appellatives: I would gladly wrap them up in their titles as a pill is enveloped in its tinsel; but it often happens, that, while I am writing, the monsieur becomes count, the count prince, and the prince knæz, the counsellor general, and the valet-de-chambre excellence. Under the creative hand of Paul every thing changes with such rapidity that I am obliged to confine myself to the bare name of the personages.

feet. The application succeeded at first, and she joined with Lambro in ridiculing the prescriptions of her physicians: but the swellings soon returned, and from late hours and much motion her disorder greatly increased. When the king's refusal was announced to her, and she was obliged to dismiss her court after having summoned it to celebrate the betrothing of her grand-daughter, she experienced a slight stroke of apoplexy. From the constraint which for several days after she imposed on herself, that she might appear with her wonted serenity, and betray no symptom of the vexation she felt at the refractoriness of *the little king* *, the blood and humours rushed still more to the head; her face, which was before highly inflamed, became at this period additionally red and livid, and her indispositions returned with greater frequency.

I should not perhaps have mentioned here the signs and prognostics of her death: but, miracles being still in vogue in Russia, it may not be amiss to observe, that on the evening of her visit

---

* This was the derisory epithet which she gave him. The young prince was ambitious from his infancy of the title of grown man, which he strove by his actions to merit. Walking one day in a park, two women cried, " Let us run into the " road to see our little king." Gustavus, hearing them, replied, somewhat piqued: " Little king! pray, ladies, have " you then a greater?"

with the king at the house of Samoïlof, a bright star shot from the sky over her head, and fell into the Neva; and for the honour of truth and funereal omens, I must add, that this fact was the common talk of the whole city. Some would have it, that this beautiful star was a prognostic of the young queen's journey into Sweden; while others, remarking that it made its descent near the spot where the citadel and tombs of the sovereigns were situated, tremblingly whispered that it was the harbinger of the approaching dissolution of the empress. I say, *tremblingly whispered*; because in Russia *death* and *empress* are two words that cannot be coupled together without danger of being charged with blasphemy.

But, to return, it is certain, that on the 4th of November 1796, Catharine, having what was called her *little hermitage* (small party), displayed an uncommon share of spirits. By a vessel from Lubeck, she had received the news of the French under Moreau having been obliged to repass the Rhine, and she wrote, upon this occasion, to the Austrian minister Cobenzel a very humorous note[*]. She amused herself greatly with Leof. Narishkin, her grand ecuyer and first buffoon,

---

[*] The note, which was in everybody's hands, was this: "I hasten to inform your excellent excellence, that the excellent troops of the excellent court have given the French an excellent drubbing."

trafficking with him for all sorts of bawbles, which he usually carried in his pockets to sell to her, like an itinerant pedlar, whose character he attempted to personate. She rallied him with great pleasantry upon the terrors to which he was subject upon hearing of any obituary intelligence, by informing him of the death of the king of Sardinia, which she had also just learned; and she spoke of this event in a free and jocular manner. She retired, however, somewhat earlier than usual, assigning as a reason, that too much laughing had given her slight symptoms of colic.

The next morning she arose at her accustomed hour, and sending for her favourite, gave him a short audience. She afterwards transacted business with her secretaries, but dismissed the last that came, bidding him wait in the antichamber, and she would presently call for him to finish what he was about. The valet, Zachary Constantinovitch, waited for awhile; but, uneasy at not being called, and hearing no noise in the apartment, he at last opened the door, when he saw, to his surprise and terror, the empress prostrate on the floor between the two doors leading from the alcove to her water-closet. She was already without sense or motion. The valet ran for the favourite, whose apartment was above; physicians were sent for; and consternation and tumult prevailed about the empress. A mattrass was spread near the window; she was laid upon it; bleeding, clysters, and all the means usually resorted to upon such occasions, were employed, which produced their ordinary effect. She was still alive: her heart was found to beat; but there was no other perceptible sign of motion. The favourite, seeing her in this alarming state, sent to the counts Soltikof and Bezborodko, and some others. Every one was eager to dispatch, on his own part, a messenger to the grand-duke Paul; and the person employed in this service by Zubof was his own brother. Meanwhile the imperial family, and the rest of the household, were ignorant of the situation of the empress, which was kept secret. Till eleven o'clock, her accustomed hour of summoning the grand-dukes, it was not known that she was at all indisposed; the circumstance of her being seriously ill did not transpire till one; and was then mentioned with a timid and mysterious caution, through fear of the consequences of mistake. You might see two courtiers meet each other, both perfectly acquainted with the circumstance of the apoplexy, yet questioning one another, answering in turn, watching each other's looks, and cautiously advancing step by step, that they might arrive both together at the terrible point, and be able to talk of what both already knew. A man must have frequented a court, and especially the court of

Russia, for being able to judge of the importance of these things, and for exculpating the historian from the charge of absurdity in relating such particulars as actually occurred.

In the meantime, those whom chance, or their connexion with office, placed in the way of being early informed of the truth, hastened to communicate it to their families and friends; for the death of the empress was looked to as the epoch of some extraordinary revolution in the state, as well from the character of Paul as from the projects and dispositions of which Catharine was suspected. It was, therefore, of importance to be able to take precautions in time; and the court first, and presently the city, were in an alarming state of agitation and anxiety.

Five or six couriers arrived nearly at the same instant at Gatshina, but the grand-duke was absent. He was gone to the distance of a few versts with his court to inspect a mill, which he had ordered to be constructed. Upon receiving the intelligence, he appeared affected, either with great joy or great grief, as extremes so nearly approach and resemble each other that it is sometimes difficult to distinguish their effects. He soon, however, recovered from his emotion, asked a thousand questions of the messengers, and gave orders for his journey, which he performed with such expedition, that in less than three hours he was at

Petersburg, which is twelve leagues from his residence at Gatshina. He arrived at eight in the evening with his wife, and found the palace in the greatest confusion.

His presence attracted about him some courtiers and ministers, while others disappeared. The favourite, a prey to grief and consternation, had relinquished the reins of empire: the great, occupied with the consequences of this event, arranged their affairs in private: all the intrigues of the court were disconcerted in a moment, and, like the spokes of a wheel when the stock is destroyed, were without point of union.

Paul, accompanied by his whole family, repaired to the chamber of his mother, who gave, however, no sign of recognition at the appearance of her assembled children. She was lying on the mattrass, perfectly still, and without any appearance of life. The grand-duke Alexander, his wife, and the young princesses, burst into tears, and formed round her a most affecting groupe. The grand-duchesses, the gentlemen and ladies of the court, were up all night waiting the last sigh of the empress. The grand-duke and his sons were frequently by her side to witness this event; and the next day passed in the same anxiety and expectation.

Paul, whose grief for the loss of a mother by whom he had been so little beloved, could not be expected to be extremely overwhelming, was occupied in giving directions and preparing every thing for his accession: and he bestowed on this grand event of his life the same care and attention as the director of a pantomime bestows on his scenes and machinery previous to the rising of the curtain. In fact the death of a sovereign seemed in this instance to be scarcely anything more than an interlude between the acts of a play; so little was the person of Catharine regarded by those about her, and even by her children. She still breathed, although nothing was thought of but the changes that were about to take place, and the individual who was on the point of succeeding her.

By degrees the apartments of the palace were filled with officers who had come with expedition from Gatshina, and were dressed in a manner so novel and grotesque that they seemed the apparitions of a former century, or ghosts from another world. In the pale and haggard countenances of the old courtiers, wherever they were seen, mortification, terror, and grief, were depicted; and they successively retired, to give place to the new comers. The palace was surrounded with carriages, obstructing the streets that led to it; and he who could claim the flightest acquaintance passed the day there, waiting the effect of this sudden event. Orders were given, that no person should quit the city, and no courier was suffered to pass the gates.

It was generally believed that Catharine had expired the preceding evening, but that her death, for reasons of state, was still concealed. The fact however is, that she was all this time in a kind of lethargy. The remedies which were administered produced their natural effect, and she had even moved one of her feet, and pressed the hand of a waiting woman : *but, happily for Paul, the power of speech was gone for ever.* About ten in the evening she appeared suddenly to revive, and began to rattle in the throat in a most terrible manner. The imperial family hastened to her; but this new and shocking spectacle was too much for the princesses, who were obliged to withdraw. At last she gave a lamentable shriek, which was heard in the neighbouring apartments, and died, after having continued for thirty-seven hours in a state of insensibility. During this period she gave no indication of pain, till the moment before she expired, and her death appears to have been as happy as her reign.

If the love that monarchs have deserved from their subjects has been sometimes estimated by the impression produced by their death, Russia is not the country to which we can apply the observation, unless indeed the court be taken for the whole empire. The individual who was the greatest loser by the death of the empress, and whom it hurled at once from the pinnacle of greatness and power into the obscurity from which favour had raised him, was also the individual who was most afflicted at the event; and there was something in the expression of his grief that was truly affecting. The young grand-duchesses, who had a tender regard for their grand-mother, with whom they had lived on terms of greater familiarity than with their own parents, paid her also the unfeigned tribute of their tears; they considered her as their provident patroness, and as the source from which flowed all their enjoyments and felicity. Those ladies and courtiers too, who had experienced the kindness of her disposition and enjoyed the pleasure of her private society, where she displayed a most captivating amenity, in like manner lamented her death. Even the young persons of her court, both male and female, regretted the happy evenings of the Hermitage, and that cheerful ease and pleasure which Catharine so well knew how to inspire, and contrasted with them the military constraint and etiquette that were likely to succeed. The wits and banterers of Petersburg lamented in secret, that they must now respect the very persons whom they had so long been accustomed to ridicule and despise, and submit to a course of life that had been the constant and inexhaustible topic of their sarcasms and jests. The menial servants of Catharine sincerely bewailed a good and generous mistress, whose mild and even temper, and noble and dignified character, were above those daily bickerings, those gusts of petty passion, which are the poison of domestic life. In truth, if we judge of Catharine as of the mother of a family, consider her palace as her house, her courtiers as her children, she was entitled to lamentations and tears.

There were other personages on this disastrous occasion of a pale and woeful aspect; but these were incapable of weeping. In them it was an air of guilt rather than of sadness, and their grief would bear no construction favourable to Catharine. I refer to those creatures of the favourite, those hypocritical ministers, those dastardly courtiers, that crowd of wretches of all states and conditions, whose fortunes and hopes were derived from the easy disposition of Catharine, and the abuses of her reign. In this desponding train must also be included those who had a share in the revolution of 1762: these men appeared to awake as from a long dream, which had suspended reflection, to be delivered up to the influence of terror, and perhaps of remorse.

As to the opinion of the people, that pretended touchstone of the merit of sovereigns, and which in Russia is no better than the clod of the highway, trampled under foot like the pavement of the streets, nothing could equal their indifference as to what was going on in the palace. It was rumoured, indeed, that provisions would be cheaper, and the power of masters over their slaves be restrained and limited; but it will presently be seen how this popular report was belied by Paul. The principal inhabitants of the city were in a state of silent consternation; and the horror inspired by the character of the grandduke seemed at this moment to call forth the love and respect that were due to Catharine.

In so brilliant a capital, and especially in so gay and polite a court, some extraordinary changes were quickly visible. The air of freedom, of ease, and of gallantry, which had so lately prevailed, was succeeded by an intolerable constraint. In the apartments in which Catharine had just fallen into the sleep of death, the word of command, the clattering of swords and of soldiers, and the stamping of enormous boots, already resounded. From the sombre garb of the ladies, the grotesque habiliments of the men, the strange phraseology which all were eager to adopt, and the general contrasts with what had existed before, those who had been acquainted with each other met without being known, spoke without being understood, and asked questions without receiving an answer. The day of St. Catharine, hitherto celebrated with so much pomp and rejoicings, arrived at this interval, as if to depict with greater horror the desolation of this fairy lace, which, lately the scene of so many pleasures and entertainments, was becoming that of as many absurdities.

Though seventy years of age, Catharine still retained some remains of beauty. Her hair was always dressed in an antique simplicity, and in a peculiar taste, and never did a crown sit better on any head than hers. She was of the middle stature, and corpulent; few women, however, with her corpulence, would have attained the graceful and dignified carriage for which she was conspicuous. In her private life, the good-humour and confidence with which she inspired all about her, seemed to keep her in perpetual youth, playfulness, and gaiety. Her engaging conversation and familiar manners placed all those who had constant access to her, or assisted at her toilette, perfectly at their ease; but the moment she had put on her gloves to make her appearance in the neighbouring apartments, she assumed a sedate demeanour and a very different countenance. From an agreeable and facetious woman, she appeared all at once the reserved and majestic empress. Whoever had seen her then for the first time would have found her not below the idea he had previously formed, and would have said,

" This is indeed the Semiramis of the north!"
The maxim, *Præsentia minuit famam*, could no
more be applied to her than to the great Frederic.
I saw her once or twice a week for ten years, and
every time with renewed admiration. My eagerness to examine her person caused me successively to neglect prostrating myself before her
with the crowd; but the homage I paid by gazing at her, was surely more flattering. She walked
slowly, and with short steps; her majestic front
lofty and serene, her look tranquil, and frequently
cast downwards. Her mode of saluting was by
a slight inclination of the body, not without grace;
but with a smile at command, that came and vanished with the bow. If, upon the introduction
of a stranger, she presented her hand to him to
kiss, she did it with great courtesy, and commonly
addressed a few words to him on the subject of
his journey and his visit: but then all the harmony of her countenance was instantly discomposed, and for a moment the great Catharine was
forgotten in the sight of the old woman; as, on
opening her mouth, it was apparent that she had
lost her teeth, and her voice was broken, and her
inarticulation bad. The lower part of her face
was rather rude and coarse; her grey eyes, though
clear and penetrating, evinced something of hypocrisy, and a certain wrinkle at the base of the
nose gave her somewhat of a sneering look. The

celebrated Lampi had lately painted a striking likeness of her, though extremely flattering: Catharine, however, remarking that he had not entirely omitted that unfortunate wrinkle which characterized her physiognomy, was greatly dissatisfied at it, and said that Lampi had made her too serious and too roguish. He was accordingly obliged to retouch and spoil the picture, which appeared now like the portrait of a young nymph; though the throne, the sceptre, the crown, and some other attributes, sufficiently indicate that it is the picture of an empress. In other respects, the performance well deserves the attention of the amateur, as also does a portrait of the present empress by the same hand *.

As to the character of Catharine, in my opinion, it can only be estimated from her actions. Her reign, for herself and her court, had been brilliant and happy; but the last years of it were particularly disastrous for the people and the

* The celebrated Le Brun, who was at Petersburg, and who could not obtain the honour of taking her likeness when living, saw her after she was dead, and drew it from his memory and fancy. I saw the rough draught of this portrait, which was extremely like.—The following humorous advice was given to M. le Brun to render the resemblance perfect: Take a map of the russian empire for the canvas; the darkness of ignorance, for the ground; the spoils of Poland for the drapery; human blood, for the colouring; the monuments of her reign, for the outlines; and for the shading, six months of the reign of her successor.

empire. All the springs of government became debilitated and impaired. Every general, governor, chief of department, was become a petty despot. Rank, justice, impunity, were sold to the highest bidder. An oligarchy of about a score of knaves partitioned Russia, pillaged, by themselves or others, the finances, and contended for the spoils of the unfortunate. Their lowest valets, and even their slaves, obtained in a short time offices of considerable importance and emolument. One had a salary of from three to four hundred rubles a year (30 or 40 *l.*), which could not possibly be increased by any honest dealing, yet was he sufficiently rich to build round the palace houses valued at fifty thousand crowns (12,500*l.*) Catharine, so far from inquiring into the impure source of such sudden wealth, rejoiced to see her capital thus embellished under her eyes, and applauded the inordinate luxury of these rascals, which she erroneously considered as a proof of the prosperity of her reign. In the worst days of France, pillage was never so general, and never so easy. Whoever received a sum of money from the crown for any undertaking, had the impudence to retain half, and afterwards complained of its insufficiency, for the purpose of obtaining more; and either an additional sum was granted, or the enterprise abandoned. The great plunderers even divided the booty of the little ones, and thus became accomplices in their thefts. A minister knew almost to a ruble what his signature would procure to his secretary; and a colonel felt no embarrassment in talking with a general of the profits of the army, and the extortions he made upon the soldiers*. Every one, from the peculiar favourite to the lowest in employ, considered the property of the state as an harvest to be reaped, and grasped at it with as much avidity as the populace at an ox given up to be devoured. The Orlofs, as well as Potemkin and Panin, filled their places with some dignity. The first displayed talents, and an inordinate ambition: Panin had besides, a considerable share of knowledge, patriotism, and many vir-

* The colonel was the despot of his regiment, of which he had the exclusive management, in the whole and in the detail. The russian army, wherever it may be situated, whether in a subjected territory, the territory of an ally, or that of an enemy, always living at free quarters, the colonels regularly take to themselves nearly the whole of the money destined for its support. By way of indemnification, they turn the horses into the fields, and the men into the houses of the peasants, there to live free of expence. The pay of a colonel is from seven to eight hundred rubles (70*l.* or 80*l.*) only a year; but the profit he derives from a regiment amounts to fifteen or twenty thousand (1500*l.* or 2000*l.*) A minister asking one day some favour of the empress for a poor officer, she replied, "If he be poor, it is his own fault; he has long "had a regiment." Thus robbery was privileged, and probity ridiculed and despised.

tues*. In general, during the last years of Catharine, none were so little as the great. Without knowledge, without penetration, without pride, without probity, they could not even boast of that false honour which is to loyalty what hypocrisy is to virtue: unfeeling as bashaws, rapacious as tax-gatherers, pilfering as lacqueys, and venal as the meanest abigails of a play, they might truly be called the rabble of the empire. Their creatures, their hirelings, their valets, and even their relations, did not accumulate wealth by the gifts of their bounty, but by the extortions committed in their name, and the traffic made of their authority: they also were robbed themselves, as they robbed the crown. The meanest services rendered to these men were paid by the state; and the wages of their buffoons, servants,

* He did one act of generosity in particular, which has found no imitators. The education of the grand-duke Paul, to whom he was first governor, being finished, the empress, among other rewards for this service, gave him seven thousand peasants, while the aides de camp, secretaries, and others employed by count Panin as his assistants, were totally unnoticed by her. Panin immediately divided among them the seven thousand peasants; and I have seen several officers who are still rich with the boon. This generous action should not, however, lead us to forget, that the two principal measures of his administration were marked with misfortune: the exchange of Holstein for six ships, which Denmark never gave; and the first division of Poland, which excited a craving for the remainder.

musicians, private secretaries, and even tutors of their children, defrayed out of some public fund, of which they had the management. Some few among them sought out men of talents, and appeared to esteem merit: but neither talents nor merit acquired a fortune under their protection, or partook of their wealth; partly from the avarice of those patrons, but still more from their total want of beneficence. The only way of gaining their favour was by becoming their buffoon, and the only method of profiting by it was by turning knave.

Thus, during this reign, almost all the people in office and authority were lucky adventurers. At the galas given by the empress, swarms of new-created counts and princes made their appearance, and that at a time when in France all titles were about to be abolished. If we except the Soltikofs, we shall find at this period no family of distinction in favour. To any other country this would have been no evil; but in Russia, where the rich nobility is the only class that has any education, and generally speaking any principles of honour, it was a serious calamity to the empire. Besides, all these upstarts were so many hungry leeches, who must be fed with the best blood of the state, and fattened with the hard earnings of the people. A frequent change of kings is often not burthensome to a state, which continues to be their heir; but an incessant change of favourites and ministers, who must all fill their coffers and carry off their treasures, is enough to ruin any country except Russia. How many millions must it have cost to fill successively the rapacious maws of about a dozen peculiar favourites? how many, to render rich and noble the Besborodkos, the Zavadofskys, the Markofs, and the vast number of others who might be named? Have not the Orlofs, the Potemkins, the Zubofs, acquired revenues greater than those of kings; and their underlings, agents in the sale of their signatures, and managers of their petty traffic, become more wealthy than the most successful merchants*?

With respect to the government of Catharine, it was as mild and moderate, within the immediate circle of her influence, as it was arbitrary and terrible at a distance. Whoever, directly or indirectly, enjoyed the protection of the favourite, exercised, wherever he was situated, the

---

* A work has fallen into my hands, intitled, "La Vie de "Catherine Seconde," [a wretched translation whereof into english was published by Dr. Hunter.] in which the author gives a statement of the sums obtained by the favourites. But how very defective is this estimate, and how far below the truth! How is it possible, indeed, to calculate the immense sums which have enriched the Orlofs, the Potemkins, and the Zubofs, favourites who had the same access to the treasury of the state, as to their own private coffers?

most undisguised tyranny. He insulted his superiors, trampled on his inferiors, and violated justice, order, and the *ukases**, with impunity.

It is to the policy first, and next to the weakness of Catharine, to which in part must be attributed the relaxed and disorganized state of her internal government: though the principal cause will be found in the depraved manners and character of the nation, and especially of her court. How was a woman to effect that which the active discipline of the cane, and the sanguinary axe of Peter I. were inadequate to accomplish? Having usurped a throne, which she was desirous to retain, she was under the necessity of treating her accomplices with kindness. Being a foreigner in the empire over which she reigned, she strove to identify herself with the nation, by adopting and even flattering its tastes and its prejudices. She often knew how to reward, but never could resolve to punish; and it was solely by suffering her power to be abused, that she succeeded in preserving it.

She had two passions, which never left her but with her last breath: the love of the other sex, which degenerated into licentiousness; and the love of glory, which sunk into vanity. By

---

* Edicts of the monarch, which in Russia hold the place of laws.

the former of these passions, she was never so far governed as to become a Messalina, but she often disgraced both her rank and her sex; and continued to be by habit what she had been from constitution: by the second, she was led to undertake many laudable projects, which were seldom completed, and to engage in unjust wars, from which she derived at least that kind of fame which never fails to accompany success.

The generosity of Catharine, the splendor of her reign, the magnificence of her court, her institutions, her monuments, her wars, were precisely to Russia what the age of Louis XIV. was to Europe; but, considered individually, Catharine was greater than that prince. The French formed the glory of Louis, Catharine formed that of the Russians. She had not, like him, the advantage of reigning over a polished people; nor was she surrounded from infancy by great and accomplished characters. She had some subtle ambassadors, not unskilled in the diplomatic art, and some fortunate generals; but Romanzof, Panin, and Potemkin excepted, she could not boast a single man of genius: for the wit, cunning, and dexterity of certain of her ministers, the ferocious valour of a Suvarof, the ductile capacity of a Repnin, the favour of a Zubof, the readiness of a Besborodko, and the assiduity of a Nicholas Soltikof, are not worthy of being mentioned as exceptions. It was not that Russia did not produce men of merit; but Catharine feared such men, and they kept at a distance from her. We may conclude, therefore, that all her measures were her own, and particularly all the good she did.

Let not the misfortunes and abuses of her reign give to the private character of this princess too dark and repulsive a shade! She appeared to be thoroughly humane and generous, as all who approached her experienced: all who were admitted to her intimacy were delighted with the good-humoured sallies of her wit: all who lived with her were happy. Her manners were gay and licentious, but she still preserved an exterior decorum, and even her favourites always treated her with respect*. Her love never excited disgust, nor her familiarity contempt. She might be deceived, won, seduced, but she would never suffer herself to be governed. Her active and regular life, her moderation, firmness, fortitude, and even her temperance, are moral qualities which it would be highly unjust to ascribe to hypocrisy. How great might she not have been, had her heart been as well governed as her mind! She reigned over the Russians less

* The reports circulated in Europe concerning her intemperance in champagne and brandy, and a number of other extravagancies, are down-right calumnies.

despotic than over herself; she was never hurried away by anger, never a prey to dejection, and never indulged in transports of immoderate joy. Caprice, ill-humour, and petulance, as they formed no part of her character, were never perceived in her conduct. I will not deside, whether she were truly great, but she was certainly beloved*.

Imbued, from her youth, with the corrupt maxims by which courts are infected; enveloped,

---

* A variety of quatrains have been composed, either to serve as an epitaph, or be placed under the portrait of Catharine, but none have been struck off so happily, or describe her so truly, as the following. They are from the pens of two young Russians, the agreeable qualities of whose mind are enhanced by those of an admirable character, and a generous heart.

> Elle fit oublier, par un esprit sublime,
> D'un pouvoir odieux les énormes abus,
> Elle se maintint par ses vertus
> Sur un trône acquis par le crime
>> " Bless'd in her sway, her subjects might disown
>> " Th' unnumber'd evils of despotic rule ;
>> " And tho' a crime had fixed her on the throne,
>> " She reign'd by precepts drawn from Virtue's school."

The next is more flattering, but inferior in merit:

> Dans le sein de la paix, au milieu de la guerre,
> A tous ses ennemis elle dicta la loi :
> Par ses talens divers elle étonna la terre,
> Ecrivit comme un sage, & regna comme un roi.
>> " Amid the train of Peace, or din of War,
>> " Each foe appall'd her sov'reign will obey'd ;
>> " Her mighty genius held the world in awe ;
>> " Like sages wrote, like Jove the sceptre sway'd."

on her throne, in a cloud of incense, through which it was hardly possible for her to see clearly, it would be too severe to apply at once the searching torch of reason to her character, and try its defects by so strict an inquest. Let us judge her now as we should have done some twenty years ago, and consider that Russia, as to the people, is still in the age of Charlemagne. The friends of liberty ought to render to Catharine the same justice as is rendered by all rational theologians to those great and wise men who did not enjoy the light of revelation. Her crimes were the crimes of her station, not of her heart: the terrible butcheries of Ismail and of Praga appeared to her court to be humanity itself. All she wanted was to have once known misfortune, and she would perhaps have possessed the purest virtues; but she was spoilt by the unvaried prosperity of her arms. Vanity, that fatal rock to women, was so to Catharine; and her reign will ever bear the distinguishing characteristic of her sex.

Meanwhile, in whatever light she is considered, she will ever be placed in the first rank among those who, by their genius, their talents, and especially their success, have attracted the admiration of mankind. Her sex, giving a bolder relief to the great qualities she displayed on the throne, will place her above all comparison in history; and the fabulous ages of an Isis and a Semiramis must be resorted to, to find a woman who has executed, or rather undertaken, such daring projects.

The ten last years of her reign carried her power, her glory, and perhaps her political crimes, to their height. The great Frederic, dictator of the kings of Europe, dying, she was left the foremost of the crowned heads; and if we except perhaps Joseph and Gustavus, all those heads taken together were not equal to her's: for she surpassed them as much in understanding, as she exceeded them in the extent of her territories; and, if Frederic was the dictator of these kings, Catharine became their tyrant. It was then that the end of that political thread, by which poor Europe had been moved like a puppet, and which had slipt from France to Berlin, and from Berlin to Vienna and to London, became fixed in the hands of a woman who drew it as she pleased. The immense empire, an empire almost of romance, which she had subjected to her sway; the inexhaustible resources she derived from a country and a people as yet in a state of infancy; the extreme luxury of her court, the barbaric pomp of her nobility, the wealth and princely grandeur of her favourites, the glorious exploits of her armies, and the gigantic views of her ambition, threw Europe into a stupefying admiration; and those monarchs, who had been too proud to pay each other even the slightest deference, felt no humiliation in making a lady the arbitress of their interests, and the regulatrix of their measures.

But the French revolution, so unfriendly to sovereigns in general, was particularly so to Catharine. The blaze, which suddenly darted from the centre of France as from the crater of a burning volcano, threw a stream of light upon Russia vivid as that of lightning; and injustice, crimes, and blood were seen, where before all was grandeur, glory, and virtue. Catharine shuddered with horror and indignation. The French, those trumpeters of fame, those flattering and brilliant historians, who were one day to transmit to posterity the wonders of her reign, were suddenly transformed into so many inexorable judges, at whose aspect she trembled. The phantoms of her imagination were dispelled. That empire of Greece she was so desirous of reviving, thofe laws she would have established, that philosophy she intended to inculcate, and those arts which she had patronised, became odious in her sight. Like many other crowned philosophers, Catharine valued the sciences so far only as they appeared the instruments for disseminating her glory. She wished to hold them as a dark lantern in her hand; to make use of their light as should suit her convenience; to see without being seen: but when they dazzled her all at once with their bright emanations, she wished to extinguish them. She, who had been the friend of Voltaire, the admirer of Buffon, and the disciple of Diderot*, now wished to be re-enveloped in the ages of barbarism: but her wishes were vain; the light was not to be resisted: she had fallen asleep on laurels, she awoke on the carcases of the dead: that glory, which in illusion she embraced, was changed in her arms into one of the furies: and the legislatrix of the north, forgetting her own maxims and philosophy, was no longer any thing more than an old sybil. Her dastardly favourites, everywhere pointing out to her Brutuses, jacobins, and incendiaries, succeeded in inspiring her with suspicions and terrors. Her delirium was even carried so far, that in her manifestos she bestowed the epithets of rebels and traitors on a king, who was actually extending his regal prerogatives, and a nobility meliorating

* Upon the breaking out of the revolution, Catharine ordered the bust of Voltaire to be taken from her gallery, and thrown among the lumber. She had requested a bust of Mr. Fox at the period when that eloquent senator, at the head of the british opposition, prevented, by his exertions the government of his country from declaring war against Russia. When the same senator, however, opposed with equal strenuousness a war with France, his bust also, which a year before she had so highly honoured, was served in the same manner as Voltaire's.

its government: the Poles were treated as jacobins, because they had not the misfortune to be Russians*.

Had Catharine been asked, in an interval of calmness, if she had not herself considerably advanced and helped to strengthen this revolution now so odious to her, what would she have answered? Yet such is the fact: since, if she had not been so eager to seize upon the unfortunate country of the Poles, and afterwards to raise dissensions in Prussia and Sweden, she would not have disgusted, as she did, all Europe and the combination of princes; Prussia would not have been induced so speedily to make peace, that he might be at leisure to watch her proceedings; nor would she have excited the indignation of Spain, by employing against a catholic king and a catholic nobility the same arms and the same insults as were employed against the French. In this view, France may erect a statue to her memory; for she has rendered the system of the enemies of that country odious and absurd even to monarchs themselves; and has done the

---

* Even the Americans, at this period, became hateful to Catharine. She condemned a revolution which she had formerly pretended to admire, called Washington a rebel, and said publicly, that a man of honour could not wear the order of Cincinnatus. Accordingly Langeron, and some other emigrants, who had been invested with this order, immediately renounced it and wore it no longer.

republic the same service as demagogues have by their enormities, and Mr. Pitt by his intrigues.

Catharine never effectually patronised letters in her country. It was the reign of Elizabeth that had encouraged them; which was distinguished by many productions capable of proving to Europe that the Russians may lay fair claim to every species of excellence *. Catharine, indeed, purchased libraries and collections of pictures, pensioned flatterers, flattered such celebrated men as might be instrumental in spreading her fame, and readily sent a medal or a snuff-box to a german author who dedicated some encomiastic work to her: but it must have come from afar to please her, and have already acquired a great name to be entitled to her suffrage, and particularly to obtain any recompense. Genius might be born at her feet without being noticed †, and

---

* The author of these Memoirs may perhaps one day obtain both the materials and the leisure for exhibiting to his countrymen a view of russian literature. They will be astonished to find how nearly, in delicacy of wit, as well as in sentiment, sprightliness and taste, it resembles their own. The russian theatre is particularly formed upon that of the french. Government, manners, and language, alone have stamped some difference on the character of the two nations.

† Many architects, painters, sculptors, mechanics, and other artists of great talents, have lived and died in obscurity and wretchedness, merely because they were Russians.

still more without being encouraged; yet, jealous of every kind of fame, and especially of that which Frederic the *unique* had obtained by his writings, she was desirous of becoming an author, that she might share in it. She accordingly wrote her celebrated *Instructions for a Code of Laws*; several moral tales and allegories for the education of her grand-children; and a number of dramatic pieces and proverbs, which were acted and admired at the Hermitage. Her grand and futile undertaking, of collecting a number of words from three hundred different languages, and forming them into a dictionary, was never executed.

Of all her writings, her letters to Voltaire are certainly the best. They are even more interesting than those of the old philosophical courtier himself, who sold her watches and knitted stockings for her*; and who repeats in his letters the same ideas and compliments in a hundred different forms, and excites her continually to drive the Turks out of Europe, instead of advising her to render her own subjects free and happy. If the code of laws drawn up by Catharine bespeak a mind capable of enlarged views and a sound policy, her letters announce the wit, graces, and ta-

---

Their names can only be found in certain topographical descriptions, or the accounts of foreign travellers, by whom more justice has been done them than by their own country.

* This he says himself in one of his letters to her.

lents of a woman of still greater merit, and lead us to regret that she was an autocrate and an usurper.

When she published her Instructions*, all Europe resounded with her applause, and styled her by anticipation the legislatrix of the north. Catharine convened deputies from the different nations of her vast empire; but it was only that they might hear this celebrated performance read, and that she might receive their compliments: for as soon as this was done, they were all sent back to their distant homes, some in disgrace for their firmness, others decorated with medals for their servility. The manuscript was deposited in a magnificent casket, to be exhibited to the curiosity of strangers. A sort of committee was appointed to compile these laws; and if a favourite or minister had any dependent for whom he wished to provide, or any buffoon whom he wanted to maintain free of expense, he was appointed a member of this committee, in

---

* It is known, that her Instruction for a Code was put into the *index expurgatorius*, and was prohibited in France: Catharine and Voltaire were witty on the occasion. Who would have thought that, twenty years after, all french publications whatever would be proscribed in Russia, and that a lieutenant of police of the very same Catharine would confiscate at Petersburg, in the shop of Gay, the bookseller, *L'Avis au Peuple par Tissot*, " Tissot's Advice to the People;" alleging that the people wanted no advice, and that it was a dangerous book.

order to give him a salary*. Yet all Europe vociferated that Russia had laws, because Catharine had written a preface to a code, and had reduced a hundred different nations to the same system of bondage †.

Among the dramatical pieces of her composition ‡, and which she caused to be acted in the theatres of Petersburg, one was of a novel species: it being neither tragedy, nor comedy, nor opera, nor play, but a miscellany of all sorts of scenes, and intitled: OLEG, *an historical representation*. Upon the celebration of the last peace with the Turks, it was got up by her

---

* The author of these Memoirs knew, among other personages, one Mitrophane Popof, a buffoon, bigot, and interpreter of dreams to a lady of the court, who was a member of this committee: he had never heard of the Instruction for a Code, and was unable to read it.

† The Instruction for a Code is so literally taken from Montesquieu and Beccaria, that Mr. F. de B. who undertook to translate it, thought he could not do better than copy the text of these celebrated writers. The curious may be satisfied of this fact by examining the translation, which was printed for Grasset, at Lausanne. I had my information from this respectable man himself.

‡ They are written in russ. M. Derjavin, secretary to the empress, and known by some other works, was considered as the maker, or at least the mender, of them. It is certain, however, that she never had about her a man capable of writing her letters to Voltaire in french. Odart and Aubri, her secretaries at the time, did not write so well as herself: she is unquestionably the author of them.

direction with extraordinary pomp and the most magnificent decorations: upwards of seven hundred performers appearing on the stage. The subject is entirely drawn from russian history, and comprises an entire epocha of it. In the first act, *Oleg* lays the foundation of Mosco: in the second, he is at Kief, where he marries his pupil *Igor*, and settles him on the throne. The ancient ceremonies observed upon the marriage of the tzars furnish an opportunity for introducing some striking scenes, and the national dances and fports, which are exhibited, produce a number of pleasing pictures. *Oleg* then sets out upon an expedition against the Greeks: he is seen filing off with his army, and embarking. In the third act, he is at Constantinople. The emperor Leo, obliged to sign a truce, receives the barbarian hero with the greatest magnificence. He is seen feasting at his table, while various companies of young Greeks, boys and girls, sing in choirs to his praise, and exhibit before him the ancient dances of Greece. The next scenic decoration represents the hippodrome, where *Oleg* is entertained with the spectacle of the olympic games. Another theatre then rises at the far end of the stage, and some scenes from Euripides are played before the court. At length *Oleg* takes leave of the emperor, fastening his shield to a pillar in testimony of his visit, and to invite his successors to return one day to Constantinople.

The piece is truly russian, and particularly emblematical of the character of Catharine: her favourite projects are represented in it, and the design of subjugating Turkey is alluded to, even when celebrating a peace with that country. Properly speaking, the performance is nothing more than a magic lantern, exhibiting different objects in succession to the eyes of the spectator: but to me such exhibitions, in which the great events of history are introduced as in a picture on the stage, are more interesting than the strainings of the throat of our opera singers, and the amorous intrigues of our tragedies.

Catharine was neither fond of poetry nor of music; and she often confessed it. She could not even endure the noise of the orchestra between the acts of a play, and therefore commonly silenced it. This defect of taste and feeling in a woman, who appeared in other respects so happily constituted, is astonishing, yet may serve to explain how, with so extraordinary a capacity and genius, she could become so impassible and so sanguinary. At her tauridan palace, she constantly dined with the two pictures of the sacking of Otchakof and Ismaïl before her eyes, in which Cazanova has represented, with hideous accuracy, the blood flowing in streams, the limbs torn from the bodies and still palpitating, the demoniac fury of the slaughterers, and the convulsive agonies of the slaughtered. It was upon these scenes of horror that her attention and imagination were fixed, while Gasparini and Mandini were displaying their vocal powers, or Sarti was conducting a concert in her presence.

This same empress, who wrote plays herself; who admired Ségur for his wit, and heard him sometimes repeat his verses; who had the most ridiculous farces played before her by her old courtiers, and particularly by count Stackelberg*, and

* In the small parties of Catharine, all sorts of frolics and games of questions and answers, cross purposes, with forfeits, &c. were played. The old gouty courtiers were seen making their whimsical efforts to frisk and caper; and the grand-duke Constantine one day actually broke the arm of the feeble count Stackelberg, by rudely jostling against him, and throwing him down. Heretofore Ségur had acted a part in those societies more worthy of his rank and understanding. Among the verses he wrote in compliment to the empress, the following, which are the epitaph on a dog, have often been cited, and are worth preserving. They are in the true spirit of french gallantry:

> Pour prix de sa fidélité,
> Le ciel, témoin de sa tendresse,
> Lui devoit l'immortalité;
> Pour qu'elle fût toujours auprès de sa maîtresse.

> " Her fond fidelity Heav'n saw, and priz'd,
>   " And to reward her tenderness bestow'd
> " The precious gift to live immortaliz'd,
>   " Enjoying still her mistress's abode."

the austrian minister*, recalled and disgraced one of her own ministers, because he wrote his dispatches facetiously, made pretty french verses, had composed a tragedy, and was desirous of illustrating the genius of his country by publishing the historical eulogies of the great men of Russia. This was prince Beloselsky, envoy at the court of Turin, a man of taste and merit, who had expended a fortune in patronising the arts,

---

* No ambassador, perhaps, was ever so long at a court, and upon such good terms, as Cobenzel at the court of Russia. He had been sent originally by Maria Theresa, and was afterwards confirmed in his office by all her successors. He was of a mean and clumsy figure, but had a considerable share of wit, and of that peculiar sort in particular that is amusing to women. He was for ten years the assiduous admirer of the handsome princess Dolgoruka, and Catharine was fond of his company. He took great pleasure in theatricals, and accordingly plays were often got up at his house, in which he acted a part, and acquitted himself well. At the age nearly of sixty, he was absurd enough to take regular lessons in singing; and often, when a courier arrived with some important intelligence from Vienna, some defeat perhaps, he was found before his mirror, practising his part, disguised as the countess of Escarbagnas, of Croupillac, &c. The unfavourable dispatches which he was continually receiving during the war, never interrupted the entertainments, balls, and plays that were regularly given at his house. When news arrived of a french victory, it was jestingly said, " Well, well, we shall have a ball " on Saturday at the ambassador's." Catharine, offended at this dramatic mania, one day said, " You will find that he re- " serves his best piece for the news of the entrance of the " French into Vienna."

and much of his time in cultivating them himself*.

If we except the travels of the celebrated Pallas, the historical researches of the laborious Müller, and some other works upon natural history, no literary production worthy of notice has distinguished Russia during the reign of Catharine †. Natural history and mathematics are the only sciences which the Russians have contributed in some measure to advance, by the help of Germans ‡; yet no country is so fortunately

---

* He is known by several poetical productions, and particularly by an Epistle to the French, in which he seems to be a Frenchman himself; and Voltaire wrote him a very flattering letter, paying him the same compliment which he had paid before to the celebrated author of the Epistle to Ninon.

† It is the same Müller who wrote so judicious a critique of the pretended history of Peter I. and of whom Voltaire said, " He is a German: I wish him more wit, and fewer " consonants." Voltaire was astonished that the Russians should pretend to know their own names, and the names of their towns, better than the dictionary of Martiniere, and should complain at seeing them mutilated. He persisted in writing Roumanow, Schouvalow, &c. instead of Romanof and Schuvalof; as if the termination of *philosophe* were more barbarous than that of *Chanteloup*. He would never write the russian names as they were pronounced; yet, to shew us that he was acquainted with a single Chinese appellative, he had often the affectation to write Confutzée, where we should say Confucius.

‡ Many celebrated men of letters in Germany, as Klinger, for instance, who has a bold and caustic mind, and Kotzebue,

situated for rendering the sciences more essential services. Natural and ancient history have a right to expect from her the most astonishing discoveries. The ruins of a score of cities attest that Tartary and Mongolia were once inhabited by polished nations, and the monuments which are still discovering realise the sublime conceptions of Buffon and Bailli. Whole libraries have been discovered under the ruins of Ablai-Kitt, and amid the ruinous heaps that skirt the Irtish. Thousands of manuscripts in unknown languages, and many others in chinese, in kalmuc, and in mantschou, are mouldering in the deserted cabinets of the academy: had they remained under the rubbish till a government or people less barbarous had brought them to light, they would have been better preserved.

The best history of Russia, in french, is certainly that of Lévêque. Catharine detested this work as much as she did that of the abbé Chappe; and she bestowed extraordinary pains in scruti-

---

a dramatic author, whose plagiarisms often disgrace his talents, wrote in Russia; but they took care, particularly the former, not to publish their works in that country. Kotzebue, however, deserved to be pardoned for his good performances, for the sake of his Langhans, a bad imitation of Candide, and his translation of the works of Derjavin, and his Flight to Paris. The topographical and statistical works of the elegant Storch would also have merited an exception, had he dared to print as he wrote.

nising the ancient chronicles, that she might discover in this estimable historian some blunders and mistakes: because he had the courage (it is now twenty years ago) to glance at the murderer of Peter III. and of Ivan. In other respects, Lévêque has merited the thanks of the russian nation; as, by his talents, industry, and perseverance, he succeeded in rendering a history, so disgusting and detached as that of Russia till the reign of Peter I. in some degree interesting to foreigners*. But who will hereafter worthily write the history of Catharine †? To the present day history has been only a collection of selected events, artfully wrought up so as to render pro-

---

* In order to surpass him, instead of badly criticising his work, as *Le Clerc* has done, a man should reside ten years in Russia, learning the language, studying the manners, consulting the ancient annals of the country, the histories of Tatischtschef, of prince Scherbatof, and especially the immense materials left by Müller, Bachmeister, &c.

† This will be some Russian, and I know one or two competent to the task: but he must quit his country to write it. Meanwhile some foreigner, unacquainted with persons, manners, and places, may collect together some historical facts, give them a form half real, half fabulous, and call his work Histoire de Catharine II. But this will be no history. Were the emperor of China the subject, such accounts might pass. However, the anonymous author to whom I allude, has obtained, respecting certain epochs, some good materials; but if those from whom he received them had read the work before it was printed, fewer errors, as to persons, places, and dates, would be found in it.

minent a few individuals, and to form a striking picture. Facts ascertained are pearls and garnets, which the historian selects at his pleasure, and threads on a black string or a white, as shall best suit the complexion of his work: truth never appears but when it is convenient. Even the author of the History of Charles XII. of Peter I. and of the Age of Louis XIV. was of opinion, that it was of greater importance to say what is useful than what is true; as if what was false could ever be useful! And in a letter to count Schuválof, he says, *" Till I have leisure to metho-* *" dise the terrible event of the death of the tzare-* *" vitch,* I have begun another work." Is this the language of a philosophic historian? Alas! if you have not the courage to assert the truth, why not abandon the pen of history? It is only in a tragedy, or an epic poem, that the licence can be pardoned, of *arranging a terrible event.* The true end of history is not to celebrate an individual, but to instruct the governed, and give a lesson to governors.

Previous to the death of Catharine, the monuments of her reign resembled already so many wrecks and dilapidations: codes, colonies, education, establishments, manufactories, edifices, hospitals, canals, towns, fortresses, everything had been begun, and everything given up before it was finished. As soon as a project entered her head, all preceding ones gave place, and her thoughts were fixed on that alone, till a new idea arose to draw off her attention. She abandoned her code, to drive the Turks out of Europe. After the glorious peace of Kaïnardgi, she appeared for awhile to attend to the interior administration of her affairs; but all was presently forgotten, that she might be queen of Tauris. Her next project was the re-establishment of the throne of Constantine: to which succeeded that of humbling and punishing the king of Sweden. Afterwards the invasion of Poland became her ruling passion; and then a second Pugatshef might have arrived at the gates of Petersburg without forcing her to relinquish her hold. She died, again meditating the destruction of Sweden, the ruin of Prussia, and mortified at the successes of France and republicanism. Thus was she incessantly led away by some new passion still stronger in its influence than the preceding, so as to neglect her government both in its whole and its parts.

Medals are in being that were struck in honour of numerous edifices that have never yet been built; and, among others, the marble church, which, undertaken some twenty years ago, is still on the stocks*. The shells of other edifices, which have never been completed are falling into

---

* The emperor Paul has since caused it to be finished of brick.

ruins; and Petersburg is encumbered with the rubbish of a variety of large mansions fallen to decay before they have been inhabited. The projectors and architects pocketed the money; and Catharine, having the plan or medal in her cabinet, concluded the undertaking to be finished, and thought of it no more.

The Petersburg almanac gives a list of upwards of two hundred and forty towns founded by Catharine,—a number inferior, perhaps, to what have been destroyed by her armies; but these towns are merely so many paltry hamlets, that have changed their name and quality by an *immennoi ukase* *, the supreme order of her imperial majesty; somewhat like that by which Paul has since ordered a yacht to be promoted to the rank of a frigate †. Several of these towns are even nothing more than stakes driven into the ground, containing their name, and delineating their scite; yet, without waiting till they shall be finished, and particularly till they shall be peopled, they figure in the map as if they were the capitals of so many provinces ‡.

* An edict under the sign manual.
† This is a well-known fact.
‡ Catharine built, at an enormous expence, near Tzarkoselo, the town of Sophia, the circumference of which is immense; but the houses are already tumbling down, and have never been inhabited. If such be the lot of a town immediately under her eyes, what must be the fate of those cities

Prince Potemkin did actually build some towns, and construct some ports in the Krimea: which are very fine cages, but contain no birds; and such as might be allured thither would shortly mope and pine to death, if they had not the power of flying away. The russian government is subjugating and oppressive; the russian character, warlike and desolating. Taurida, since it was conquered, has become a desert *.

founded by her in remote deserts? But the most ridiculous town in being is unquestionably that of Gatshina, of which Paul has the honor to be founder. These personages look upon mankind as storks, who are caught by placing a wheel on the top of a house, or on a steeple. But all these forced erections, from the superb Potsdam to the contemptible Gatshina, prove that the real founders of cities are cultivation, commerce, and freedom: despots are only the destroyers of them; they know nothing of building and peopling anything except prisons and barracks.

* A friend of mine, a man of learning, was travelling in Taurida under the protection of government, for the purpose of investigating the country. One day coming to the habitation of a Tartar, who led a patriarchal life, and treated him with becoming hospitality, my friend, perceiving that his host was dejected, asked him the cause of his sadness: " Alas!
" I have great reason," said he. " May I not be permitted
" to know it?"—" The russian soldiers, who are in the neigh-
" bourhood, come every day and cut down my fruit-trees,
" that serve me both for shade and nourishment, to burn them;
" and shortly my bald head will be exposed to the parching
" heat of the sun."—" Why do you not complain of this
" treatment to their commander?"—" I have done so."—
" Well!"—" He told me that I should be paid two rubles
" a foot for such as they had already cut down, *and the same*

This mania of Catharine, of planning everything and completing nothing, drew from Joseph II. a very shrewd and satirical remark. During his travels in Taurida, he was invited by her to place the second stone of the town of Ekatarinoslaf, of which she had herself, with great parade, laid the first. On his return, he said, " I have finished in a single day a very important business with the empress of Russia: she has laid the first stone of a city, and I have laid the last."

Of all the monuments erected by her at Petersburg that will remain as long as they shall not be swallowed up by the swamps, are the superb quay of the Neva, and the equestrian statue of Peter I*. The last, however beautiful, is greatly

---

" *for as many as they may cut down hereafter.* But I am not in want of their money. Only let me die in peace under the shadow of the trees which my fathers have planted! or I must follow my unhappy brethren, and flee my country, as they have been forced to do." As he spoke the tears trickled down the beard of this venerable patriarch.

* D'Orbeil addressed some verses to Catharine, in which was the following handsome quatrain:

> C'est par tes soins que le bronze respire
> Sur ce rocher de Thétis aperçu,
> Et que le tzar découvre son empire
> Plus vaste encore qu'il ne l'avoit conçu.

> " 'Twas thou that bid yon rock-built statue's pride
>   " In breathing bronze o'erlook the distant main;
> " Surveying hence his realms extended wide,
>   " The tzar still wonders at his vast domain."

inferior to the accounts which hyperbolical travellers have given of it. The following verses from Delille may be applied to it:

> Du haut d'un vrai rocher, sa demeure sauvage,
> La nature se rit de ces rocs contrefaits.
>
> " On a wild rock nature contemptuous sits,
> " And laughs to scorn these idle counterfeits."

The idea of placing the great tzar upon a stupendous and rugged rock, over which he had climbed, was certainly new and sublime; but it has been badly executed. The rock, which was brought from Finland to the bank of the Neva with infinite labour, was twenty-one feet in height, forty in length, and covered with moss several inches thick, which must have been ages in accumulating. It was deprived of its wild and primitive form to give it a more regular appearance; and, what with hewing and polishing, was at last reduced in size nearly one half; so that it is now a little rock beneath a great horse; and the tzar, who ought to be surveying from it his empire, more vast even than he had conceived, is hardly able to peep into the first floor of the neighbouring houses. By another absurdity, Peter appears in the long russian caftan, which he obliged his subjects to quit by cutting them round at the knees. If this statue had a pedestal proportionate to its size, it would be an admirable performance.

A picture of Petersburg and its manners under the reign of Catharine, written in the spirit of the Picture of Paris by the penetrating Mercier, would be an interesting performance. But this, like all works of genius, has produced none but bad imitations, from the description of Berlin, conceived and executed by Nicolai, to that which a professor Georgi has given of Petersburg: they are all as poor in ideas, and as destitute of utility, as they are replete with minute details. Count Anhalt has given in the same way a description of the imperial house of the Cadets, of which he was director-general; wherein he tells us how many stair-cases, stairs, windows, doors, and chimnies there are in this immense building: which may do very well for a person intending to contract for the sweeping of them; but what instruction does it convey to the public *?

M. Storch, an industrious and well-informed young Livonian, has published a work under the title of a *Picture of Petersburg*, which ought not

---

* This description of Petersburg is even not exact in its details. The author of these memoirs has the honour of being mentioned in it among the literary characters then resident in the city; but, by a strange confusion of names, titles, and works, he makes but one person of general Melissino, major M——, and his brother; yet the writer was actually at Petersburg, and knew these men. After this, what faith can be placed in descriptions?

to be confounded with that I have been speaking of; but this picture resembles Petersburg as the portrait of Lampi resembles Catharine: it is too much à la chinoise, and without shadings, as the author himself foresaw. Storch, however, only wanted one thing to render it perfect,—an opportunity for writing it any where but in Russia. He dedicated it to Catharine, who rewarded the author for his flattering delineations; but she afterwards expressed her dissatisfaction at his having adopted the roman characters, for printing in german his *Statistical Tables*, another work which gives very accurate information concerning the political state of Russia.

Petersburg, some parts of which are singularly magnificent and beautiful, is not unlike the sketch of a grand picture, in which are already delineated a face resembling that of the Apollo Belvedere, with such an eye as would be given to Genius, while the rest is faintly chalked out in confused touches or dotted lines.

Petersburg being inhabited by colonies of different nations, nothing can be more heterogeneous than its manners and customs; and, in general, it is difficult to ascertain what is the prevailing taste or fashion. The french tongue serves as the connecting tie between these various people, but many other languages are equally spoken. In a company by no means numerous, you will find in turn three languages used, the russian, the french, and the german; and it is not uncommon, in the same society, to hear Greeks, Italians, English, Dutchmen, and Asiatics, all conversing in their peculiar tongues.

In Petersburg, the Germans are artists and mechanics, particularly taylors and shoemakers; the English, saddlers and merchants; the Italians, architects, singers, and venders of images; but it is difficult to say what the French are. The greater part change their occupation every year: one arrives a lacquey, is made *utschitel* (a tutor), and becomes a counsellor; others have been seen alternately actors, managers, shopkeepers, musicians, and officers. There is no place so convenient as Petersburg for observing how much the Frenchman is inconstant, enterprising, ingenious, and adapted for every thing.

For discerning the manners and customs of each nation distinctly, you must see them in their houses—in the street they all appear like Russians. The French play off their witticisms, sup gaily, and sing some of the vaudevilles, which they have not forgotten: the English dine at five o'clock, drink punch, and talk of commerce: the Italians practise music, dance, make grimaces and gestures, and the subjects of their conversation are the theatres and the arts; in the houses of the Germans, the discourse turns on science, they smoke, dispute, eat heartily, and make abundance of compliments : in the russian houses you have everything indiscrimately, and especially gaming, which is the soul of their parties and pleasures; but it does not exclude any of the other amusements. A foreigner, and particularly a Frenchman, after winding along the inhospitable shores of Prussia, and traversing the wild and uncultivated plains of Livonia, is struck with astonishment and rapture at finding again, in the midst of a vast desert, a large and magnificent city, abounding in the sociality and amusements, the arts and the luxury, which he had supposed to exist no where but in Paris.

In a climate like that of Petersburg, where the fine weather of the whole year scarcely lasts above a few weeks, and under a government like that of Russia, where politics, morals, and literature are excluded from conversation, the pleasures of society must be very contracted, and the enjoyments of domestic life proportionably increased. The luxury, however, and studied conveniences, the splendor and good taste of the apartments, the profusion and delicacies of the table, the cheerfulness and frivolity of the conversation, repay the man of pleasure for the constraint in which nature and the government hold both his body and his mind. Balls and entertainments are given in infinite succession; every day may be a festival to him; and he finds collected in one great house chefs d'œuvres of all the arts, and the productions of every country; and frequently even, in the midst of winter, the gardens, the fruits and the flowers of spring.

Tzarsko-selo is an immense and dreary palace, begun by Anne, finished by Elizabeth, inhabited by Catharine, and forsaken by Paul. Its situation is a swamp, the country round it a desert, and the gardens are uniformly dull. The monuments with which it has been adorned by Catharine, like the buildings at Petersburg, are so many emblems of her character. By the side of obelisks, rostral columns and triumphal arches erected to the Orlofs, Romanzofs, and the russian warriors who subjected the Archipelago, and for a moment reconquered Lacedemon, are seen tombs consecrated to some of her favourite dogs; and not far from these is the mausoleum erected to the amiable Lanskoï, the most beloved of her favourites, and the only one whom death tore from her embraces. Monuments certainly of very different services, most familiarly placed together. Are we from this to imagine that a dog, a lover, and a hero, are of equal importance in the eyes of an autocrat? These monuments, however, from the neglect to which they are doomed, will shortly disappear in the dreary swamps which serve for their foundation.

The Ægyptians, who set the people they conquered to labour, and the Romans, who stripped every nation to embellish Rome, executed immense works. The Greeks while free distinguished themselves by the taste and elegance, rather than the magnitude of their buildings; and Russia was lately the only state that could undertake those astonishing edifices which we so much admire in antiquity; because in Russia men are slaves, and, as in Ægypt, cost only a few onions. It is for this reason we see in Mosco and Petersburg such gigantic edifices. At the same time there is not so much as a proper highway to unite these two capitals, which are only about two hundred leagues asunder. This also was one of the abortive projects of Catharine; for the road she begun is only an incumbrance, and renders travelling still more tiresome and impracticable than before. But Catharine preferred expending two or three millions of rubles in building a gloomy marble palace for her favourite, to the forming of a road: this latter was too common an undertaking for her genius *.

* Paul, so far from finishing the most useful of those works begun by his mother, as the quays, canals, and high roads,

O Catharine! dazzled by thy greatness, of which I have had an intimate view; charmed with thy beneficence, which rendered so many individuals happy; seduced by the thousand amiable qualities that have been admired in thee, I would fain have erected a monument to thy glory: but the torrents of blood thou hast shed rush in and overthrow it: the chains of thirty millions of slaves ring in my ears, and deafen me; and the crimes which were perpetrated in thy name call forth my indignation. I throw away my pen, and exclaim, " Let there be henceforth no glory " without virtue! Let injustice and depravity be " transmitted with no other wreath to posterity " than the snakes of Nemesis!"

has built, in his turn, churches and palaces, though there were already of both in Petersburg more than enough for all the imperial highnesses in the world, and all the saints of paradise. But the monuments he has erected in greatest number, are houses for military exercise, barracks, guard-houses, and particularly centry boxes. Happily, however, all these constructions are of wood, and will hardly outlast their founder.

CHAP. III.

OF THE FAVOURITES.

Their office made a distinct place at court—The Empress's generosity in this point—Installation of Zubof—List of the twelve who enjoyed in succession the title of favourite—Little Hermitage—Little Society.

ELIZABETH of England, Mary of Scotland, Christina of Sweden, all the empresses of Russia, and most women who have been their own mistresses, have had favourites or lovers. To consider this as a crime might be thought too rigid and ungallant. Catharine II. alone, however, availed herself of her power to exhibit to the world an example, of which there is to be found no model, by making the office of favourite a place at court, with an apartment, salary, honours, prerogatives, and, above all, its peculiar functions; and of all places there was not one, the duties of which were so scrupulously fulfilled: a short absence, a temporary sickness of the person by whom it was occupied, was sometimes sufficient to occasion his removal. Nor perhaps was there any post, in which the august sovereign displayed more choice and discernment: I believe no instance occurred of its having been filled by a person incapable of it; and, except the interregnum between Lanskoï and Yermolof, it was never twenty-four hours vacant.

Twelve favourites succeeded each other in this post, which became the first of the state. Several of these favourites, confining themselves to the principal duty it prescribed, and having little merit, except the performing that duty well, had scarcely any influence beyond the immediate sphere of their peculiar department. Some, however, displaying ambition, audacity, and, above all, self-sufficiency, obtained vast influence, and preserved an ascendancy over the mind of Catharine after having lost her heart; while others continued to retain her friendship and gratitude, and when dismissed from their personal attendance on the empress, were thought worthy of serving the empire in public offices.

It is a very remarkable feature in the character of Catharine, that none of her favourites incurred her hatred or her vengeance, though several of them offended her, and their quitting their office did not depend on herself. No one was ever punished, no one ever persecuted. Those whom she discarded went into foreign countries, to display her presents, and dissipate her treasures, after which they returned, to enjoy her liberalities with tranquillity in the bosom of their country, though their formidable mistress could have crushed them in a moment. In this respect Catharine certainly appears superior to all other women. Was it from greatness of mind, or from defect of passion? Perhaps she never knew what it was to be in love; perhaps she still respected in her lovers the favours with which she had honoured them.

Soltikof, Orlof, and Lanskoï, were all of whom she was deprived by death; the rest surviving her love, though they might have exposed her weaknesses, still possessed quietly such places or wealth as rendered them objects of envy to the whole empire. She contented herself with dismissing Korsakof, whom she surprised even in her own apartments with one of her maids of honour; and she resigned Momonof to a young rival. Assuredly these are very extraordinary features, and very rare, in a woman, a lover, an empress. This great and generous conduct is very distant from that of an Elizabeth of England, who cut off the heads of her favourites and her rivals; and from that of a Christina of Sweden, who caused one of her lovers to be assassinated in her presence.

But Catharine, with all that superior sense and understanding which she evinced, notwithstanding the exterior decency she affected, must have thoroughly known and despised the Russians, since she ventured so frequently to place beside her young men taken from the crowd, and hold them up to receive the respect and homage of the whole nation, without any other title to this distinction than one for which she ought to have blushed.

It will be sufficient to relate how Zubof, her last favourite, was installed, to shew my indignant readers in what manner these affairs were managed.

Plato * Zubof was a young lieutenant in the horse-guards, patronised by Nicholas Soltikof, to whom he was a distant relation, and to whom my friend, who furnished me with part of these memoirs, was at that time aide-de-camp. In this post he frequently found himself by the side of Zubof, and even sought this advantage at table. Zubof spoke french fluently; he had some education, was of a polite and pliant disposition, could converse a little on literary subjects, and practised music. He was of a middle size, but supple, muscular, and well made. He had a high and intelligent forehead, with fine eyes, and his countenance had not that downcast, cold, and supercilious air, which it afterwards assumed. When the empress went to Tzarsko-selo, in the spring of 1789,

* This name led the courtiers to say, that Catharine ended with platonic love.

he solicited from his patron the favour of being appointed to command the detachment that attended her; and, having obtained it, dined with Catharine. The court had scarcely arrived, before the rupture with Momonof took place. This favourite was married and dismissed. Zubof was the only young officer in sight; and it appears that he was indebted rather to this fortunate circumstance, than to the deliberate choice of Catharine, for the preference he obtained. Potemkin being absent, Nicholas Soltikof, at that time in high credit, introduced and served the young Zubof with so much the more zeal, as he hoped to find in him a support against the haughty Potemkin, of whom he was the only contemner at court. After some secret conferences in presence of the Mentor*, Zubof was approved, and sent for *more ample information* to Mademoiselle Protassof and the empress's physician†. The account they gave must have been favourable, since he was named aide-de-camp to the empress, received a present of an hundred thousand rubles (20,000l.) to furnish himself with linen, and was installed in the apartment of the favourites with all the customary advantages.

* He was governor to the grand-dukes, and minister at war.
† Mademoiselle Protassof was commonly called *l'eprouveuse*, from her functions.

The next day, this young man was seen familiarly offering his arm to his sovereign, equipped in his new uniform, with a large hat and feather on his head, attended by his patron and the great men of the empire, who walked behind him with their hats off, though the day before he had danced attendance in their antichambers.

In the evening, after her card-party was over, Catharine was seen to dismiss her court, and retire, accompanied only with her favourite: sometimes her son and her grandsons were present.

Next day the antichambers of the new idol were filled with aged generals, and ministers of long service, all bowing the knee before him. He was a genius discerned by the piercing eye of Catharine: the treasures of the empire were lavished on him, and the conduct of the empress was sanctioned by the meanness and shameful assiduities of her courtiers *.

Perhaps the reader may have some curiosity to peruse a list of those who enjoyed the title of favourite to Catharine, and who reigned over

* Zubof being one day hunting, stopped with his suite on the road from Petersburg to Tzarsko-selo. The courtiers who were going to court, the couriers, the post, all carriages, and all the peasants, were stopped: no one daring to pass till the young man thought proper to quit the road; and he staid there more than an hour, waiting for his game.

Russia with various degrees of authority in the name of their august lover.

1. SERGIUS SOLTIKOF.

It is whispered that he received Catharine's first favours when she was only grand-duchess; a happiness said to have been denied by nature to the unfortunate Peter III. Soltikof, beloved and happy, grew indiscreet, and excited jealousy. Elizabeth civilly banished him from court, and he died in exile *.

2. STANISLAUS PONIATOFSKY

soon occasioned him to be forgotten. He was at that time envoy from Poland at Petersburg. Handsome, gallant, and lively, he engaged the affections of the young Catharine. Peter III. sometimes interrupted them, though he was little addicted to jealousy, and preferred his pipe, his bottle, his soldiers, and his mistress, to his lovely wife. It is well known that Catharine, when seated on the imperial throne, rewarded

* Soltikof had all the wit, the agreeable qualities, and the vanity of a young russian nobleman. He was the only one of Catharine's favourites selected from a powerful family. Her heart was not at that time guided by her politics.

her lover with the crown of Poland. His disastrous reign evinced, that love, in bestowing a crown, is as blind, as favour in distributing places and honours. Stanislaus was the most amiable of men, but the weakest of kings. How has it been possible that so pusillanimous a being should for a moment have gained the esteem of Europe? Yet by whom was he not admired? What contradiction between his sentiments, his language, and his conduct! at the last diet, the generous nuncio Kamar said to him publicly on perceiving him waver, " What, sir! are you no " longer the same who said to us, when signing " the constitution of the 3d of May, ' May my " hand perish rather than subscribe anything " contrary to this?' All Europe charges you " with being Catharine's king: justify her at " least for having put the sceptre into your hand, " by showing that you are capable of wielding " it*." Yet, only a few days after, the unworthy Stanislaus signed that compact which

* This brave Pole was interrupted in the midst of this spirited speech, and carried off by the russian satellites Rothenfeld and Pistor, worthy counterparts of the barbarous Kretschetnikof and Kakofsky. Heavens! what names! yet they who bore them were still more rugged: and these were the two men who conquered Poland in one campaign, and overturned the constitution of the 3d of May, which all the nation seemed to defend! Koschiusko! where wert thou at the time?

dismembered Poland for the second time; and by which he formally acknowledged himself factious and rebellious, in establishing a rational constitution, which gave him, as a king, more authority, and promised his nation more happiness and freedom*. If at this period he had at least abdicated his dignity, he would have excited some concern. He had not the resolution either to remain a king, or to cease from being one: he had not even the wit and pride of Harlequin, who, when his pursuers are struggling to get from him his wooden sword, and he can defend it no longer, throws it on the ground, saying, " There, take it!" Stanislaus chose rather to drag on an old age of disgrace, and go and die at Petersburg in a state of humiliation †.

* It was not, however, without reluctance, that he signed. He said to Sievers, who conjured him to repair to Grodno to head the confederates, " I will never be guilty of such baseness. Let the empress take back her crown: let her send me to Siberia, or let me quit my kingdom on foot, with my staff in my hand—but I will not sully my honour." He was confined, kept fasting, threatened, and then placed himself at the head of the confederacy. It was colonel Stackelberg, nephew of Igelstrœm, who finally brought him the treaty of partition. Stanislaus, on reading it, burst into tears, and said, " O sir, have mercy on me! let me not be forced to sign my own disgrace!" Stackelberg told him, that after this sacrifice he might enjoy a happy and tranquil old age. Wiping his eyes, he replied, " Well, I will hope so;" but his niece entering he again wept bitterly with her.

† At one of those court ceremonies in which Paul amuses himself in strutting about with the sceptre in his hand, the

Of all the favourites of Catharine, Stanislaus was the only one whom she took pleasure in humbling, after having exalted. Fidelity and patriotism, which appeared for an instant to contend with gratitude and submission in the heart of the king, were crimes in the eye of the haughty tzaritza. She was indulgent in love, but implacable in politics: ambition was her ruling passion, yet she always made the lover subservient to the empress.

3. GREGORY ORLOF,

who enjoyed such long and distinguished favour, and whose history is so intimately connected with that of Catharine, seemed to share in the throne on which he had placed her[*]. He en-

---

crown on his head, and the imperial mantle on his back, as the jewish kings are represented in the old tapestry, Stanislaus, who was in his train, bending under age and fatigue, was obliged to sit down in a corner while three or four hundred court-slaves were kissing the hand of Paul. The emperor perceiving that the old king had seated himself during this august ceremony, sent an aide-de-camp to him, to order him to keep on his legs.

[*] If no mention be made of the revolution of 1762 in these Memoirs, it is because Europe is sufficiently acquainted with it from the history left by Rhulières, which agrees in every point with what is universally known and believed at present. I have repeatedly heard the particulars in Russia from persons who were actors in the business, and they were very nearly the same with those which I have since read in Rhulières.

joyed all the power and honours united, which were afterwards seen to adorn Potemkin and burden Zubof. He had much of the haughtiness and firmness of Potemkin. Though he was young and robust, his brother Alexius, a Hercules in strength and a Goliath in stature *, was associated with him in his office. The empress was then in the bloom of life. She had an acknowledged son by Gregory, who was named Vasily Gregorievitch Bobrinsky, and educated in the corps of cadets; admiral Ribas, then tutor to that corps, being afterwards appointed his governor †. Two pretty maids of honour, whom

* It was this Alexius Orlof, who, with Passek and Baratinsky, was concerned in strangling Peter III. He afterwards made himself famous by his expedition to the Archipelago, and particularly by the battle of Tchesmè, from which he received the surname of Tchesminsky. His infamy in carrying off from Italy a daughter of the empress Elizabeth*, served to render him completely odious and execrable, in spite of his surreptitious laurels. He is at present banished to Germany, where he vainly endeavours to obtain consequence by his luxury and expensive manner of living, and is universally avoided and detested.

† This Bobrinsky strongly resembles his mother in the face, and whoever sees the head of Catharine on a ruble, beholds the likeness of her son. He has distinguished himself by his disorderly life, though he has sense, and is not void of information. He was banished to Esthonia, but Paul recalled him at his accession, and made him a major in the horse-guards. Not long after, however, he fell into disgrace.

* See Life of Catharine II. vol. ii. p. 55, 56, 57—62.

madame Protassof, first lady of the bed-chamber, educated as her nieces, are likewise reputed to be Catharine's daughters by Orlof. It was for this celebrated favourite she erected the gloomy marble palace, the inscription on which informed all the world that it was erected by grateful friendship. In honour of him likewise she ordered a large medal to be struck, on occasion of the journey he took to Mosco to re-establish order, and being particularly instrumental in stopping the dreadful ravages of the plague. On this medal he is represented as Curtius, leaping into the gulf, with this inscription: *Russia too can boast such sons.* The palace of Gatshina, now inhabited by Paul, is another monument to prince Orlof. Twelve years intimacy, added to the haughtiness of this lover, at length wearied his sovereign, now firmly established on the throne; and, after a long contest, Potemkin bore away the laurel. The triumph of his rival, and the inconstancy of Catharine, whom he openly accused of ingratitude, had such an effect on him, that his health was destroyed, his mind deranged, and the once proud, powerful, and magnificent Orlof died in the most horrible state of insanity and human infirmity*.

---

* It is pretended by some that Potemkin poisoned him with a herb, which possesses the quality of turning the brain, and which the Russians call *piannia trava,* "the intoxicating "plant."

4. VASSILTSCHIKOF,

whom Panin introduced during an absence of Orlof, filled up the interval that took place between the two haughty rivals. He was merely the instrument of Catharine's pleasures.

5. POTEMKIN

came one day, and boldly took possession of the apartments of his predecessor; thus proclaiming his victory, by making himself master of the field of battle, so long disputed with him. His love, his valour, and his colossal stature, had charmed the heart of Catharine. He was the only one of her favourites who dared become enamoured of her, and to make the first advances. He seemed to be truly and romantically captivated by her*.

---

* There is a russian song of his extant, beginning *K'ak skora ya tébè vidal,* &c. which he composed when first in love. It breathes sentiment, and deserves to be translated. The following is the sense of what I recollect of it: " As soon as " I beheld thee, I thought of thee alone: thy lovely eyes cap- " tivated me, yet I trembled to say I loved. To thee, love " subjects every heart, and enchains them with the same " flowers. But, O heavens! what torment, to love one to " whom I dare not declare it! one who can never be mine! " Cruel fate! why have you given her such charms? or why " did you exalt her so high? Why did you destine me to " love her, and her alone? her, whose sacred name will " never pass my lips, whose charming image will never quit " my heart!" &c.

He first adored his sovereign as the object of his passion, and then cherished her as that of his glory. These two great characters seemed formed for each other: their affection was mutual; and when they ceased to love, they still continued to esteem each other: when emancipated by love, they were still united by policy and ambition.

I leave to travellers the office of describing the pomp of his entertainments, the laborious luxury of his house, and the value of his diamonds; and to german scribblers, to relate how many bank-notes he had bound up as books in his library, and what he paid for the cherries, a plate of which he was accustomed to present every new year's day to his august sovereign; or the cost of his sterlet-soup, which was his favourite dish; or how many hundred miles he would send a courier for a melon, or a nosegay, to present to one of his mistresses *. They who wish to see a cha-

* Potemkin had in his suite an officer of high rank, named Bauer, whom he sent sometimes to Paris for a dancer, then to Astrakhan for a water-melon; now to Poland, to carry orders to his tenants; to Petersburg, to deliver news to Catharine; or to the Krimea, to gather grapes. This officer, who thus spent his life travelling post, requested an epitaph to be ready for him in case he should break his neck, and one of his friends gave him the following:

    Cy git Bauer sous ce rocher:
     Fouette, cocher!
   " Here Bauer lies, beneath this stone !
    " Coachman, drive on !"

racteristic portrait of him, may find one drawn in a superior manner in the work intitled *Life of Catharine* II.*; as to relate all the particulars of Potemkin's life would carry me too far.

He created, destroyed, or confused, yet animated everything. When absent, he alone was the subject of conversation; when present, he engaged every eye. The nobles, who detested him, and who made some figure when he was at the army, seemed at his sight to sink into the earth, and to be annihilated before him. The prince de Ligne, who wrote flatteries and tales to him †, said, "There is something gigantic, "romantic, and barbaric, in his character:" and it was true. His death left an immense vacuity in the empire, and that death was as extraordinary as his life. He had spent nearly a year at Petersburg, rioting in all kinds of pleasure and even debauchery, negligent of his fame, and displaying his wealth and influence with insulting pomp. He received the greatest men of the em-

---

* In three volumes, 8vo. printed for Longman and Rees, Paternoster Row.

† He told him, in one of his letters, which the prince's vanity induced him to make no secret: "Your august and "amiable sovereign is indebted to you for more marks of gal- "lantry than Louis XIV. was to all his courtiers together." The duke de la Feuillade, however, erected a superb statue to his master at his own expense. Potemkin never paid Catharine a compliment equal to this.

pire as though they were his footmen, scarcely deigned to notice the *little Paul*, and sometimes entered Catharine's apartments with his legs bare, his hair about his ears, and in a morning gown. Old marshal Repnin availed himself of his absence from the army to beat the Turks, and force them to sue for a peace, accomplishing more in two months than Potemkin had done in three years. The latter, who wished still to prolong the war, was roused at the news, and set off*; but he carried death in his veins. Being arrived at Yassy, where his head-quarters had long been established, or, to speak more properly, his capital and his court, he became gloomy, melancholy, a prey to vexation, and impatient under his disease. He determined to struggle with it, and overcome it by his iron constitution; laughing at his physicians, and

---

* His interview with Repnin was a curious scene: " You little martinist priest (1)," said he, " how dared you undertake so many things in my absence? Who gave thee any such orders?" Repnin, enraged at this speech, and emboldened by success, dared for once to behave to him with firmness. " I have served my country," he answered: " my head is not at thy disposal, and thou art a devil whom I defy." Saying this, he flung out of the room in a rage, shutting the door on Potemkin, who followed him with his clenched fist. The two heroes of Russia were within an ace of going to loggerheads.

(1) Repnin is a zealous apostle of martinism.

eating salt meat and raw turnips. His disease grew worse: he would be conveyed to Otchakof, his beloved conquest; but he had scarcely advanced a few versts, before the air of his carriage seemed to stifle him. His cloak was spread by the road-side; he was laid on it, and there expired in the arms of his niece Branicka, who accompanied him. Catharine fainted three times on hearing of his death: it was found necessary to bleed her: she was thought to be dying; and she expressed almost as much grief as at the death of Lanskoï. But it was not the lover she regretted; it was the friend, whose genius was assimilated with her own, whom she considered as the stay of her throne, and the executor of her vast projects. Catharine, holding an usurped sceptre, and hated by her son, was a woman, and consequently timid: she was accustomed to behold in Potemkin a protector, whose fortune and glory were closely allied with her own. She appeared to feel herself again a stranger; she began to dread her son, and now leant for support on her grandson Alexander, who was just rising out of infancy, and began to oppose him to his father.

What a contrast, what a lesson, does the death of the three greatest personages in Russia offer! Orlof, who reigned twelve years by the side of

Catharine, died in a state of deplorable insanity. Potemkin, the powerful, the magnificent Potemkin, the founder of so many palaces and cities, the conqueror of a kingdom, expired by the wayside; and Catharine herself fell down in her water-closet, and died on the floor with a lamentable shriek!

The wealth of Potemkin has been exaggerated: it was far short of that of Mentchikof, and still farther of what the unworthy Biren amassed. Even the last favourite is in possession of more. It is true Potemkin drew immediately from the imperial coffers; but he also spent a great deal for the empire, and shewed himself as much grand-prince of Russia as the favourite of Catharine. Zubof had equal command over the public treasury, and never expended a ruble for the public.

What distinguishes Potemkin from all his colleagues is, that after losing the heart of the empress, he still retained her entire confidence. Ambition succeeded love in his breast, and preserving the same unbounded influence, every succeeding favourite was appointed by him, and remained subordinate to him.

6. ZAVADOFSKY

was the man whom Potemkin presented to Catharine, to succeed in fulfilling the office of private favourite. He was young, athletic, and well made; but Catharine's inclination for him was soon at an end. He had been secretary: his disgrace made no noise; he continued to be employed in the affairs of the cabinet, and was appointed a privy counsellor. He is still living, rich with the former bounties of his mistress.

7. ZORITCH,

on whom the inconstant Catharine next cast her eye, is the only foreigner whom she ventured to create favourite during her reign. He was a Servian, who had been taken prisoner by the Turks, and made his escape from Constantinople, where he was confined as a slave. He appeared at court for the first time in the dress of a hussar. His beauty dazzled every eye, and the old ladies in Russia still speak of him as an Adonis. Protected at first by Potemkin, he wished to shake off his yoke, quarrelled with him, and challenged him to a duel. His mind was not sufficiently cultivated to captivate that of Catharine, who dismissed him at the end of twelve months loaded with favours. He obtained the town of Schklof, which was erected into a kind of sovereignty for him, the only instance of the kind in Russia. There he lives as a prince, holding a court and receiving strangers. If he be enriched with the spoils of the country, he returns part of them very nobly. He has founded at Schklof a corps of cadets, where two hundred young officers are educated at his expense. Notwithstanding these occupations, his gaming, his theatrical exhibitions, and other amusements which he follows to his ruin, he is tired of his principality. Some years ago he is said to have solicited permission to make his appearance at Petersburg: it was not granted. Paul, however, has just called him to court.

8. KORSAKOF,

a sort of russian fop, was raised to the rank of favourite from that of serjeant of the guards at the palace, where Catharine noticed him. He was either faithless or ungrateful. Catharine herself surprised him in the arms of the handsome countess Bruce, her maid of honour and confidant. Struck with astonishment she withdrew, and would never again see her lover or her friend. This was all the revenge she took.

9. LANSKOI,

of the horse-guards, had already drawn some attention[*]. He was soon the most beloved of Catharine's lovers, and seemed the most worthy of being so. He was handsome, graceful, and accomplished, an admirer of the arts, a friend to talents, humane, and beneficent. Every one seemed to take an interest in the sovereign's predilection for him. Perhaps he might have acquired as much influence by the qualities of his mind, as those of his heart procured him partisans. Potemkin feared him; and, from the circumstance of his dying with horrible pains in his bowels, it was pretended that he gave him poison. Catharine in vain lavished on him the most tender cares: her lips received his last breath. She shut herself up for several days, which she passed in all the violence of grief. She accused heaven, would die, would cease to reign, and swore never to

[*] All the officers who had, or thought they had, fine persons, endeavoured on every occasion to throw themselves in Catharine's way. Even at court, the nobles would sometimes give place to a handsome man, knowing that nothing pleased their sovereign so well as to traverse her apartments between two rows of handsome youths. It was a situation which men eagerly sought after, and exhibited themselves to the greatest advantage; and, indeed, many families founded their hopes on some young relation, whom they strove to bring forward in this way.

love again. She really loved Lanskoï, and her affliction turned into rage against the physician, who could not save him, and who was obliged to throw himself at his sovereign's feet, to implore her pardon for the impotence of his art. A decent and afflicted widow, she went into mourning for her lover, and, like another Artemisia, erected for him a superb mausoleum in the gardens of Tzarsko-selo. She suffered more than a year to elapse before she filled his place; but, like a second ephesian matron, she gave him an unworthy successor. This was

10. YERMOLOF,

the least amiable, and least striking in figure of all she had chosen, who at length consoled her for the handsome, the tender Lanskoï. He displeased Potemkin, however, before he ceased to please Catharine; and the haughty prince demanded, and obtained, the dismissal of this favourite, who was in office not quite two years.

11. MOMONOF,

who had disputed the place with Yermolof, succeeded to it. Momonof was amiable, and his bust was a perfect model; but downwards he was not well made. Catharine approved and loved him, and would have done so long; but he was soon disgusted with the faded charms of a mistress of threescore.

He became enamoured of the young princess Scherbatof, and had the courage to avow it, demanding permission to marry her. Catharine had pride and generosity sufficient to grant his request, without any reproaches. She saw him married at court to the object of his honourable attachment, and sent him to Mosco loaded with presents.

12. ZUBOF.

The rise of this last favourite has been explained at the beginning of this chapter. He was not quite five and twenty, and the empress upwards of sixty *. She finished by treating him as much like a son as a lover, took upon herself the care of his education, and grew more and more attached to her own work, which became her idol. Yet even at this advanced period of her life she revived the orgies and lupercalia, which she had

* Catharine was two years older than the almanac expressed. As she was older than Peter III. Elizabeth graciously took off these two years when she sent for her into Russia; and there are old german calendars, which prove that she was born in 1727. This is but an opinion, however, which several dispute, and which I have it not in my power to ascertain.

formerly celebrated with the brothers Orlof. Valerian, a younger brother of Zubof, and Peter Soltikof, their friend, were associated in office with the favourite. With these three young libertines did Catharine, the aged Catharine, spend her days, while her armies were slaughtering the Turks, cutting throats with the Swedes, and ravaging Poland; while her people were groaning in wretchedness and famine, and devoured by extortioners and tyrants.

It was at this juncture she formed a more intimate society, composed of her favourites, and most trusty ladies and courtiers. This society met two or three times a week, under the name of the little hermitage. The parties were frequently masqued, and the greatest privacy prevailed. They danced, represented proverbs, played at little games with forfeits, joked, romped, and in short there was no kind of gaiety which was not permitted. Leof Narishkin acted the same part there as Roquelaure at the court of Louis XIV; and that egregious fool Matrona Danilovna, seconded him. This was an old gossip, whose wit entirely consisted in uttering the most absurd vulgarities; and as she enjoyed the common right of fools, that of saying anything, she was loaded with presents by the lower order of courtiers. Such foreign ministers as were in favour with the empress, were sometimes admitted to the little hermitage.' Segur, Cobenzel, Steding, and Nassau, chiefly enjoyed this distinction; but Catharine afterwards formed another assembly, more confined and more mysterious, which was called the small party. The three favourites just mentioned, Madame Branicka, Madame Protassof, and some confidential women, and valets-de-chambre, were its only members.

I might have enlarged this chapter with the surnames, titles, and dignities of each favourite; but they would not be worth printing, as not deserving even to be mentioned. It is sufficiently known that Catharine, after having heaped upon her minions all the places, titles and orders of knighthood in Russia, wrote to Vienna to obtain for them successively patents of count and prince of the holy roman empire. The orders of Poland and Prussia bedaubed also the favourites of the favourites. Potemkin and Zubof, when they displayed all their decorations, looked like the hawkers of ribands and trinkets at a fair.

Paul is more russian than his mother: being of opinion, that a count or prince of the holy greek empire is superior to a count or prince of the holy roman empire. Under Catharine, the russian kniaz was made a german prince; under Paul, the german prince is raised to the dignity of a russian kniaz. I shall not take upon me to decide the question of precedence.

In like manner I shall pass over the gifts and presents bestowed on the favourites. I could mention only what they have received publicly as recompenses; and however enormous the sum may appear*, it was not equal to the gifts lavished on them in secret. Who can calculate what the Orlofs, Potemkin, and the Zubofs received? Had they not the imperial treasury at command, without giving any account of the sums they took out? and were not places, rank, justice, impunity, nay, even foreign alliances, peace and war, purchased of them and of their creatures †?

* I have a pretty accurate list: the sum is greater by one third than that given in the *Histoire de Catharine II*.

† Valerian Zubof, a few months after he had shared with his brother the favours of Catharine, staked thirty thousand rubles (3000l.) on a single card at faro; and this young man possesses, as has been observed, part of the immense domains of the dukes of Courland.

CHAP. IV.

ACCESSION OF PAUL.

Conduct and projects of Catharine with regard to her son—He is proclaimed—His first steps as Emperor—Funeral honours paid to his father and mother—Rigorous proceedings towards the guards—The wacht-parade—Graces and disgraces—His occupations—Proscription of round hats and russian harness—Re-establishment of etiquette—Its ridiculous or cruel consequences—Alterations in the army, and in the civil department—Peasants—Soldato-mania—Office of punishment—Finances—A valet-de-chambre becomes favourite.

ONE of the greatest crimes of which Catharine was guilty, was her conduct to that son in whose right she governed Russia five-and-thirty years. In his infancy he evinced qualities which were stifled by her ill treatment. He had sense, activity, a disposition for the sciences, and sentiments of order and justice: but all these perished for want of cultivation. Her dislike towards him has been urged as a proof of his being the son of Peter III. and this proof is of considerable weight *. She could not bear him, kept him at

* It is an opinion generally adopted at the court of Russia, that Paul is the son of count Soltikof, one of the earliest favourites of Catharine. He has no physical resemblance to Peter III. and is still more unlike his mother. He had the ill luck to be disowned by one and detested by the other.

a distance from her, surrounded him with spies, held him in restraint, exposed him to every kind of humiliation; and while her favourites, inferior to her son in years, governed Russia and wallowed in wealth, he was living retired, insignificant, and in want of necessaries. Thus she soured his temper, and rendered him capricious and mistrustful, savage and cruel. Assuredly a mother must be highly culpable who inspires her own child with hatred and contempt. But what other sentiments could he entertain? Not satisfied with depriving him of the affection and the prerogatives that he ought to have enjoyed as a son, she resolved to take from him likewise the rights and pleasures of a father. His wife came almost every year to lie in at Tzarsko-selo, and left her children there in the hands of strangers. They were brought up under Catharine; neither the father nor mother having the least concern in their education, or authority over their conduct. Latterly, they were even whole months without seeing them. Thus she strove to alienate the hearts of these children from parents whom they scarcely knew. Here, however, Paul ceases to inspire interest; here he no longer appears the timid and respectful child, but the fearful, imbecil father. What man is base enough not to claim the sacred rights of paternity? Why had he not the spirit to say to his mother, "You have my crown;

" keep it; but restore me my children: leave me
" at least an enjoyment which you do not deny to
" your meanest slaves." He who finds not in his heart sufficient motives to hold such language, and to act conformably to it, deserves not praise as a respectful son, but rather blame as a contemptible, unfeeling father*: he is a slave; and on becoming master, cannot fail of being a tyrant.

Death took Catharine by surprise. It is evident to those who were acquainted with her court, and the unfortunate estrangement between the mother and son, that she entertained a wish to have another successor. The dread of reflecting on the period of her days, and on that of her reign, which she feared still more, together with the death of Potemkin †, prevented her from accomplishing this project, while she had time for it, or from confirming it by a will. The youth of the grand-duke Alexander, and especially the excellence of his head and heart, were afterwards

---

* The duke of Wurtemburg, brother to the present empress, acted in a more becoming manner. Catharine being desirous of taking charge of his children, he declared that he would rather die than give them up. She durst not venture to proceed to extremities, and he took them with him out of the country.

† It is thought by many that she entertained a design of making Potemkin king of Taurida, in order to have his support in disinheriting Paul, and proclaiming Alexander heir to the crown.

obstacles to the execution of her design. Her predilection for the young prince, however, worthy no doubt of a purer source, was very striking; and her private conferences with him began to be frequent and mysterious. Perhaps she might in time have succeeded in her endeavours to stifle in him the voice of nature, have corrupted his understanding and his morals, and driven him imperceptibly to act a detestable part towards his father. After l'Harpe had quitted him, after a separate court was established for him, and some persons of merit removed; he was the worst attended and least occupied of princes. His days were spent alone with his wife, or with his valets, or in the society of his grandmother. He lived more effeminate and obscure than the heir of a sultan in the harams of the seraglio. This kind of life would infallibly at length have stifled all his excellent qualities. Had he been willing, or had Catharine but been able to speak one word before she died, Paul probably would never have reigned. Who would have declared for him? and to what rights could he have appealed *? If

* I am aware that Paul was proclaimed heir to the throne though his birth is so equivocal. Since his accession, he has attempted to remove the confusion that prevails in the succession of the tzars, by an act which he promulgated at his coronation, and which he had framed in concert with his wife, in the form of a will, so early as the year 1788; consequently when he was only grand-duke, and of course could dispose of

the russians have no fixed rights, still less have their sovereigns. Since Peter I. who arrogated to himself the power of nominating his successor, the throne of the tzars has been occupied by scarcely any other than usurpers, who have overturned each other with more barbarity and confu-

nothing. The year 1788 was the time when Potemkin was in the zenith of his power. It appears that Paul, at that juncture, apprehended some unhappy catastrophe, since he made these arrangements: in fact, it was then in agitation to disinherit him, and divide the empire between his eldest son and Potemkin.—In this act, Paul, though merely grand-duke, arrogates to himself the same right as Peter I. that of nominating his successor. Accordingly he bequeaths the empire to his eldest son, and his male descendants; on failure of these his female descendants were to succeed in an order which Paul laid down, endeavouring to prevent and adjust all the inconveniences that may happen to the end of time.— That the son should be heir to his father is a natural right, but there can be no right by which an emperor shall nominate his successor, and bequeath an empire like a field. Let us suppose, however, that this power has been, *by the grace of God*, conferred on the russian autocrates, how can one take it from the rest, or restrict it, by nominating the successor of his successor? Is not Alexander or Constantine to enjoy the same power as Paul? Is it not treasonable to imagine the contrary? Such are the inconveniences in which they involve themselves who build upon errors and prejudices, and contemn the laws of nature and nations. The laws which issue from their brains having no support but the power that promulgates them, perish with it. A hundred years hence a russian emperor will not tumble over the old papers of Paul, to know how he shall act; for before that time, perhaps, events may take place which will bring the Russians to adopt ideas more clear and simple.

sion than the successors of Ottoman. Catharine I. became empress, because Mentchikof had the boldness to proclaim her *; Peter II. reigned by virtue of a will; Anne was elected by a council, the senate, and the army; Ivan was made emperor by an ukase; Elizabeth said, in her manifesto, that she ascended the throne of her father because the people willed it, and the guards were revolting; and on these grounds she condemned a prince in the cradle to a perpetual prison; and his relations, as innocent as himself, experienced the same fate. Peter III. reigned by favour of Elizabeth; and when he was dethroned by Catharine II. she, on mounting the throne of Russia, declared, that it was God himself who called her to it. A son supplanting his father would not have added greatly to the horror excited by these acts of despotism: but the sudden death of Catharine happily prevented that catastrophe. The horrid shriek she gave as she expired, was the dreadful sound that proclaimed Paul emperor of all the Russias. His wife was the first who fell at his feet, and paid him homage with all her children: he raised her up, embracing her and

* It was pleasantly said on that occasion, that a journeyman pastry-cook proclaimed a servant-maid empress of all the Russias. See what it is to be proud of their birth! Mary, conceiving the houses of Holstein and Wurtemburg not good enough, makes her daughters sign themselves *Romanof!*

them, and giving them assurance of his imperial and paternal kindness. The court, the chief officers of the different departments and of the army, all who were on the spot, came next to prostrate themselves, and take the oath of allegiance severally according to rank and seniority. A detachment of guards conducted him into the palace, and the officers and soldiers arriving in haste from Pavlofsky and Gatshina, swore fealty to him; as did the heads of the different colleges. The emperor repaired himself to the senate to receive it, and that memorable night passed without disturbance or confusion.*

The next day, Paul was proclaimed emperor everywhere, and the *tzarevitch* Alexander, heir presumptive to the throne. Thus, after five-and-thirty years spent under restraint, denials, injuries, and contempt, the son of Catharine, at the age of forty-three, found himself at length his own master, and that of all the Russias. His first steps seemed to contradict the reports of his stern and capricious disposition. He had long suffered by the abuses and disorders of the court: bred in the school of misfortune, the crucible in which great minds are refined, and little ones evaporate; a distant spectator of affairs, the scrutator of the plans and conduct of his mother, he had had thirty years of leisure to regulate his own. Accordingly he seemed to have in his pocket a multitude of regulations ready drawn up, which he only pulled out and put in execution with astonishing rapidity *.

Far from imitating the conduct which his mother had held with respect to him, he immediately called his sons about him, entrusted each with the command of one of the regiments of guards, and made the elder military governor of Petersburg, an important post, which chained the young prince to his father's side. His first behaviour towards the empress, who was pitied for her lot and position, surprised and delighted every one: suddenly changing his conduct towards her, assigning her a considerable revenue, increasing those of his children in proportion, and loading his family with caresses and kindnesses.

His conduct towards the favourite likewise wore every appearance of generosity. He seemed moved at his affliction; and, approving the attachment he shewed to his mother, continued him in his offices in flattering terms; saying, as he delivered to him the cane of command, which is borne by the general aide-de-camp upon duty: " Con-
" tinue to execute those functions about the

* His intimates had long been in possession of his military regulations, which he put in execution at Gatshina and Pavlofsky, and which in a moment became those of all the russian armies.

" corpse of my mother: I hope you will serve
" me as faithfully as you have served her."

The ministers, and the heads of the several departments, were likewise confirmed in their posts in condescending terms; and the most powerful were even promoted, and loaded with additional favours.

The first ukase he issued announced pacific dispositions, and were particularly adapted to attach the nobility to him. A levy of recruits recently ordered by Catharine, which was to take one peasant in every hundred, was suspended and annulled by this ukase. This levy, however, was a few months after renewed.

Every hour, every moment announced some wise alteration, some just punishment, or some merited favour; insomuch that both court and city were struck with astonishment. If the first steps of Paul had not been dictated by policy, fear, and joy, he would have appeared, for three or four hours, to be born to repress abuses and to restore order. People began to imagine that they had all along mistaken his character, and that his long and melancholy pupillage had not entirely depraved it. All men thought themselves happily deceived in their expectations, and the conduct of the grand-duke was at once forgotten in that of the emperor. He soon, however, brought it back to their remembrance.—But let us bestow a few minutes more on the too transient hopes of happiness which he promised to his empire.

The first two political steps taken by Paul inspired confidence, gained the nobility, and suspended two horrible scourges which Catharine, at her death, seemed to have bequeathed to Russia—war, and a public bankruptcy. She had at length resolved to act directly against France, by succouring the emperor of Germany, and attacking Prussia* : and had actually issued orders for raising near a hundred thousand recruits. The coffers of the state being emptied, and assignats multiplied to such a degree, that they were threatened with the same fate as those of France†; she devised the method of doubling her current coin, by giving every piece of money twice its real value. Paul quashed these two disastrous measures, which were already begun to be carried into execution. At the same time he broke off the treaty of subsidy with England which was on the carpet; not that it was his intention, as had been published abroad, to acknowledge the *odious* french republic, but because his imperial pride was, not without reason, above entering

---

* This scheme of Catharine is incontrovertible: she resolved to drive the king of Prussia back to the borders of the Rhine with her cannon. To make him feel the absolute necessity of returning to the coalition, she fomented revolts in Prussia, at Dantzic, and in Silesia.

† At this juncture they fell sixty per cent.

K

into the pay of England like a petty state, by selling the blood of the Russians.

The brave Koschiusko, the last of the Poles, as Philopœmen was the last of the Greeks, was made prisoner of war, as all the world knows, when defending his country and her natural rights against the attacks of foreign oppressors. He was, however, in contempt of all laws and of common sense, detained as a state criminal, though he was always better treated * than Ignatius Pototski, and his other companions in glory and misfortune, who were more rigorously

* He was in the house of the late count Anhalt. For a guard he had a major, who sat at table with him. People were permitted to see him; he had several rooms at his command, and he employed himself in reading, drawing and turning. The colonel, to whom he was conducted as prisoner by the chasseurs, who found him wounded in a swamp, is a young man, a friend of mine, equally brave and humane. He kept a pocket-book of Koschiusko's, which we looked over together. We found in it several notes, in french and italian, taken during a tour in Italy, philosophical observations, extracts from authors, effusions in French verse, and rough draughts of various small compositions. Every thing shewed that the pocket-book had belonged to a man of merit, knowledge, taste, and feeling. There were in it likewise several letters sealed, and addressed to ladies at Warsaw, in the french and polish languages, with sketches of some of the manifestoes he published, all in his own hand-writing. My friend kept this pocket-book as a relic of a celebrated man whom he had admired while forced to fight against him. When he was set at liberty, I suggested to my friend the idea of returning these papers to their owner, and I believe he did so.

confined in the fortress, and at Schlusselburg. Paul was equitable enough to set them all at liberty, and generous enough to go himself to deliver Koschiusko. It was interesting to see this brave man, still sick of his wounds and his sufferings, carried to the palace, where he was introduced to the emperor and empress, to testify his gratitude. He is a little thin person, pale and emaciated: his head was still surrounded with bandages, and his forehead could not be seen: but his mien, his eyes, still brought to remembrance what he dared attempt with such feeble means. He refused the peasants that Paul would have given him in Russia, but accepted a sum of money to go and live independent in another country.*

This circumstance made a great and favourable impression on the public. Unquestionably it did honour to Paul; but, to appreciate his conduct on this occasion, it must be remembered, that Koschiusko had not personally offended him, though he had the empress Catharine. Her son is certainly not more prompt to pardon than she was: Koschiusko is indebted for his liberty only

* America was the place he chose for his residence. When he was in England, on his way thither, a model of him was taken by Miss C. Andras, which is said to be a striking likeness, and from which an elegant whole length engraving has been made by Sharpe.—*Tr.*

to Paul's hatred of his mother, and his affectation of acting contrary to her views in every respect.

The funeral honours to be paid to the empress, were again a fortunate circumstance to engage the mind of Paul; by suspending or interrupting the torrent of new regulations and capricious ordinances continually starting from his head; but, what was not expected of him, he considered it as a filial duty to remove the ashes of his unfortunate father. The name of Peter III, which no one had dared to pronounce for five-and-thirty years, appeared on a sudden at the head of the ceremonial of mourning and interment; wherein the services and funeral honours to be paid to Peter and Catharine, were prescribed at the same time. On reading the *prekase*, one would have supposed that the husband and wife had just departed together. Paul repaired to the convent of Alexander Nefsky, where the body of his father had been deposited. Causing the old monks to shew him the private grave, and open the coffin in his presence, he paid the sad remains that still presented themselves to his eyes, a tribute of respectful and affecting tears*. The coffin was placed on tressels

---

* He took one of the gloves, that still covered the bones of his father's hand, and kissed it several times with tears. O Paul! thou hadst then the heart of a son; sometimes thou hast appeared a good father! What might not have been ex-

in the middle of the church, and the same service was performed over it as over that of Catharine, which was exposed to view on a bed of state in the palace.

Paul then caused enquiry to be made after those officers who were attached to his father at the time of his unhappy catastrophe, and who had since been living in disgrace or unknown at court. Baron Ungern Sternberg, a respectable old man, who had long lived in retirement amid a small circle of friends, and who had not even a wish to be brought forward again upon the stage of the great world, was at once made general in chief, and sent for to the emperor, who ordered him to be ushered into his closet. After accosting him in the most gracious manner, he said, " Have you heard what I am doing for my " father?—" Yes, Sir," answered the old general, " I have heard it with astonishment."— " With astonishment! why? is it not a duty I " had to fulfil? See," continued he, turning to a picture of Peter III. which was already placed in the cabinet*, " I will have him to witness my

pected from thee, if thou hadst had another mother, and a different education!

* All the pictures of Peter III. had been proscribed, both in the imperial palaces and private houses. How Paul contrived to conceal this I cannot tell. Happy, at this period, he who could find one of these portraits in a lumber-room, to which it had been banished; it presently became the chief

"gratitude toward his faithful friends." Saying these words he embraced general Ungern, and invested him with the riband of St. Alexander. The worthy old man, though above being dazzled with this vanity, could not resist so affecting a scene, and retired with his eyes swimming in tears.

Paul then directed him to do duty by his father's body, enjoining him to provide for the ceremony the same uniform that he had worn when aide-de-camp to Peter III. Ungern was lucky enough to find such a one in the possession of an old acquaintance. Paul wished to see and to keep this relic himself, which likewise made the fortune of him who had so well preserved it*.

ornament of his house. The painters of Petersburg could not supply the demand for copies.

* General Ungern Sternberg is a Livonian, and was formerly the friend and comrade of general Melissino. The writer of these memoirs was very intimate with him, which he mentions here, to give more weight to what follows. Ungern was one of those german officers who stood highest in Peter's esteem, and was his aide-de-camp. It was he whom he chose to accompany him in a secret visit to the unfortunate Ivan at Schlusselburg, where he had been confined by Elizabeth, who dethroned him. They found this wretched young man in a dungeon, the window of which admitted but a faint gleam of day, the light being intercepted by piles of wood heaped up in the court. He was in a dirty white jacket with a pair of old shoes on his feet. His hair was very light and cut short like that of a russian slave. He was tolerably well made, and his complexion

Several other officers, and among them the only one who had attempted to make any resistance in favour of Peter III. at the revolution in 1762, had a paleness which shewed that the sun had never shone on his face. He was then upwards of twenty, and had been confined ever since he was fourteen months old; but he had received some impressions and ideas which he still retained. Peter III. affected at his condition, put several questions to him, among the rest, " Who are you?"—" I am the emperor."—" Who put you into prison, then?"—" Vile, wicked " people."—" Would you like to be emperor again?"—" To " be sure: why not? I should then have fine clothes, and " servants to wait upon me."—" But what would you do if " you were emperor?"—" I would cut off the heads of all " those who have wronged me." Peter III. having then asked whence he learned what he told him; he answered, that he had it from the virgin and the angels, and began to enter into long stories of these pretended visions. Though alone, and confined from his infancy, he did not appear terrified at the sight of the emperor and his officers. He examined his dress and weapons with much curiosity and pleasure, as a forward child would have done. The emperor asked him again what he wished for, and he answered in his vulgar russian dialect, " To have more air." Ungern was left some time at Schlusselberg to gain his confidence, and find out whether his apparent imbecility were real or only assumed. He was soon convinced, however, that it was the natural consequence of his mode of life. He gave him, from the emperor, a silk morning gown. Ivan put it on with transports of joy, running about the room, and admiring himself as a savage would have done who had never been dressed before. As all his wishes centred in the requisition of more air, Peter III. sent the plan of a little circular palace, in the centre of which was to be a garden, with orders to have it built for Ivan in the court of the fortress. It was cruel that this act of humanity towards an innocent man

were found out in their retirement, and recalled to court to be loaded with favours.

These particulars are affecting, and do honour to the heart of Paul; but we see clearly from the answer of Ungern, that they astonished every one. They were attributed as much to Paul's opposition to his mother as to his love for his father; and several ascribed this part of his conduct to a politic design of thus proclaiming him for his father, who would not, when alive, acknowledge him for his son. The parade and ostentation with which he caused the sad remains of Peter to be disinterred, and then held up to the admiration of the public, were particularly blamed. The coffin that contained them was crowned*, and removed in great pomp to the palace, to be exhibited there, in a temple constructed for that purpose, by the side of the corpse of Catharine, with which it was afterwards to be conveyed to the citadel. Never till then did the husband and wife rest together in peace. People came with great respect to kiss the coffin of the one, and the cold and livid hand

should have served as a pretext against the unfortunate Peter. He was charged with having intended to build a prison for his wife and son, and this was made a pretext for his own assassination.

* Peter III. had never been crowned, and this was the reason assigned for not burying him in the church of the fortress with the other russian emperors.

of the other; they made a genuflection, and were obliged to descend the steps backwards. The empress, who had been badly embalmed, soon appeared quite disfigured: her hands, eyes, and lower part of her face, were black, blue, and yellow. Those who had seen her only in public, could not know her again; and all the pomp with which she was still surrounded, all the riches that covered her corpse, served only to augment the horror it inspired.

If, by restoring the honours of his father, Paul might be thought to throw disgrace on the memory of his mother, in bringing to mind the scenes which a silence of five-and-thirty years had nearly consigned to oblivion, yet the vengeance he took on some of the assassins of Peter III. possessed a degree of sublimity which was approved by all. The celebrated Alexius Orlof, the conqueror of Tchesmè, once so powerful, remarkable for his gigantic stature and antique dress, and whose age and military honours would have entitled him to respect, if such a man could be respected, was obliged to follow the sad remains of Peter. Every eye was turned upon him, and the performance of this just, but cruel task, must have awakened in him that remorse which his long prosperity had doubtless lulled asleep. As to prince Baratinsky, he durst not appear before Paul, who could never bear his sight, but had fled from Petersburg. Passek, who owed his fortune solely to the same crime, and whose physiognomy, not less brutal than that of Baratinsky, seemed to betray it, was fortunately absent from court, and survived the funeral but a few days.

Such was the good that Paul did in the first days of his reign; and I have collected the whole of it together, lest these instances of reason, justice, and feeling, should be lost and forgotten in the heap of violences, whims, and meannesses with which they were always offuscated, and which I shall now proceed to relate.

The guards, that dangerous body who had overturned the throne of the father, and who had long considered the accession of the son as the term of its military existence, was, from the very first day, by a bold and vigorous step, rendered incapable of injuring him, and treated without the least management. Paul incorporated in the different regiments of guards his battalions that arrived from Gatshina*, the officers

* Paul waited for these battalions with evident impatience and anxiety. They marched all night, and arrived in the morning. Ratikof, a subaltern, who had no other merit than the good fortune of announcing to him their wished-for arrival, was instantly created a knight of St. Anne, and made aide-de-camp to the grand-duke. It was not till Paul saw himself surrounded with his little army, that he began to act as he had done at Gatshina.

of which he distributed among the various companies, promoting them at the same time two or three steps; so that simple lieutenants or captains in the army found themselves at once captains in the guards, a place of importance, and hitherto much honoured, and which gives the rank of colonel, or even of brigadier. Some of those ancient captains, and they the first families in the empire, found themselves under the command of officers of no birth, who but a few years before had left their companies as serjeants or corporals, to enter into the battalions of the grand-duke. This bold and hasty change, which at any other time would have been fatal to its author, had no other effect than that of inducing a few hundreds of officers, subalterns and others, to retire. Most of these were such as had sufficient to live upon beside their commissions, or could neither digest the putting others over their heads, nor support the harassing discipline which the intruders were about to establish*.

* Of these obtruded officers, no one made his fortune so rapidly as Araktscheief. Seven years before, the grand-duke, willing to have a company of artillery at Pavlofsky, asked general Melissino for an officer capable of forming one. Araktscheief, who had been brought up in the corps of cadets, and who had gotten himself noticed by the progress he made and particularly for the ardour and passionate zeal he displayed for the minutiæ of discipline, was given him. In spite of his indefatigable attentions, severity, and exactitude in the service, it was some time before he could establish

Many of these young officers, however, felt no other affront than that of being obliged to quit

himself thoroughly in the good opinion of Paul. Several pretty fireworks, which he composed with the assistance of his old master for the entertainments at Pavlofsky, but, above all, the rage for exercising with which he burned, and which induced him to harass the soldiers day and night, at length gained him the favour of the grand-duke. At his accession to the throne, Araktscheief was created a major in the guards, with the rank of general, and appointed military governor of Petersburg. He received the order of St. Anne, with some thousands of peasants, and became the emperor's right-hand. Araktscheief, with whom major M. has served in the corps of cadets, where he was serjeant, was truly commendable for the talents, acquirements, and zeal which he displayed at that time: but he is disgusting by his brutality, which he exercised even towards the cadets. Never was pindaric poet more imperiously tormented by his muse, than this man is possessed by his military demon. His fury and his cane have already cost more than one unfortunate soldier his life, even under the eye of Paul. This wretch has revived a barbarity, which had long been a stranger to the russian service: he abuses and strikes the very officers when exercising. However, while in favour, that he might have the appearance of being grateful, he recommended general Melissino, his former master, with whom he was at variance. He was lately disgraced, but since recalled, and baronized. It was he who reviewed the troops sent into Germany.—The history of another of these officers deserves to be mentioned for its singularity. It will prove how a man sometimes makes his way in the world. One of the friends of major M. taking a walk on the quay, met with a youth of sixteen, who appeared to have lately landed, and walking in despair along the water-side as if intending to throw himself in. He went up, and spoke to him. The young stranger said, that he was a Frenchman by descent,

their brilliant uniforms, and to alter their dress according to the grotesque and fantastical

but born in Russia; that the grand-duke had been his godfather; that his father had sent him in his infancy to France, to be educated in a seminary there, from which he eloped, to return to Russia, where he could learn no news of his father: that he was without money, without acquaintances, and that he had no alternative but to make away with himself. The major's friend endeavoured to console him, took him to his own house, and set on foot some enquiries. He learned that his father, baron Bilistein, had in fact been preceptor to the grand-duke, but that he had since married in Moldavia, where he died. Major M. and his friends exerted themselves to get the young man admitted into the guards as a subaltern officer. In the swedish war, he went with his regiment, and was made prisoner at the defeat of the russian galleys. A year after he came back in a more deplorable condition than ever; and, to add to his misfortunes, the major's friend and his other patrons being no longer at Petersburg, he had no resource but major M. to whom he came every day to relate his misfortunes. One morning he found him reading the life of Jamerai Duval, and his correspondence with mademoiselle Sacalof, afterwards the wife of admiral Ribas. M. knew that this lady was a friend of mademoiselle Nelidof, the mistress of the grand-duke, which suggested to him the following thought. He dictated to Bilistein a letter to madame Ribas, wherein he told her, that having accidentally been reading one of her charming letters to Duval, it had given an interval to his despair, from conceiving that a lady who could paint the sentiments of benevolence and humanity so well, must possess them in her heart: he therefore proceeded to lay before her his sad situation, and solicited her influence to be recommended to the grand-duke. Madame Ribas sent for him and recommended him to mademoiselle Nelidof, who presented him to the grand-duke. A few hundred rubles were given him to equip

clothing of those battalions which had so long excited their ridicule.

Paul, alarmed and enraged at this general desertion, went to the barracks, flattered the soldiers, appeased the officers, and endeavoured to retain them, by excluding from all employ, civil and military, those who should retire in future, and who besides were no longer to wear their uniform. He afterwards issued the ridiculous and cruel order, that every officer or subaltern who had resigned, or should give in his resignation, should quit the capital within four-and-twenty hours, and return to his own home. It never entered the head of Paul, or of him who drew up the ukase, that it contained an absurdity; as several of the officers were natives of Petersburg, and had families residing in the city. Accordingly some of them retired to their homes without quitting the capital, not obeying the first part of the order, lest they should be found guilty of disobedience to the second. Arkarof, who was to see it put in force, having informed the emperor of this contradiction, he directed that the injunction to quit Petersburg should alone be obeyed. A number of young men were con-

himself, and through the means of count Soltikof he obtained a lieutenant's commission in the battalions at Pavlofsky. From that time he has lived somewhat less wretchedly, and always appeared extremely grateful. At the accession of the grand-duke he was made a lieutenant-colonel in the guards.

sequently taken out of their houses as criminals, conveyed out of the city, with orders not to reenter it, and left on the road without shelter, and without pelisses, in a very intense frost. They who belonged to remote provinces, for the most part wanting money to carry them thither, wandered about the neighbourhood of Petersburg, where several perished of cold and want.

These measures were extended to all the officers of the army; and those on the staff as generals were equally obliged to join their regiments, or resign, because these staffs were abolished. And it was by this impolitic step that he pretended to commence a reform, and gain the goodwill of the army. But what soon shewed that Paul, on becoming emperor by no means renounced the military frivolities which had entirely occupied him while grand-duke, was his devoting all his attention, from the morning of his ascending the throne, to the trifling changes he was about to introduce into the dress and exercise of the soldiers. For a moment the palace had the appearance of a place taken by assault by foreign troops; those who began to mount guard there differing so much in dress and style from those who had been seen there the day before. He went down into the court, where he was manœuvring his soldiers three or four hours, to teach them to mount guard after his fashion, and establish his *wachtparade* (guard-parade), which became the most important institution and the central point of his administration. Every day since he has dedicated the same time to it, however cold the weather. Here, in a plain deep green uniform, great boots, and a large hat, he spends his mornings in exercising his guards*: here he gives his orders, receives reports, publishes his favours, rewards, and punishments; and here every officer must be presented to him. Surrounded by his sons and aides-de-camp, stamping his heels on the pavement to keep himself warm, his bald head bare, his snub nose cocked up to the wind, one hand behind his back, and with the other raising and falling his cane in due time, and crying, *raz, dva; raz, dva;* one, two; one, two; he prides himself in braving a cold of fifteen or twenty degrees of Reaumur without furs. Presently, none of the officers dared any longer to appear in pelisses; and the old generals, tormented with coughs, gout and rheumatism, were obliged to form a circle round Paul, dressed like himself †.

---

* See the print of him, which though intended perhaps as a caricature, is nevertheless a striking likeness, published in St. James's-street, having under it, " Our magnanimous ally. "—Painted at Petersburg."

† A Hogarth, who should see the emperor and his younger son busy about a poor recruit, turning him to the right and to the left, marching him forward and backward,

The first impressions of fear and joy being deadened in the heart of Paul, punishments and disgraces succeeded in the same rapidity and profusion with which he had lavished his favours. Several persons experienced the two extremes within the space of a few days. It is true, that most of these punishments at first appeared to be just: then, however, it must be allowed, that Paul could scarcely strike any where but on the guilty, so corrupt were all who beset the throne.

Notwithstanding the assurances he had just given to Zubof, one of the first orders that followed was, to seal up his chancery and that of Markof, and to expel their officers and secretaries from the court with disgrace. One Tersky, master of requests, and reporter to the senate, who publicly sold justice to the highest bidder, and, with a shocking effrontery, was at first gratified with an order of knighthood, and obtained some lands, which he said the late empress had promised him a few days before her decease;

raising up his chin, tightening his belt, and placing his head properly, with every now and then a blow, would have a fine subject for a caricature. An emigrant named Lami conceived the humorous idea of dedicating to Paul a bad translation he made of the explanation of Hogarth's prints. I know not whether he did it out of simplicity, or as a stroke of satire; but the name of Paul is very happily placed at the head of that work, which wanted only the ridicule of such a dedication to make it complete. Paul, however, suspected no joke in it, for he sent abbe Lami a present of a snuff-box.

was next morning dismissed from his offices. This respect of Paul to the pretended will of his mother, and his care farther to enrich a rascal before he discarded him, excited a stupid admiration. Surely he ought rather to have brought to trial this despoiler of the widow and orphan, and made him an example of public justice!

Samoïlof, the procureur-general, whom likewise he had honourably confirmed in his office, with a present of four thousand peasants, amounting in value to more than twenty thousand rubles (2000l.) a year, was displaced a few days after, put under arrest, and his secretary was sent to the fortress. In short all was reformed in this manner, except Besborodko, Nicholas Soltikof, and Arkarof *.

This uncertain and fluctuating conduct, which characterised the first steps of Paul, clearly proves that his favours were the effects of policy; and the disgraces that followed them were to be ascribed to passion rather than to justice. But what confounded all who had admired him, was to see him, at the very moment when he was entering such an intricate labyrinth of business and abuses, and the importance whereof to the state would have found him work enough at least for some days, was, I say, to see him applying the very morning of his

* See the next chapter.

accession with the same eagerness to the most trifling details of the military service. The shape of a hat, the colour of a feather, the altitude of a grenadier's cap, boots, spatterdashes, cockades, queues, and sword-belts, became the affairs of state that absorbed his astonishing activity. He was surrounded by patterns of accoutrements and uniforms of all kinds. If Louis XIV. was of all the princes of Europe the most expert at making a lock, verily Paul I. is the best hand at scouring a button, and employs himself at it with the same assiduity as formerly Potemkin did in brushing up his diamonds. The greatest proof of zeal and merit any one could give him during the first days of his reign, was to appear before him in the uniform he had last introduced. An officer, who could give his tailor a hundred rubles to have a dress of the new fashion made in a few hours, and appear in it the next morning at the *wacht-parade*, was almost certain of obtaining some post, or at least a cross. Several had no other merit, and employed no other means to gain the good graces of their new emperor [*].

[*] General Meyendorf being mentioned to him as a good officer of horse, he dispatched a courier to him; and Meyendorf, in his eagerness to obey the command, presented himself at the parade in his ancient uniform. Paul, enraged, uttered some severe reproaches to those who had recommended such a man, called him one of *Potemkin's soldiers*, and banished him to his estate.

Another fancy, which caused no little surprise, was the imperial prohibition of wearing round hats, or rather the sudden order of taking them away, or tearing them to pieces on the heads of those who appeared in them; which occasioned some scandalous scenes in the streets, and particularly near the palace. The kozaks and soldiers of the police ran up to the passengers and snatched off their hats, beating those who, not knowing the reason, attempted to defend themselves. An english merchant, going through the street in a sledge, was thus stopped, and his hat snatched off. Supposing it a robbery, he leaped out of his sledge, knocked down the soldier, and called the guard. Instead of the guard, arrived an officer, who overpowered and bound him; but as they were carrying him before the police he was fortunate enough to meet the coach of the english minister, who was going to court, and claimed his protection *. Sir Charles Whitworth made his complaint to the emperor; who, conjecturing that a round hat might be the national dress of the English, as it is of the Swedes †, said, that his

---

* Another Englishman was met by an officer of the police, who took from him his round hat. The Englishman, folding his arms, and surveying him from head to foot, said with a look of compassion, "My friend! how I pity thee for being a Russian!"

† It is likewise the national hat of the Russians, a little difference in the crown excepted, which it was well to be ap-

order had been misconceived, and he would explain himself more fully to Arkarof. The next day it was published in the streets and houses, that strangers, who were not in the emperor's service, or naturalized, were not comprised in the prohibition. Round hats were now no longer pulled off: but they who were met with this unlucky head-dress were conducted to the police to ascertain their country. If they were found to be Russians, they were sent to be soldiers; and woe to a Frenchman who had been met in this dress, as he would have been condemned as a jacobin *. It was reported to Paul, that the chargé d'affaires of the king of Sardinia, in raillery at this singular proscription of round hats, had said, that such trifles had often been on the point of occasioning seditions in Italy; the chargé d'affaires received orders, through Arkarof, to quit the city in twenty-four hours. Thanks to the distance and situation of the king of Sardinia, he could not demand an explanation of such an insult, otherwise round hats might have become

prised of, as it prevented the wearer from insult. The hatters' shops being soon emptied of cocked hats, they who had neither time nor means to procure one, cocked up their little round hats with pins, that they might walk the streets with safety.

* Perhaps the reader may suppose that these round hats were considered as some party sign. By no means: it was a singular aversion which Paul had for them; and he had declared war against them at Pavlofsky four years before.

the motive of a war between two monarchs: the rights of the throne and the altar, the dignity of the crown and the happiness of the people, would doubtless have figured in the several manifestos *.

A regulation altogether as incomprehensible was the sudden prohibition of putting to and harnessing the horses after the russian mode. A fortnight was allowed for procuring harness in the german fashion; after the expiration of which, the police was enjoined to cut the traces of every carriage to which the horses were harnessed in the ancient manner. Almost as soon as it was made public, several persons dared not venture abroad, still less appear in their carriages near the palace, for fear of being insulted. The sadlers, availing themselves of the occasion, asked as far as three hundred rubles (30l.) for a plain harness for a pair of horses. To dress the *isvoschtschiki*, or russian coachmen, in the german fashion, was attended with another inconvenience. The generality of them would

---

* It was fortunate that it did not happen to the swedish or prussian ambassador. The latter, however, fell into disgrace with Paul for a motive equally noble. He gives out that the hat, the tail, the bag, the spatterdashes, and the sword behind the back, are in the prussian mode. M. van Tauenziehn appeared to protest against the fidelity of the translation, by coming to court in a more modern and more elegant uniform. This was the crime for which Paul demanded his recal.

neither part with their long beards, their *kaftans*, nor their round hats; still less would they tie a false tail to their short hair, which produced the most ridiculous scenes and figures in the world. At length the emperor had the mortification to be obliged to change his rigorous order into a a simple invitation to his subjects gradually to adopt the german fashion of dress, if they wished to merit his favour.

Another reform with respect to carriages: the great number of splendid equipages that swarmed in the streets of Petersburg, disappeared in an instant. The officers, even the generals, came to the parade on foot, or in little sledges, which also was not without its dangers *.

It was anciently a point of etiquette for every person who met a russian autocrate, his wife, or son, to stop his horse or coach, alight, and prostrate himself in the snow, or in the mud †. This barbarous homage, difficult to be paid in a large

---

* An officer, walking the streets in a large pelisse, had given his servant his sword, which incommoded him, intending to put it on again, and to take off his pelisse, when he got near the palace. Unfortunately, before this took place, the emperor met him, and in consequence he was reduced to the ranks, and his servant made an officer in his place.

† Peter I. ordered those who prostrated themselves before him in this manner to be caned, and even caned them himself.

city, where carriages pass in great numbers, and always on the gallop, had been completely abolished under the polished reign of Catharine. One of the first cares of Paul was to re-establish it in all its rigour. A general officer, whose coachman passed on without observing the emperor riding by on horseback, was stopped, and immediately put under arrest*. The same disagreeable circumstance occurred to several others; so that nothing was so much dreaded, either on foot or in a carriage, as to meet Paul. What befel a lady of the name of Likarof, however, deserves to be recorded, for the sake of inspiring that horror which is due to tyrants.

This lady being in the country, at a small distance from Petersburg, with her husband brigadier Likarof, he happened to be taken ill; and, from the tenderness of her affection, not caring to trust to others, she set out herself to fetch a physician and the necessary assistance from town. Her country servants, not knowing the new emperor, and still less his new regulations, and she,

---

* When his sword was returned him, he refused to take it, saying, that it was a gold-hilted sword received from the empress, with the privilege of its never being taken from him. Paul sent for him, returned the sword to him himself, and said, that he had resolved to make an example, and had no particular ill-will towards him: at the same time he ordered him to repair immediately to the army.

absorbed in the apprehensions of her husband's danger, ordered them to drive to the physician's house as fast as possible. Unfortunately her carriage passed, without stopping, at some distance from Paul, who was taking the air on horseback. Enraged at this, he immediately dispatched an aide-de-camp to stop the coach, commanded the four servants to be sent off as soldiers, and the lady to be conveyed, for her impertinence, to the prison of the police. These orders were executed on the spot, and the unfortunate lady of the brigadier was kept in confinement four days. This shocking treatment, with the condition in which she had left her husband, wrought so forcibly on her feelings as to throw her into a violent fever, which brought on a delirium. She was at length removed to an inn, that some care might be taken of her; but her reason she never recovered. Her husband, deprived of his wife and servants, and left without assistance, died in a state of the deepest affliction, without ever seeing her more.

The etiquette established within the palace became equally strict, and equally dreaded. Woe to him, who, when permitted to kiss the rough hand of Paul, failed to make the floor resound by striking it with his knee as loud as a soldier with the butt-end of his firelock. It was requisite too, that the smack of the lips on his hand should be heard, to certify the reality of the kiss, as well as of the genuflexion. Prince George Gallitzin, the chamberlain, was put under arrest on the spot by his muscovite majesty himself, for having made the bow and kissed the hand too negligently*.

Another of Paul's first regulations, was a strict injunction to all tradesmen to efface from the front of their shops the french word *magazin*, and substitute the russian word *lavka* (shop); assigning as a reason, that the emperor alone could have magazines of wood, flour, corn, &c. while a tradesman ought not to be above his condition, but to stick to his shop.

To report all the ordinances of similar weight and importance that succeeded each other in the course of one week, would be descending into particulars too tedious †. What can be said,

---

* Paul, when grand-duke, had a great predilection for etiquette. Being once at Montbelliard, he suddenly took by the arm a young officer of his suite, who was playing at cards, and turning him out of the room, said to those who were playing with the officer, " Gentlemen, that young coxcomb " is not of a proper rank to make one of your party." At the court balls, the dancers were obliged to twist themselves every possible way, that they might not turn their backs upon him when dancing, wherever he might happen to be. Paul will allow none to turn their backs but his enemies. Whether they will avail themselves of the permission, if he should give them an opportunity, I will not pretend to say.

† He has since issued different ukases, prohibiting the wearing of frock coats, waistcoats without sleeves, and pantaloons. He has forbidden the academy to use the word *revolution* when speaking of the course of the stars; and has

what can be hoped, of a man, who, succeeding Catharine, could consider the regulating such things as his most urgent business? Frequently these new and important regulations contradicted or frustrated one another, and what was ordained one day was often obliged to be modified or annulled the next. In a word, we may say that Paul, when he wrapped himself in the imperial mantle, let the grand-duke peep out; that he thought to govern a vast empire as he had governed his Pavlofsky; his capital, like his house; and thirty millions of men of all ranks and all nations, like a score of lackeys.

Of all the unforeseen changes which he introduced without any preparation, those which he made in the army were the most extensive, and the most impolitic. Unquestionably there was room for great reforms and great amendments in the military department. To improve the condition of the brave russian soldier; to settle that of the officer, which was still more wretched; gradually to diminish the number of supernumeraries; to restore order and discipline, which the reign of so many women and so many favourites had destroyed; opened a fine field to the military

enjoined the players to employ the word *permission* instead of *liberty*, which they had been accustomed to put in their bills. He has forbidden the manufacturers to fabricate any tricoloured ribands or stuffs whatever.

genius of Paul. All he was capable of doing was to multiply irregular promotions, increase a staff already too numerous, and alter uniforms, ranks, terms, and titles. The russian army offered a pattern to be followed, in the beauty, simplicity, and convenience of its dress, equally adapted to the climate, and to the genius of the country.* A large *charvari*, or pair of pantaloons of red cloth, the ends of which terminated in boots of pliable leather, and which was fastened by a girdle over a red and green jacket; a little helmet well adapted to a soldier, with the hair cut short in the neck, but long enough to cover the ears, and easily kept in order; constituted the whole of the military uniform. The soldier was dressed in the twinkling of an eye, for he had but two garments; and their size was such, as allowed him to defend himself from the cold by additions underneath, without infringing upon the uniformity of his external appearance. This neat and warlike equipment is now changed for the antiquated dress of Germany, which the russian soldier abominates: his flaxen locks, which

* Accordingly the soldier imagined himself much superior to his neighbours, and not without reason. Paul deprived him of this national pride, by compelling him servilely to imitate the Germans of the last century, whom the Russians imagined they had far outstripped. Paul has acted like a pedant, who should turn a scholar back to his *a, b, c,* for having presumed to learn to read too rapidly.

he loved to wash every morning, he must now bedaub with grease and flour; and must spend an hour in buttoning his black spatterdashes, which he curses for pinching his legs. He complains so bitterly, that probably the false tail which he is forced to suspend from his poll, will occasion as many desertions as the catogans of St. Germain *. That old original, marshal Suvarof, when he received orders to establish these novelties, with little sticks for measures and models of the soldiers tails and side-curls, said, " Hair-powder is not gunpowder; curls are not " cannons; and tails are not bayonets." This sarcasm, which is not destitute of wit, and forms in the russian language a sort of apophthegm in rhime, soon spread from mouth to mouth through the army, and was the true reason that induced Paul to recal Suvarof, and dismiss him from the service. This old warrior was the idol of the russian soldiery.

It was the same with the changes which he made in civil affairs. His wish was to alter, not to improve. For anything to have subsisted un-

* Before the reign of Paul, desertion was almost unknown to the Russians: now they desert in parties, and repair to Prussia, where whole regiments are formed of them. I asked some of them, why they deserted. " Why, Sir," said they, " we are forced to be at our exercise from morning till night " without having anything to eat; our cloaths are taken from " us, and we are beaten black and blue."

der the reign of his mother, was a sufficient reason why it should cease under him. All the tribunals, all the governments of the empire, have been fresh modelled, and their boundaries altered. That which had been consecrated by its name (*Ekaterinoslaf*) to the glory of Catharine was abolished, and this public affront to the memory of his mother is not less so to the heart of Paul*.

* There is nothing so trifling to which this *microphilist* does not descend, to shew disrespect to his mother's memory. The persons belonging to her wore rings, on which the date of her decease was enamelled. The emperor expressed his dissatisfaction at it; and they were obliged to wear rings with the motto of, *Paul consoles me.* He is indeed such a comforter as to make all the world laugh at him.—He carried his want of filial regard so far, as to check, by his disapprobation, a society of opulent Russians, who had united at Hamburg under the auspices of the russian minister, to erect a poetical monument to the memory of Catharine. The situation in which major M. stood at that time, and particularly what he owed to two of his friends, induced him to exert his talents on the occasion. The judges of the Lyceum at Hamburg had the courage to adjudge the second prize to the piece he sent, notwithstanding the proscribed sentiments that beamed through the manner in which he spoke of Catharine, and his silence respecting the comforter she left behind, or his allusions to him (1). The secretary of the embassy, when he

(1) The motto of the piece was, *Fuit illa et ingens gloria Russorum*; and in it were the following verses:

* Mais j'entends retentir une voix gemissante;
Je vois l'Humanité plaintive et menaçante:
Barbares! arrêtez: eh! pour qui cet autel?
Voyez ces combattans, ces fers, ces feux, ces armes;
    Ah! mon sang et mes larmes
Vont éteindre à vos yeux cet encens criminel!

The reader may judge of the confusion, injustice, wretchedness, and ruin, that such placing and displacing must occasion in Russia: no revolu-

announced to him the success of his piece, informed him, that they were going to send it to the emperor, and pay his majesty the compliment of this monument, which would be magnificent, and cost vast sums of money. At the same time he requested him to write an ode in honour of Paul, to be placed at the head of the pieces that had been approved. M. positively refused this new tribute, which would have been a piece of meanness in him, as he had just been torn from his family, and unjustly proscribed by the emperor. Not receiving the medal, however, which had been adjudged to him, he sent to the secretary to demand it, saying, he would otherwise make a public protest in the newspapers against such an unworthy proceeding. He knew that his piece had spread through the court at Petersburg, where his name had been discovered, though he had taken the precaution to disguise it in an *anagram*; and this contributed not a little to bring Paul's anathema upon the society at Hamburg. The threat of such a public affront had its effect, and the medal was at length sent, with some excuses for the delay of more than a year, and a confession that the emperor, having disapproved of this

" But hark, a voice that wildly groans and shrieks!
" Humanity bewailing, threat'ning speaks:
" ' Barbarians, halt! for whom those blood-stain'd fanes?
" ' Behold yon combatants, yon arms and chains!
" ' My blood, my tears, e'en now shall quench the fire,
" ' And save each hero from the funeral pyre."

Likewise

L'aigle puissant du nord, frappé dans sa carrière,
   Se rabat sur la terre:
Il erre dans la nuit; son astre s'est eteint.

" Behold the threat'ning eagle of the north,
  " That soar'd exulting in resistless pow'r,
" Struck in his mid career, descends to earth,
  " Wandering in night. His sun shall rise no more."

tion ever caused so much for the reforming of every thing, as the accession of Paul to render all things worse. Upwards of twenty thousand gentlemen were thrown out of employ.

If this new reign has been fatal to the army and to the poor gentry, it has hitherto appeared still more so to the unhappy peasantry, whose chains it tends to rivet. If Paul were determined to borrow an example from Prussia, assuredly it should have been that of her treatment of the Poles, whom treachery had subjected to her dominion *. It would not be too much to say, that

---

monument to his mother, the illustrious society was afraid of his indignation. Major M. himself communicated to me these particulars, as well as the letters of the secretary.

* Let the reader compare the ukase of Paul, which enjoins all his subjects to prostrate themselves at his sight, with the order which the young king of Prussia has just given to his ministers, on his return from Poland, where it was with indignation he found a people debased almost to as low a degree as the Russians. The following is a translation of some fragments of this memorable order, as it appears in the *Jahrbücher der Preussischen Monarchie*, " Annals of the Prussian
" Monarchy," for January 1799:

" My dear ministers of state von Voss and von Schroeter:
" During the tour I have lately made in the new provinces of
" Prussia, I have seen that the lowest class of my subjects in
" those countries is in a state of civilisation far beneath that
" of the other provinces. These miserable beings are de-
" gradingly distinguished by the dirtiness of their houses and
" clothes, but still more by their servile manners, and a pre-
" posterous humility——In my eyes, and in those of the law,
" the lowest of my subjects possesses the dignity of a man.

the prussian government grants the polish vassals more liberty than Koschiusko could have bestowed on them, had he been victorious. The king of Prussia, far from imitating Catharine, or Paul, who distributes these slaves among his courtiers, thus exposing them to more insupportable private tyranny, has annexed them to his domains, and they experience an infinitely milder lot than formerly *.

A report being spread, that Paul was about to restrict the power of masters over their slaves,

" The people of these new provinces are still ignorant of this
" dignity, for which they are indebted to the prussian sceptre,
" because the inferior officers of government are ignorant of
" their duty, and abuse their authority. It is become a pro-
" verb among them, that the Polanders must be governed by
" the whip; and I have several times heard complaints of
" such treatment being exercised towards my subjects, while
" changing horses," &c. This is the manner in which a king expresses himself who, feeling as a man, is shocked at the sight of a nation of slaves prostrating themselves at his feet. He enjoins his ministers to raise up this degraded nation, by instructing it, civilising it, and punishing abuses of power.

* All those princes who have wished to raise the people and depress the great, the better to establish the authority of government, have endeavoured to annex all seignorial rights and estates to their own domains. The russian autocrates take the opposite course: they distribute the domains of the crown among the nobility, to render them more zealous supporters of a government more severe than ever was that of the feudal system. By this ill-judged policy they render themselves incapable of restoring liberty to their slaves at a future period.

and give the peasants of the lords the same advantages as those of the crown, the people of the capital entertained great expectations from the change. At that juncture an officer set off for his regiment, which lay at Orenburg. On the road he was asked about the new emperor, and what new regulations he was making. He related what he had seen, and what he had heard; among other things mentioned the ukase which was soon to appear in behalf of the peasants. At this news, those of Tver and of Novgorod indulged in some tumultuous movements, which were considered as symptoms of rebellion. Their masters were violently enraged with them; and the cause that had led them into the mistake was discovered. Paul immediately dispatched old marshal Repnin at the head of some troops against a few villages, whose inhabitants had given scope to their joy in a manner somewhat tumultuous on hearing that their new emperor intended to alleviate their bondage; and the officer, who had unwittingly given rise to this false hope, by retailing the news of the town on his road, was soon brought back in custody as a criminal, the promoter of rebellion, and a preacher of liberty. The senate of Petersburg judged him deserving of death, and condemned him to be cashiered, to undergo the knoot, and, if he survived that punishment, to labour in the mines: and this for having mentioned at a few post-houses on the road between Petersburg and Orenburg, that the new emperor, from sentiments of humanity, was about to restrict the authority of masters over their vassals. The emperor confirmed this absurd and atrocious sentence. This is the first criminal trial that was laid before the public; and assuredly it justifies but too well those remains of shame which have hitherto kept secret similar outrages. The senate had the effrontery to affix the seal of justice and law to this sanguinary act, which might no doubt have taken place under the reign of Catharine, yet would have been accompanied with that silence and mystery in which guilt envelopes itself.—But let us quit the cruelties of Paul, to return to his absurdities.

The most prominent of these is that mania which, from his infancy, he has displayed for the military dress and exercise, and which has ever since been increasing. This passion in a prince no more indicates the future general or hero than a fondness for dressing and undressing her doll forebodes the good mother in a girl, who passes her days in those amusements. Frederic the Great, the most accomplished soldier of his time, is well known to have had from his infancy the most insuperable repugnance to all those minutiæ of a corporal to which his father would have subjected him: this was even the first source of that disagreement which ever subsisted between the father and son. It was only by stealth that the young Frederic could indulge himself in studying history and literature with his preceptor du Han. Frederic William considered every book, except the Psalms of David and his military regulations, as useless or dangerous; and when he saw the young Frederic, not confining himself to the guard's march, but wishing to exchange his little drum for a harpsichord, and his fife for a german flute, he forbad him music. This paternal tyranny had the opposite effect to what his father intended: it gave more energy to Frederic's repressed desires. He acquired information; he became a hero: his father was never anything more than a corporal *.

Peter III. carried likewise his soldatomania to a ridiculous excess, fancying he had taken Frederic for his model. He was fond of soldiers and arms, as it is common to be fond of horses and dogs. He knew nothing but how to exercise a regiment, and never went abroad but in a captain's uniform. And, after all, this Peter III. at the head of a regiment so well drilled by himself, had not the courage to face a young woman, on her march to meet him with a few companies of

---

* I know some young Russians, whose genius the same causes have only served to display: thus a good bow springs from under the hand that bends it.

the very same guards who were totally ignorant of the prussian exercise. He lost both his crown and his life, without daring to defend them. Certainly a more local, strong, and recent example cannot be adduced against this mania, which seems rather to exclude courage and military talents than to be a sign of them. It is very easy to put on a coarse surtout buttoned over the belly, to wear a greasy hat*, and a sword behind the back: a man may even spend the whole day on the parade, caning the soldiers and abusing the officers:—but this would be a satirical caricature of a great king; it would be to represent him as a recruiting officer, affecting to give himself airs. But, says Molière :

> Quand sur une personne on prétend se régler,
> C'est par les beaux côtés qu'il lui faut ressembler:
> Et ce n'est pas du tout la prendre pour modèle
> . . . . . . que de tousser et de cracher comme elle.

> " When Admiration bids us mimic others,
>   " We in their virtues should the semblance hit,
> " Nor will the sage and fool e'er pass for brothers,
>   " Because forsooth alike they cough or spit."

There is one part of this great king's conduct of far more utility, and almost as easy to imitate,

---

* Paul affects to wear a dirty hat: but where lies the merit of this? Since he will have every one do his duty, why not make his *valets-de-chambres* do theirs, in beating and brushing his old beaver? and, by this important service give them an opportunity of sooner meriting the rank of privy-counsellors?

since it requires neither talents nor genius, but merely good will, patience, and a love of justice; this is for a sovereign to receive, like him, the petitions and letters of his subjects, but particularly to answer them. The perseverance and exactness with which he always adhered to this resolution, which he adopted at the commencement of his reign, cannot be too much admired. Whether he granted or refused, whether he found the petition reasonable or unreasonable, he answered every man who addressed him. I have seen several of those answers, admirable for their precision and sagacity; yet Frederic found time to do and to write other things beside answering letters. He did not rise earlier than Paul; but he staid only a quarter of an hour on the parade, and often did not go to it at all.

Nothing could be more worthy of a russian autocrate than to establish a similar correspondence between himself and his subjects, since arbitrary acts and public violences are nowhere so frequent or so enormous. Hitherto, every man who had the audacity to present a request immediately to the sovereign, even under the reign of Catharine, was sent to prison. Paul appeared to have abolished this atrocious custom from the day of his accession, and took some papers that were offered him. He even ordered a sort of office to be constructed on the stairs of the palace, into which any one might put letters; and gave public notice, that he would read them all, make the necessary inquiries, and then answer them. In consequence, he forbad any one to disturb him in future on the *wacht-parade*, and ordered those to be arrested who should thenceforth approach him with a paper in their hand. In the meantime, the box of the letter-office was soon filled; and Paul, contrary to his expectation, finding more petitions than accusations, became tired of entering into the merits of them; and was frightened at their number. He did not reflect that they would necessarily diminish in proportion as he employed more readiness and method in answering them *. Things returned to their former chaotic state; and the secretaries directed to examine these pieces are, as before, arbiters of the fate of those unfortunate persons who apply to their master.

The finances of the empire, exhausted by the prodigalities, and still more by the waste of Ca-

---

* Paul has sometimes given orders respecting the letters he has received, but he does not answer them. I myself have drawn up a few very brief, clear, and just requests, for some oppressed persons, which remained unanswered. He now causes his refusals to the petitions he receives to be printed in the Petersburg gazettes. By this means the sovereign, who ought to be in regard to his people what a confessor is to his penitent, publishes himself the secrets of families, and betrays the confidence of his subjects.

tharine's reign, required a prompt remedy; and to this Paul seemed at first to turn his thoughts. Partly from hope, partly from fear, the paper money of the crown rose a little in value. It was to be supposed, that the grand-duke of all the Russias, who for thirty years had been obliged to live on an income of a hundred thousand rubles (10,000*l*.) per annum, would at least have learned economy perforce; but he was soon seen to heap wealth upon some, and lavish favours upon others, with as much profusion as his mother, and with still less discernment. The spoils of unhappy Poland continued to add to the riches of men already too wealthy*. A man must be

* I am informed that the emperor, on his coronation, among other gratuities, distributed eighty-two thousand *souls* among about a score of people; that is to say, in the language of mortals, that he has made presents of tracts of land inhabited and cultivated by eighty-two thousand male slaves; for in Russia a woman is not a soul yet. By these donations the emperor cedes the private rights which he claims over these wretched beings, and the lands they are obliged to cultivate, reserving to himself only the sovereignty. Now if we suppose the *slave-soul*, or peasant, to bring the *body*, or gentleman who possesses it, only seven rubles clear per annum, which is a very moderate computation, it follows that the emperor has given away so much of the domains of the crown as would produce a neat income of five hundred and seventy-four thousand rubles (57,400*l*.) which, considering the nature of the property, is a capital beyond estimation. Catharine, by her profusion in this way, had nearly disposed of all her domains; but the confiscated estates and starosties in Poland constitute the fund to which the present emperor has

acquainted with the inexhaustible sources whence a russian autocrate can draw his means, not to be struck at the immense presents he bestowed on his courtiers, and at the same time disgusted at the little he has dedicated to the public, to justice, to merited rewards and true beneficence *.

The eagerness with which Paul seized the reins of government, and the terror inspired by his known rigor and activity, at first disappointed the dark intrigues of the knaves and villains, who had misapplied the treasures of the state to their own profit. The prevention of the scandalous dilapidations of these treasures would double the amount of them; and it is to be presumed, that, every thing being re-modeled, the robbers will be obliged to suspend their operations for a time; but, when once they are acquainted with the emperor's course, they will regulate their own accordingly; they will dig other mines, and contrive new channels; pillage and collusion will revive, and be reduced to a system, as before.

recourse. It need not be mentioned, that a population of eighty-two thousand males in Russia or Poland must occupy an immense district.

* All that Paul's talents have enabled him to do for the restoration of a sort of equilibrium between his receipts and disbursements, is reduced at last to an exorbitant tax, which he has just laid on all the classes of his slaves. The poll-tax of the wretched vassals has been doubled, and a new tax has been imposed upon the nobles, which however the vassals must ultimately pay.

Theft is a vice inherent in the russian government, and springs from the character of the nation, to which morals, probity, and public spirit are strangers*.

It must be confessed that, morally speaking, the people about Paul are better than those that were about his mother, and that he will be more culpable than she if he allow the same disorders to prevail. It is true that Catharine pretended to lead her cattle, and that Paul, on the contrary, will suffer himself to be led by footmen rather than by statesmen; he would feel himself humbled because of his vulgar self-love, in following the advice of a man who should seem better informed than himself. The person who has more immediate influence on his actions than his ministers, or even his mistress will ever have, is a *valet-de-chambre*, by birth a Turk, made a slave in his infancy, and brought up in his house. It is to this Turk, named Ivan Pavlovitch Koteitzof, the generals and great men are eager to pay their court, as the real fountain of Paul's private favour. Love is the strongest and most excusable of passions: its excesses and abuses, therefore, appear less odious, and the reign of

---

* The French author confesses, that while he was writing this, he scarcely expected to find the same infamous conduct triumphing under a *republican form* of government, and in a *regenerated* nation.

favourites, or of mistresses, will never be so humiliating as that of valets. Beside their bad education, which gives a strong prepossession against them, the influence a prince allows them has always something mean and repulsive, and savours strongly of the water-closet *.

* This Ivan Pavlovitch is at present counsellor of state, and has the title of excellency. Many lackeys, *Hof,* or *Kammer-fouriers,* gentlemen of the bed-chamber, are every day rising to the highest posts. Thus extremes meet each other: the muscovite licentiousness leads to that equality of rights which it considers with horror: but here it is a real calamity. A great russian lord was accustomed to hold out his hand familiarly to every scullion or shoe-black that he met at court, styling them *brat,* or *batiuschka,* brother or father. A gentleman expressing surprise at this familiarity, the lord said, " It is from policy, sir: between this and to-morrow, these " fellows may become my colleagues." Such is russian equality: it is that of Tarquin cutting off the heads of his tallest poppies, or of a sultan creating his water-carrier prime vizier. This is quite in order: the sultan and the turkish water-carrier, the russian kniaz and estopnik (1) are generally on an equality in knowledge and merit.

(1) The menial servant that lights the fires at court.

CHAP. V.

HAS PAUL REASON TO FEAR THE FATE OF PETER III?

Parallel between Paul and his father—Portrait of the present empress—The grand-duke Alexander—The grand duke Constantine—Zubof—Nicholas Soltikof—Markof—Arkarof—Repnin—Suvarof and Valerian Zubof—Traits of the character of Paul, and his principal courtiers or ministers—His portrait—Anecdotes of his conduct when grand-duke.

PAUL, both in his mode of life while grand-duke, and in his conduct since his accession, so strongly resembles his father; that, changing names and dates, the history of the one might be taken for the history of the other. Both were educated in a perfect ignorance of business, residing at a distance from court, where they were treated as prisoners of state rather than as heirs to the crown; making their appearance there from time to time as ghosts or aliens. The aunt of the father [Elizabeth] acted precisely as the mother of the son has done since. The endeavours of each were directed, to prolong their infancy and to perpetuate their insignificance, and even to render them odious and contemptible to the nobles and people. The young princes were both distinguished by great vivacity of body and a great apathy of mind, by an activity which, for want of proper object and aliment, degenerated into turbulence; that of the father was sunk in debauchery: that of the son, lost in the most insignificant trifles. An unconquerable aversion to study and reflection gave to both that singular infatuation for military puerilities, which would probably have displayed itself less forcibly in Paul had he been a witness of the ridicule they drew upon Peter*. The education of Paul, however, was much more attended to than that

---

* A singular opposition may commonly be observed between father and son, if any striking feature exist in their characters. A well-disposed son will frequently possess that virtue which is directly opposite to his father's vice, particularly if he has seen its folly, or fallen its victim. I could adduce private instances particularly interesting to myself; but those of three or four successive kings of Prussia are particularly striking. Frederic I. was as remarkable for his politeness and munificence as his son for his roughness and parsimony. The great king of Prussia avoided both extremes. The grandfather protected and honoured the sciences ostentatiously; the son persecuted them, and endeavoured to render them contemptible. The grandson cherished them, and cultivated them himself. The first was a royal courtier; the second, a royal corporal; the third, a royal hero. This contrast between father and son has not been observable for a long time in Russia, as one has not been the other's successor; but it is now about to appear in a very striking manner. Catharine and Paul are the two extremes, and the grand-duke Alexander promises fair to be at some future day the happy mean between both.

of his father. He was surrounded in his infancy by persons of merit, and his youth promised a capacity of no ordinary kind*. It is even probable that the eccentricities he has since contracted are to be ascribed rather to the modes of life which he has in a manner been obliged to adopt, than to any natural defects. It must also be allowed, that he is exempt from many of the vices which disgraced Peter: temperance and regularity of manners are prominent features of his character; features the more commendable, as having hitherto been rarely found in a russian autocrate. To this education and his knowledge of the language and character of the nation, it is owing that he differs from his father in other valuable qualities. If he has the wisdom to profit by these advantages, he will not fall into the same errors and misfortunes.

The similarity which, in some instances, has marked their conduct towards their wives, is still more striking; and in their amours, a singular coincidence of taste is observable. Catharine and Mary were the finest women of the court, yet both failed in gaining the affections of their

---

* Louis XIV. and Frederic the Great, loaded with favours and honours those who had superintended their education. The aged Æpinus, Paul's tutor, is threatened with the fate of Seneca and Burrhus. That of colonel L'Harp and major Masson, who were tutors to his son, would be still less mild, should they fall again into the hands of Paul.

husbands. Catharine had an ambitious soul, a cultivated mind, and the most amiable and polished manners. In a man, however, whose attachments were confined to soldiers, to the pleasures of the bottle, and the fumes of tobacco, she excited no other sentiment than disgust and aversion. He was smitten with an object less respectable and less difficult to please. The countess Vorontzof, fat, ugly in her person, and vulgar in her manners, was more suitable to his low guard-house taste; and she became his mistress*.

In like manner, the regular beauty of Mary, the unalterable sweetness of her disposition, her unwearied complaisance, her docility as a wife, and her tenderness as a mother, have not been sufficient to prevent Paul from attaching himself to mademoiselle Nelidof, whose disposition and qualities better accord with his own. She is a little homely girl; but seems desirous, by her wit and address, to compensate for the disadvantages of her person: for a woman to be in love with Paul it is necessary she should resemble him †.

On their accession to the throne, neither the

* She got drunk with him, and swore like a trooper: she squinted, and spat when she was talking.

* He has lately proved fickle. Mademoiselle Nelidof, who lived on tolerable terms with the empress, is dismissed, and a young lady of the name of Lapukhin is now the favourite.

father nor the son were favourites either of the court or of the nation, yet both acquired momentary popularity and favour. The first steps of Paul appeared to be modelled, but improved, on those of Peter. The liberation of Koschiusko and other prisoners brought to public recollection the recal of Biren, Munich, and Lestocq, with this difference, that Peter III. did not disgrace those acts of clemency or justice, by ridiculous violences, or by odious and groundless persecutions. Both issued ukases extremely favourable to the nobility, but from motives essentially different, and little to the honour of the son. The father granted to the russian gentry those natural rights which every man ought to enjoy; while the object of the son was merely to revive those distinctions which in the present day are become obsolete and ridiculous [*]. In the conduct which he has observed towards the clergy, Paul, however, has shewn himself a superior politician: instead of insulting the priests, and obliging them to shave their beards, he has bestowed the orders of the empire on the bishops,

---

[*] Paul has now taken it into his head to create an heraldic nobility in Russia! Formerly this gothic institution was unknown there. The tzar Fedor even ordered the patents, of which some families would have availed themselves, to be burned. Have the Russians but now reached the twelfth century? They were the only nation in Europe, who, in their rapid progress to civilization, bounded over this folly.

to put them on a footing with the nobility, and flattered the populace and the priesthood by founding churches from divine inspiration*.

* A soldier in the guards having stood sentry at a door of the summer palace (an old wooden house in which Elizabeth resided), went to his captain, pretending he had a secret to communicate. He informed him, that while he was on duty, he saw a light in the uninhabited apartments of the palace, and presently some person knocked at the door at which he stood, and called him by name. He had the courage to look through the chinks in the door, and there beheld St. Michael. The saint ordered him to go to the emperor, and tell him that he must build him a church on that spot. In consequence, the soldier begged him to speak to the emperor, or he must take the liberty to do it himself, in obedience to his mission. The officer treated the visionary as a madman, and sent him about his business; he, however, mentioned the adventure to the major, who thought proper to relate it to Paul. The soldier was called, and ordered to repeat the account of his vision. The emperor told him, that St. Michael should be obeyed, for he had already been inspired with the design of building him a church, and had even the plan prepared. On this he sent for the model of a church, which he had ready in his closet. Does not this sound like a legend? yet this farce took place at the court of Russia in the month of December 1796, and the author was, in part, a witness to it. The palace is pulling down, and a church and a new palace are begun, dedicated to *monseigneur* Michael.—*Gospodi pomiloï* (1)!—The miracle is unravelled, when it is known that a cousin of the soldier was one of Paul's valets-de-chambres; and that the soldier, by way of recompense, was promoted to the same post. We may expect soon to see him counsellor of state.

(1) The usual exclamation which the Russians make, crossing themselves at the same time, when they see any thing extraordinary. It is one of the burdens of the litanies; " Lord have mercy!"

From all which it follows, that Peter had a sounder mind and a better heart, but that he was imprudent; and that Paul has more subtlety and prejudices, and that he is a hypocrite.

In his military operations, however, his grand policy appears to have failed him, because here he was hurried away by his ruling passion. The quick and total change of discipline he has introduced in his armies has created him nearly as many enemies as there are officers and soldiers. The preference he gives to the old Germans in his service may prove as fatal to him as it did to his father. In the distrust and suspicions which incessantly haunt him, his inferiority to his father is also apparent. One of the first acts of Peter III. was to abolish the political inquisition established by Elizabeth; whereas Paul has prosecuted no scheme with greater alacrity than that of establishing a system of spies, and devising means for the encouragement of informers. The blind confidence of the father was his ruin, but it flowed from a humanity of disposition always respectable. The distrust of the son may not save him: it is the offspring of a timorous mind, which by its suspicions is more apt to provoke than to elude treason.

From the conformity of character observable, in so many particulars, between these two princes, we might be led to conclude that the catastrophe of the one will be that of the other: but this seems at present not at all probable; for striking as the resemblance is between Peter and Paul, the persons who compose their courts, and the circumstances of the times, are no less strikingly different.

In the first place, the character of Mary, as a wife, is wholly opposite to that of Catharine: sweetness of disposition is her chief characteristic. Her mildness, patience and modesty, have been severely proved by the most rigorous and inconsistent treatment; and, perhaps, by the persevering exercise of these qualities, she may finally triumph. Her time is employed in a succession of duties and occupations suitable to her sex and her station. The education of her children, from whom she has too long been reluctantly separated, is at present a source of happiness to her. Her attention to her husband has enabled her to endure fatigues and exercises the least suitable to her sex and her character. How often has she been seen to attend him on horseback, at the wearisome reviews of Gatshina and Pavlofsky? Though exhausted with heat and fatigue, sometimes drenched with rain, or covered with snow, she has still, by her smiles, expressed her acquiescence*. She is, perhaps, more care-

* He frequently posted the grand-duchess on an eminence, to serve as a mark or point of attack to his troops, while he

ful of her time, and dedicates it to more useful purposes, than any lady in Russia. Music, paint-

defended the approaches. One day, I remember, he placed her thus in the ruinous balcony of an old wooden mansion, round which he disposed his troops for defence. One party of troops he had given to major Lindener, with orders to make the attack according to his own plan. This plan was to establish the reputation of the major, and Paul prepared for the most able resistance. The princess, meanwhile, remained fixed on the turret, exposed to a heavy rain. Paul hastened to every point where he expected the enemy, and pranced about amid the rain as proudly as Charles XII. in a shower of musket-balls. One hour passed after another; the rain redoubled its violence, and no enemy appeared. Paul, entertaining a high opinion of his Prussian, presumed that he had made a skilful march behind the wood, to surprise him more effectually. Accordingly he visited, changed and reinforced his advanced posts every moment, and sent out parties to reconnoitre and scour the country. Frequently a noble impatience getting the better of him or his horse, he galloped a considerable way to meet the enemy, with whose tardiness he began to be dissatisfied. Presently his impatience was changed into rage and vexation. Lindener had taken the field early, and made a long round through the estate of Soltikof, to arrive at the village: but he had gotten his column entangled among the shrubberies of the gardens, which threw it into confusion, and he knew not how to march out, as he had not room to form his line. The aides-de-camp, who came from Paul every moment to order him to make haste, completed his perplexity; and he could find no resource but to pretend he was seized with a violent colic, hasten home, and leave his troops to themselves. Paul, enraged at having made such an excellent disposition of his forces in vain, spurred on his horse as hard as he could gallop to the palace, there to digest his rage; leaving his wife, his army, and those whom he had invited to see this famous manœuvre, wet to the skin. They had waited from five in the morning till one in the afternoon;

ing, etching, embroidery, are the arts in which she excels, and which have alleviated the solitude in which she lived. Reading and study are with her not so much a business as a recreation; and the management of domestic affairs, and the distribution of charities, serve happily to occupy her hours. Tall, well made, and still in the prime of life, she is rather handsome than pretty; she has more majesty than grace, and less wit than sentiment. She is a dutiful daughter and an affectionate sister, as well as a faithful wife and an excellent mother. Far from forgetting her country and her relations, the splendour which surrounds her and the distance which separates them, serve but to increase the warmth of her affection and the vivacity of her remembrance. Her numerous relations are always in her mind; her correspondence with them occupies many hours of tranquil happiness, and her felicity is doubled by making those whom she loves partakers of it. She has not, like the ambitious Catharine, flattered the Russians by adopting their manners, their language and their prejudices: she has not attempted to gain the esteem of that nation by affecting to despise her own, and to be

and much in this manner did Mary spend all her mornings, with one or two young ladies at most, one of whom too was Paul's favourite, and received all the attention of him and his courtiers.

ashamed of her origin; but has made herself beloved for her goodness and respected for her virtues*. We might, perhaps, pity her as a wife, were it not that the attachment of her charming family will prove a source of sufficient happiness to her, and Russia may not improbably one day be indebted to her for national content. Her fruitfulness ensures a more tranquil and natural succession, and the generous blood which she has transfused into the branch of Holstein will mitigate, perhaps, the barbarity which remains to it from the house of Romanof†.

It appears from this sketch, that Paul would have nothing to apprehend from the empress, even though the love of the nation for her, and

---

* Nothing can be more astonishing than that such a man as Mirabeau could relate, in his Secret Correspondence, such a silly anecdote of the grand-duchess of Russia. The young man, who is represented as the hero and relater of the story, was assuredly never in the company of that princess, or even at the court of Russia; and there is no truth in the scenery of this adventure, which would appear flat, ridiculous, and undeserving of notice, had it not been related by Mirabeau.

† What I say of this princess is a homage to truth: she well knows, and I more strongly feel, that it cannot be one to gratitude. It must be confessed too, that her good qualities are singularly obscured by a petty vanity, which makes her think and act like a person raised from a low station. The princess Dorothy of Wirtemberg, become Mary of Holstein-Romanof, might dispense with this gothic haughtiness; for her children, grand-dukes as they are, are no longer chapitrable in Germany.

its aversion to him, should increase. The guards and the people would in vain entreat Mary to ascend her husband's throne; she would reject the invitation with horror. Paul, however, never treated her with becoming respect except when he seemed to stand in awe of her*. The court then saw with astonishment this husband, hitherto so harsh and untractable, change at once his conduct towards her. On his accession, he granted her the sum of five hundred thousand rubles (50,000l.) for her private expenses, promising her at the same time a more ample provision†. He solicited the return of madame Benkendorf, whom he had some years before dismissed from the service of his wife with circumstances of great indignity. To furnish Mary with occupations suitable to the benevolence of her disposition and her sex, he appointed her superior of the convent of young ladies. In fhort he treated her with the respect and attention he ought always to have shewn her. A conduct, so unexpected from Paul, caused great

---

* This period was soon at an end. I am informed, that Mary was put under arrest for twelve hours, for having given one of her women some trifling order which Paul did not approve. It appears that this warlike emperor conducts everything in a military style, even in his bed-chamber.

† As grand-duchess, she had only 60,000 rubles (6000l.) a year; and with this sum was more generous, and did more good, than at present.

sensations, and the vulgar ascribed that to his heart which was nothing but the effect of his policy and his fear. I may perhaps be in the wrong, but this at least is certain, that in his treatment of his wife, Paul wisely differs from his father; who, after his accession to the throne, behaved to Catharine with the same neglect and disrespect as before*.

We have already seen, that Catharine was prevented by death from executing another design, which would have proved more fatal to Paul, but that the youth and natural good disposition of his eldest son defeated it; who by the purity of his morals and his personal qualities inspires a high degree of admiration. That ideal character which enchants us in Telemachus is almost realised in him: however, though his mother may have the domestic virtues of a Penelope, he is very far from having had a Ulysses for his father, or a Mentor for his tutor. He may be reproached, too, with the same defects which Fenelon has allowed in his imaginary pupil †; but

---

* It must be confessed, however, that Catharine, whose amours with Stanislaus Poniatofsky were a scandal to the whole court, gave her husband strong reasons for ill treating her; and that the conduct of Mary is irreproachable.

† " With a generous and well-disposed heart, he appeared " neither obliging nor sensible to friendship, nor liberal nor " grateful for the pains taken on his account: neither was he " prompt to acknowledge merit," &c.—Telemachus, book xvi.

these are, perhaps, not so much failings as the absence of certain qualities not yet developed in him, or which have been stifled in his heart by the miserable companions that have been assigned him. He inherits from Catharine an elevation of sentiment and an unalterable equality of temper; a mind just and penetrating and an uncommon discretion; but a reserve and circumspection unsuitable to his age, and which might be taken for dissimulation, did it not evidently proceed rather from the delicate situation in which he was placed between his father and grandmother, than from his heart, which is naturally frank and ingenuous. He inherits his mother's stature and beauty, as well as her mildness and benevolence, while in none of his features does he resemble his father, and he must certainly dread him more than love him. Paul, conjecturing the intentions of Catharine in favour of this son, has always behaved coldly towards him; since he discovers in him no resemblance of character, and no conformity of taste with himself: for Alexander appears to do what his father requires of him, from a principle of filial duty rather than compliance with his own inclinations. His humanity has acquired him the hearts of the soldiers, his good sense the admiration of the officers: he is the constant mediator between the autocrat and those unhappy persons who, by some trifling neglect, may have provoked imperial wrath and vengeance. This pupil of L'Harpe requires not the dignity of grand-duke of Russia to inspire sentiments of love and interest; nature has richly endowed him with the most amiable qualities, and his character of heir to the greatest empire in the world, cannot render them indifferent to humanity. Heaven, perhaps, may have destined him to render thirty millions of people more free than they are at present, and more worthy of being so.

His character, however, though amiable, is passive. He wants the courage and confidence to discover the man of merit, always modest and unobtrusive; and it is to be feared, that the most importunate and impudent, who are generally the most ignorant and vicious, will find least difficulty in procuring access to him. Yielding too easily to the impulses of others, he does not sufficiently consult his own heart and understanding. He appears to have lost his relish for instruction, on losing his masters, and especially colonel L'Harpe, his first preceptor, to whom he owes all the knowledge he has acquired. A premature marriage may have contributed to diminish his energy; and it is probable that, notwithstanding his good qualities, he will become in time the dupe of his courtiers, and even of his valets.

From this account of his character, it cannot be supposed that he will ever undertake of himself the odious project with which Catharine wished to inspire him. However, during the last illness of the empress, and for several days after her death, he was detained about the person of his father with such marks of tenderness as seemed to betray symptoms of distrust. Scarcely was he allowed an hour in the day to visit his young duchess. The emperor surrounded him with officers on whom he thought he could rely, and removed from their places all those who were not his creatures and spies: he took from him his own regiment to give him another, and appointed him military governor of Petersburg, naming at the same time, for his assistant or guardian, the ferocious Araktscheief. The revenue of the young prince, which hitherto had not exceeded thirty thousand rubles* (3000l.) was increased to two hundred thousand (20,000l.); and his father, by employing him in many trifling concerns, which detained him about his person nearly the whole

---

* The great, the generous Catharine, whose magnificence astonished the universe, and who gave rubles by millions to her favourites, left her son and grandson in want of necessaries. Thirty thousand rubles in paper for a grand-duke of all the Russias! equal to sixty thousand livres french money (2500l.) Sometimes they were given in gold or silver: but they who had the management of the revenues of the young princes, took care to play the usurer, so that in their hands they were diminished nearly half.

day long, was manifestly desirous of watching over him himself. It is impossible not to praise the emperor for having thus brought about by means so mild and natural, the object of his unjust suspicions; and we are pleased with these marks of affection for his children, after being fifteen years without having the resolution to give them the least proof of his regard *.

The vulgar, who in general judge from the most deceitful appearances, perceiving in the grand-duke Alexander a reserve and circumspection of conduct, which they mistook for pride, were at first charmed with his younger brother Constantine. This prince does not possess the advantage of so agreeable and prepossessing a person as his brother; grimace serves him for wit, and buffoonery procures him popularity. He exhibits more than one trait of resemblance to the unhappy tzarovitch Alexius, especially in his aversion for the sciences, and the rudeness of his manners. He possessed, however, the germs of a sound heart and understanding, which his first masters neglected to cultivate, and which colonel L'Harpe attempted in vain to improve, by extir-

* I am informed that the grand-duke Alexander has just been placed by Paul in the office of Besborodko, as Frederic the Great was by his father in the office of a minister, to perform the functions of a simple clerk. Whether it be to procure him instruction, or to humble and punish him, the young prince will be one day the better for it.

pating the weeds that checked their growth. It will be happy for Constantine, when he arrives at an age of more discretion, should he revive and cultivate them himself.

In other respects, he is a son worthy of his father: the same eccentricities, the same passions, the same severity, and the same turbulence. He will never possess the information which his father has acquired, nor his capacity, though he promises in time to equal, and even to surpass him, in the art of manœuvring a dozen automatons. Can it be believed, that a prince of seventeen, lively and vigorous, would, on the morning after his marriage to a young and beautiful woman, leave his bride at five o'clock to manœuvre, by dint of blows, in the court of his palace a couple of soldiers, who were placed there as centinels? Yet such was the conduct of the grand-duke Constantine. I know not whether this military mania announces a good general, but sure I am that it is a proof of a very bad husband *.

---

* Some time before his marriage, he had a detachment of soldiers given him for his amusement. After having tormented these poor wretches for some months, he went so far as to cane the major who commanded them. The major had the courage to complain to count Soltikof, and the favourite related the story to the empress. She ordered her grandson under arrest, and took from him his soldiers, who were not

Paul, though he found in his own family no cause to fear the misfortunes of his father, or any attempt dangerous to his tranquillity, had not equal reason to be satisfied on the part of the nobility. It is certain that he was disliked by them all, and for ten years had been the object of their ridicule at the court of his mother; but Potemkin was no more. A diminutiveness in virtue as in vice, was the characteristic of all who approached the throne: no one possessed that strength of capacity which is necessary to accomplish a revolution, and all wanted that energy which great crimes demand. Catharine might, with more justice than the countess of Muralt, have bestowed on her ministers the epithet which she gave to her wits*. A slight sketch of each of these personages will be sufficient to prove the truth of what I have advanced.

---

returned to him till after his marriage.—Many other stories might be told of this young prince, but it would be only repeating the vulgar tricks of a boy without education. His grandmother perceived it too late to remedy it. In his childhood he bit and struck his masters; now he strikes the officers at their exercise, and knocks out the teeth of the poor soldiers. The king of Sweden being with all the court at a ball given by Samoïlof, he said to him, " Do you know in whose " house you are?—That of the greatest w—— in Peters- " burg." His grandmother put him under arrest.

* It is well known that she called them *mes bêtes*.

Count and prince Zubof, the last official favourite of Catharine, was thirty years of age and upwards. He was far from possessing the genius and ambition of Orlof and Potemkin, though at last he united in his person more power and credit than those celebrated favourites had ever enjoyed. Potemkin was indebted for his elevation almost solely to himself. Zubof owed his to the infirmities of Catharine. He increased in power, in riches, and in credit, in proportion as the activity of Catharine diminished, her vigour abated, and her understanding declined. During the last years of her life, this young man found himself literally autocrat of all the Russias. He had the folly to wish, or to appear, to direct everything; but, having no knowledge of the routine of business, he was obliged to reply, to those who asked him for instructions, *Sdélaïte kak prégedé*, " Do as before." Nothing equalled his haughtiness but the servility of those who eagerly prostrated themselves before him; and it must be acknowledged, that the meanness of the russian courtiers has always surpassed the impudence of the favourites of Catharine. All crouched at the feet of Zubof: he stood erect, and thought himself great. Every morning a numerous court besieged his doors, and filled his antichambers. Veteran generals and grandees of the empire did not blush to caress the lowest of his valets *. Stretched in the most indecent undress on a sofa, his little finger in his nose, his eyes vacantly turned up to the cieling, this young man, of a cold and vain physiognomy, scarcely vouchsafed his attention to those who surrounded him. He amused himself with the tricks of his ape, leaping on the shoulders of his degraded courtiers, or conversed with his buffoon; while the veterans, under some of whom he had been a serjeant, the Dolgorukys, the Gallitzins, the Soltikofs, and all who were distinguished for their exploits or their crimes, standing around him, waited with profound silence till he condescended to turn his eyes towards them, that they might again prostrate themselves before him. The name of Catharine figured in his conversation, but he scarcely deigned to pay the heir of the crown that exterior respect which the etiquette of the court required; and even Paul was forced to humble himself before a petty officer of the guards, who, but a short time before, had begged his pardon for having offended one of his dogs †. To obtain money or favours for his

---

* These valets have been frequently seen to beat back the officers and generals who crowded round the doors, and prevented them from being shut.

† Paul had a dog of which he was fond. This dog, roaming round the palace, attempted to snatch a piece of meat from a trumpeter belonging to the guards. The soldier gave him a blow over the head with his trumpet. The dog ran

dependants, the grand-duke Constantine paid him the most assiduous court. Meanwhile, none of the twelve favourites of Catharine appeared so poorly endowed in person and mind as Zubof. In his elevation, he displayed no genius, no virtues, no passions, unless we account as such the vanity and avarice which distinguished him; accordingly, when his power expired, his emptiness was apparent. The immense wealth of his family, and the vast estates extorted by his father from the landholders of his provinces, are the monuments which he has left of his administration*. The death of the empress reduced

howling and bloody to the apartments of Paul, who was in a rage on hearing the story. " So!" cried he, " everything " belonging to me, everything I love, is an object of persecu-" tion. I have but one dog, and they want to kill it. Let " the officer on guard be sent to me, and he shall be pu-" nished!" The officer on guard at that time was Zubof, who, informed of the rage of the grand-duke, went and threw himself at the feet of Soltikof, his patron, to beg he would go with him and solicit his pardon. It was with difficulty Soltikof could obtain it; for Paul was persuaded that his dog had been beaten out of hatred to him, and because he was detested by the guards. The trumpeter maintained that he did not know to whom the dog belonged; and this Paul took for a fresh insult, for which he would certainly have inflicted a severe punishment, had it been in his power.

* Zubof's father was made a senator; and, to enrich himself, he bought up all the old causes in the court, or made the parties relinquish them to him, and then in the senate decided them himself, or caused them to be decided in his favour.

him in a moment to the obscurity from which she had drawn him; as the ephemeron of a day, produced by the sun, flutters in his cheering beams, but cannot survive the passing breeze. Zubof lamented Catharine, as a son bewails the loss of his mother; and this was the only moment of his life in which he appeared at all interesting. It is also just to observe, that, mingling with the crowd, he discovered more readily the station that was suitable to his insignificance, than the courtiers did theirs, which ought to have been still by his side. They shewed themselves yet more base than he was humbled; and though for the first days his antichambers were deserted, for a long time afterwards, when he appeared at court, the stupid courtiers made way for him, and prostrated themselves before him as before a sovereign; so difficult is it for slaves to rise from their servility! We must do him the farther justice to acknowledge, that he did not, like a Mentchikof and a Biren, people the deserts of Siberia; though, at the instigation of Esterhazy and other french emigrants, he committed acts of great injustice and inquisitorial violence; and the calamities of Poland may in part be considered as his work.

The emperor, who, at the moment of his accession, had treated him with astonishing respect, confirmed him, in the most flattering terms, in all his employments; bestowed on his brother the first order of Russia, solely for having undertaken a journey to Gatshina; made him a present of one of his military uniforms;—the emperor, I say, having measured his man, perceived that he had nothing to fear from him; accordingly, the seal was suddenly put on his chancery, and it was the grand-duke Constantine, lately his most assiduous courtier, who executed this commission, as officer of the police, with all the brutality which is natural to him*. His secretaries were banished, or driven from the court †;

* It is to be observed, that Zubof, who had all the places in his hands, and the secretaries, who had all the business in theirs, were sent off in four-and-twenty hours, without making them give any account, or demanding any information. The confusion this occasioned will appear in the sequel.

† The two most famous are Altesti and Gribofsky. The former is a Ragusan, whom the russian minister Bolkunof took from a merchant's compting-house in Constantinople to employ him in his office. When war was declared, he came to Petersburg to solicit employment, and got into the service of Zubof, who was growing in favour. He understood several languages, and was not destitute of sense. He soon became the penman of Zubof, and even of the empress. A pamphlet, which he wrote in french against the king and revolutionists of Poland, and in which he treated the former as a factionary, the latter as jacobins, stuffing it with epithets, lies, stupidities, and flattery, established his reputation and his fortune. This libel was spread abroad like a manifesto. Titles, orders of knighthood, and slaves, were presently lavished on Altesti. Not contented with these gifts, he en-

his creatures exiled, or imprisoned*; and all the officers of his staff, or of his suite, upwards of two hundred in number, were obliged to join imme-

riched himself prodigiously by other means. The Polish confederates, the governments, the Kozacks, &c. were eager to purchase his protection and services by hard ducats. All the affairs of Poland were in his hands, and on him depended wealth, liberty, and life; since it was he who made out the lists of the proscribed. He grew uncommonly haughty and impudent; but an impertinent trick he played count Golovin, who had the courage to complain of it, at length ruined him. He had orders to retire to his estates; but Zubof had obtained his recal, and he was on the point of re-entering into office a few days before the death of Catharine. One of the first orders of Paul was an injunction to him to depart in twenty-four hours. Altesti has talents, but is ungrateful: he occasioned the disgrace of Bolkunof, his first benefactor.—Gribofsky, the other secretary, was a Russian. He had not the understanding of his colleague, but perhaps a better heart, and acquired nearly equal influence. He was the son of a clergyman, and began his career as a copyist in the office of Potemkin. In less than two years, under Zubof, he attained the rank of colonel, and his luxury and expensive mode of living astonished and disgusted all Petersburg. The finest ladies admired his person, and he was flattered by the greatest lords. He kept a band of music, buffoons, mistresses, and horses. In the spring he gave suppers, with desserts of fruit not to be equalled at the empress's table; and I was present at an entertainment where every one paid his shot, the dessert of which, furnished by him, was reckoned, on account of the season, at five hundred rubles (50*l.*)

* Among others, Kapief, a young man, who would have deserved a better fate had his heart been equal to his head: he was accused of having said to one of his friends, whom he met in Paul's new uniform, " Bon jour, beau masque!"

diately their respective corps, or give in their resignation. To remove him with less indignity from the palace, a large mansion was given him as a present, and all his offices were then withdrawn. He did not himself give in his resignation of thirty different employments till in reality he no longer held them. The emperor created Nicholas Soltikof field-marshal, and restored to his office the administration of military affairs, which had been taken from it by Zubof. It was then that the disorders and abuses which pervaded the service were discovered. The favourite, who, to enrich himself, carried on a war in Persia, the conducting of which was entrusted to his brother*, had not condescended to submit to the college of war the ordinary reports; and the troops which he had marched towards Gallicia were equally neglected: so that when it became necessary to make a new arrangement of the army, it was not known where the greater part of the regiments were, and still less in what condition they would be found. Officers, who had to rejoin their corps, knew not to what quarter of the world they should set

* At the empress's table, during the visit of the king of Sweden, the conversation turned on some news just brought by a courier. " It is nothing," said Zubof to a Swede: " my brother sends *us* word, that he has gained a battle and " conquered a province: that is nothing new."

off to find them, and in vain attended the offices to obtain the necessary information*.

A few weeks after, Zubof obtained permission, or rather received orders, to quit Russia. Like all his predecessors, he went into Germany to exhibit the brilliants, the orders, and the portraits which he had received from Catharine: but of all the gifts of his old mistress, the rubles are those which he has used with most discretion. After having taken with him a girl disguised as a valet, he fell in love at Tœplitz with a pretty emigrant of the name of Roche-Aimon: but he there soon became acquainted with the young

---

* This was frequently the case in Russia; but the following will excite more astonishment. A Frenchman, the chevalier Roger, having solicited count Soltikof, through the medium of major M. to give him the post of commandant of some remote place, as he wished for such a retirement, where he might live with his wife more cheaply, the minister gave orders to see whether any such place was vacant. Being informed that fort Peter and Paul in the government of Orenberg was without a commandant, Roger was appointed to the post, and set off. Some months after, major M. received a letter from Roger in the following words: "I am arrived in the country where my fort was said to be; "but judge of my surprise on being informed that it was "destroyed by Pugatshef twenty years ago, and exists no "longer. Finding myself in a desert with my family, without an asylum, and without resource, I have been obliged "to return to Orenburg." This letter was shewn to the minister, who gave Roger another post.

princesses of Courland, who, with the graces and beauty they inherit from their mother, and the immense fortunes which their father will leave them, are the greatest fortunes in Europe. He endeavoured, accordingly, to pay his court to the old duke, whom a little before he had attempted to strip of his sovereignty, and towards whom he had assumed so much haughtiness at Petersburg. The duke expressed to him his resentment and contempt; but Zubof, unaccustomed to meet with obstacles, conceived the design of carrying off the eldest princess by force. Whether, however, the duke complained to the emperor, or Paul was actuated by other motives, he dispatched an order to Zubof to return to Russia; and it is probable that the last favourite of Catharine has, by this time, acted his last part.

Count Nicholas Soltikof, field marshal, minister of war, and grand master to the young grand-dukes * * * *

The old vice-chancellor Ostermann, whom Paul eagerly advanced to the post of chancellor, in order to get rid of him, burdened with old age and infirmities, no longer appeared at court but as a memorial of past times. He was far from acting under Catharine the part which his father played in the reign of Anne, and from deserving the same disgrace from Paul which his father had merited from Elizabeth. He had the name only of vice-chancellor, and the dispatch of some passports which were given him to sign. Diplomatic and foreign affairs were divided in the office of Zubof between Besborodko and Markof, who were the actual authors of all the ministerial papers; and the first of whom particularly enjoyed an immense influence, which even balanced that of the favourite.

Besborodko and Markof were perfect contrasts to each other. The one was aukward, clownish, negligent, disorderly, with his stockings about his heels, and had the gait of an elephant; though richly habited, he appeared always as if he had dressed himself at the conclusion of a debauch, which still oppressed him with the stupidity of drowsiness: the other was so minutely attentive to dress, that he might pass for the ridiculous marquis of some of our comedies; and so absurdly affected that he never entered a room or bowed but according to the rules of a dancing-master, never walked but on his toes, and never took snuff without displaying the brilliants which sparkled on his fingers. When he spoke too, it was always in the ear of the person with whom he discoursed: his conversation consisted of bon-mots, his answers of points; and the same study and affectation were perceptible in his attempts at wit as in his dress and manners.

Besborodko, notwithstanding the depravity of his morals, is active, and occasionally laborious.

Promoted from the situation of clerk in the chancery to the rank of prime-minister*, he is well acquainted with the routine of affairs, and writes with facility; but the negligence and disorder which characterise his person are equally perceptible in all the offices under his administration, and particularly in the management of posts, of which he is director-general, and which is an office open to the inspection of every one †.

Before his appointment, it was the best conducted public institution in Russia: under his administration it will soon become the worst. His office is a devouring gulph, from which nothing returns; and the advantages which principally distinguish his house are the multitude of

---

* At first a writer in the office of Romanzof, he became secretary to Catharine, and the following is said to have been the making of his fortune. Having been ordered one day to draw up an ukase, he forgot it, and appeared before the empress without it. On her asking for it, Besborodko, without being disconcerted, took from his pocket a sheet of blank paper, in which he began to read, as if it contained the ukase in question. Catharine, satisfied with the language, asked for the paper, that she might sign it, and was much astonished to find it blank. This facility of extemporaneous composition struck her; and far from reproaching the secretary with his negligence or deceit, she made him minister of state, for knowing the style of a ukase by heart, and having had the boldness to impose it on her.

† Of all parts of the country, the estates of the director-general of the post were those where horses were never to be had, and where travellers were sure to be *taken in*.

entrances and secret stair-cases by which he contrives to escape, in quitting, or shun, in entering, the unhappy expectants, who wait whole days in the antichamber*. It is necessary to have the clue of Ariadne to reach this Minotaur; who, without doubt, would be found at the extremity of his labyrinth, engaged in preying upon some young beauty.

If the morals of Markof are not edifying, it must be admitted that he does not traverse the *Metschansky* † like Besborodko. He is attached to a tragic actress of the name of Hus, who has great influence over him, and who at least endeavours to be respectable in the character of mother, which her admirer often succeeds in conferring upon her ‡. On the talent which is

---

* It is said that an attorney, not being able to get sight of him, at length contrived to slip into his carriage, and wait for him there. Besborodko, astonished at the boldness of the scheme, heard the man's tale, and promised to make his business known to the empress: but the man would not quit his post, and remained in the carriage till Besborodko came out of the palace, that he might have an answer. Report says it was a favourable one.

† The name of that quarter of Petersburg in which girls of the town most abound.

‡ The emperor, by a refinement of vengeance, forbad la Hus to accompany Markof in his exile; saying, she belonged to the court, and not to him. This tragic actress, who possesses considerable talents, had converted the french theatre into an aristocracy, over which she presided.

ascribed to these two ministers, of being able, the one to translate impromptu into russ, the other into french, the ministerial papers, I set but little value. All the compositions I have read of the one or of the other, especially of Markof, have neither been distinguished for elegance of style, nor clearness of expression. I do not speak of logic, the details which they have had to give having been generally too absurd to assort with it. Besides, under Catharine II, russian diplomatics did not require splendid talents. She employed two means more persuasive than either argument or eloquence—threats and money, the effects of which are always fear and corruption.

The prejudice of many parts of Europe, and especially of Germany, in favour of Russia, is astonishing. It is thought, that the cabinet of Petersburg is composed of men of superior abilities: the court of Vienna crouches beneath its influence, and that of Berlin has not yet been able to dismiss its fears and respect. Doubtless, if the intelligent statesmen of Germany could have a clear view of those men who seem to dazzle their eyes, they would be ashamed of having so long mistaken the false lustre of a piece of rotten wood for the true radiance of genius, paper for money, boastings for greatness, and presumption for ability.

Besborodko, who had always worn shoes and

buckles like Paul, and who was moreover extremely rich and powerful, was at first treated with respect*. Markof, who did not possess these advantages to the same degree, was dismissed with indignity, and publicly disgraced. He is the same person who was formerly sent from Holland to Paris, where he is still remembered by the appellation of the insipid Markof.

The present count Samoïlof, procureur-general of the empire, had no other merit than that of being the nephew of Potemkin, and having a few affected resemblances of his figure. His capacity was unequal to the duties of his functions, by which he was grand-treasurer and president of the senate, and of all the courts of the empire. It was against his own inclination that he was called from the army to fill these civil employments. He acknowledged that he did not possess the necessary talents; but his deficiency was his chief recommendation, for a passive agent was wanted, unable, from incapacity, to counteract the views of Catharine or her favourites. It was at his house that the infamous inquisition reassembled which Ann erected under the name of

---

* He was made a *prince,* and was worthy of being one. He continued Paul's prime-minister; and it was he who, in the name of his master, declared war on the french republic; citing as a motive decrees, which I believe were known only to himself. He is since dead.

the *Secret Chancery*, which Peter III. thought it his duty to abolish, which Catharine revived under another form, and the worthy members of which Paul carefully distributes in the anti-chambers of particular houses. The palace of Samoïlof, which is one of the most elegant in Petersburg, contains several prisons for the detention of accused persons, where they were safely kept till otherwise privately disposed of. It was apparently on that account alone that many considered it as a public building. In other respects, Samoïlof was insignificant and like the ass carrying reliques. Paul, to reward him for the readiness with which he caused the oath of fidelity to be taken by the senate, bestowed on him four thousand peasants, under pretence that his mother had already promised them. Some days after he was suddenly removed from his place, and prince Kurakin appointed his successor.

But the man against whom the blood and tears of thousands of victims cried most loudly for vengeance, he who ought to have suffered first beneath the axe of justice, if the successor of Catharine had been endowed with firmness, equity, and humanity, was Arkarof, governor-general of Petersburg. This man, or rather this ferocious savage, had distinguished himself for a long time by a brutality worthy of an executioner in the train of Attila. He was governor of Tver, where he exercised a system of robbery, the particulars of which would excite horror, and appear incredible, when Catharine towards the end of her life, placed him near her person. This is the man whom she judged worthy to be the guardian of her crown, when the french revolution, the Zubofs, the Esterhazys, and perhaps her own remorse, began to fill her with suspicions and terror. He soon displayed, in a more extensive field, those horrid qualities which had been the scourge of the provinces of Mosco and Tver. Upon the death of Catharine, the fall of Zubof, and the accession of Paul, the punishment of this monster was expected as an event that could not fail to take place. Innumerable victims of his tyrannies cast themselves at the feet of Paul, demanding justice and vengeance. The emperor, however, granted no redress to complaints of abuse of power or oppression, but contented himself with commanding Arkarof to pay some debts. This vice-tyrant was too useful to the system which Paul was about to introduce, to have anything farther to dread. Of all those who enjoyed the confidence of the mother, he was, by a horrible exception in favour of his talents, the only one who obtained the confidence of the son. He was confirmed in all his former, and even raised to new employments. Nevertheless, the complaints of honest men, and the cries of the people, increased against him. It is said, that Paul, when on his way to Mosco to be crowned, would find the road strewed with petitions which the people would present against this new Sejanus *. Wretched inhabitants of Tver and Mosco, in vain will you run to meet your gospodar, in vain bow your heads to the dust, your cries will never touch his heart!

From this account of four or five persons, who held the reigns of government at the death of Catharine, it appears that Paul had nothing to apprehend from them: all of them were rich, their fortunes made, and none of them young. It cannot, however, be too carefully observed, with what eagerness Paul still loaded with wealth these blood-suckers of the state, before he discarded them. His motives are obvious: as soon as he thought he had no longer anything to fear from them, he disgraced them. The sudden death of his mother prevented any other party from forming at court, and there was no individual at the head of the armies in a situation to undertake anything. The three generals in chief, who then commanded the principal armies of the empire, were as remote from each other, by the difference of their manners, views, and characters, as by the immense distance which actually separated them.

* He is now in disgrace, though not for his crimes.

The most respectable was prince Nicholas Repnin, whose name has so often resounded through Europe in conjunction with that of the celebrated Romanzof*. He, with this veteran warrior, was the only general of signal merit in the armies of Catharine, whose appearance and person did not exhibit a perfect contrast to their reputation. In the last war but one against the Turks, he acted a brilliant part as a general, and displayed great abilities as a negotiator at Con-

---

* I make no mention, likewise, of that old warrior, whom the ingratitude of Catharine, who was indebted to him for her first triumphs, will render for ever celebrated, no less than his own exploits. He was himself dying at the time of the empress's decease; and, though he had the command of an army, his debility rendered him inactive. Paul wore mourning for him three days, and ordered all his army to do the same. For twenty years he had left off visiting the court; and, whether in retirement or in the camp, led a life as selfish as philosophic; for he is less to be honoured as a husband or a father, than as a general. He parted from his wife, and remained as much a stranger to his family as la Fontaine. One of his sons having finished his studies, came to the army to him to ask a commission. " Who are you?" said Romanzof. " Your son."—" O, very well! you are grown " up, I see." After a few more questions *equally* paternal, the young man asked, where he should take up his abode, and what he was to do. " Why, to be sure, you are ac- " quainted with some officer or other in the camp!" said his father. It is a fact no less singular, that his son, Sergius Romanzof, returning from his embassy to Sweden, asked Nicholas Soltikof for a letter of recommendation to his father, that he might be well received by him.

stantinople. He was afterwards distinguished in Poland by as much politeness as arrogance: He then submitted ignominiously to the ascendency of Potemkin, who treated him as a respectable character of past times. In his old age he still further obscured his early reputation by an attachment to the mysteries of martinism and the illuminés; and we are at a loss to determine, whether it was the humility of a devotee, the servility of a courtier, or the stoicism of a patriotic hero, that enabled him to bear the insolence of Potemkin and the hatred of Catharine, who, while they availed themselves of his military talents, loaded him with insults. He had incurred the dislike of Catharine by declaring in favour of Paul, and advising him to assert his rights to the crown, of which his mother had only been proclaimed guardian and regent. In the last war against the Turks, Repnin acted a very inferior part, yoking himself voluntarily to the car of Potemkin, lest he should otherwise not be harnessed at all; for he was resolved to serve, whether it were allowed him or not. In the antichambers of the favourites he prostituted his laurels and his hoary head more eagerly than a young officer who had still his fortune to make. How different was Repnin here to Repnin when ambassador at Warsaw, giving audience to the king of Poland in his dressing-gown*! or rather, it was the same character; for the haughtiest persons will always be found to be the most servile.

While Potemkin, however, was detained from the camp by the pleasures and festivities of Petersburg, as has been already mentioned, the old marshal Repnin, to whom he had left the command of the army during his absence, so far emancipated himself as to neglect the order he had received to remain inactive. He suddenly passed the Danube, and, by a skilful march, surprised and defeated the grand army of the vizir Yussuf. This gallant and successful action revived the faded laurels of Repnin. The court resounded with his praises: they compared this bold and decisive campaign with those of Potemkin, who was content every winter to attack a few fortresses, the capture of which cost torrents of blood, and who had never found a turkish army to fight

---

* One day, the king coming to pay him a visit, he ran and put on a morning-gown to receive him. After a trifling excuse, and a slight bow, he turned his back to the looking-glass, making all manner of ridiculous and insulting gestures to the king, who was facing the mirror. At Riga, he received d'Artois almost as rudely, pretending not to know him, and leaving him alone by the fire. He was piqued at the air of superiority which the french prince assumed, and at his not saluting the guard, which paid him military honours.

with. Roused from his lethargy by this blow, which disgraced and threatened him, Potemkin abandoned his pleasures, and entered Moldavia. His interview with Repnin was a terrible explosion, which the conqueror of the Turks sustained with greater firmness than was expected of him. But he was driven from the army, and obliged to acquiesce in his dismissal, for having gained a most decisive victory, and forced the Turks to solicit an ignominious peace: such was still the influence of Potemkin, and the condescension of the ungrateful Catharine! On the death of Potemkin, which shortly after happened, Repnin repaired to Petersburg, and degraded his old age and his honours in the anti-chamber of Zubof; who, flattered to see the old warrior in the number of his assiduous retainers, appointed him governor-general of Livonia. In the consternation and rage into which Catharine was thrown by the massacre of the Russians in Warsaw, he received orders to collect the regiments of his province and to invade Poland. He was at this period the only general of great reputation, and the oldest in the army: he had the further satisfaction of seeing his sovereign, contrary to her inclination, obliged to employ him. The regular and cautious march, however, of Repnin, through Lithuania, did not accord with the impatient vengeance of Catharine: she thirsted for blood, for the blood of all the inhabitants of Warsaw; and she let loose from another quarter the furious Suvarof, who strewed his route with carcases to the very gates of Praga. Repnin then received the severest insult he had ever swallowed, but he digested it as readily as former ones. Suvarof was created field-marshal, and appointed commander over the man whose orders the day before he had received, and by whom he was despised *. Catharine added even raillery to insult, by making a present of a house to Repnin, for having been passed over in this appointment. The whole army resented this treatment of the veteran commander; several generals remonstrated, and count Ivan Soltikof, with generous indignation, resigned his commission. Repnin alone, Repnin, who

* Suvarof caused the first report sent him by Repnin to be read aloud to him two or three times over, in the presence of his staff, making a thousand antics, pretending to be deaf, that the reader might raise his voice, and astonished at receiving a report from prince Repnin, whom he thus cruelly rallied. Catharine was always very despotic, and always made seniority give way to favour. At the death of Potemkin, Kamenskoi, one of her best generals, took the command of the army as a matter of right, and sent his first report accordingly. He said, " Having taken the command in conse-
" quence of my seniority, &c." against which Catharine wrote in the margin, " Who gave you orders?" He then spoke of the disorder which he found prevailing among the troops, and in the margin Catharine wrote, " He dared not say a
" word while the prince was alive." In answer to his report, Kamenskoi received orders to quit the army.

had most reason to be offended, and was most capable of making it felt, who could with impunity shew that he was susceptible of resentment and honour, like a stoic or a christian, submitted to this disgrace.

On his accession, Paul at length created him field-marshal, and the last warlike exploit of Repnin was the executing military vengeance on some villages in the government of Novgorod, who had talked of affranchisement.

Repnin, who has shewn himself a great general, as well as an imperious minister and a servile courtier, possesses some personal qualities rarely to be met with in russian generals. Not only his figure, but his manners and carriage, are noble. His heart is humane *, and he neither affects the muscovite grossness of his colleagues towards their inferiors †, nor is tainted with that rapa-

---

* Particularly towards the soldiers. Reviewing a regiment of cavalry, he said, " I inquire only about the men: as " to the horses, they are bought by the colonel, and therefore " I know better care is taken of them."

† His behaviour to his officers, however, while at Berlin, shocked the Prussians, to whom the haughtiness of the russian generals was unknown. At this place, it was matter of astonishment to see Repnin gravely stalking along, decorated with the badges of all his orders of knighthood, while a kniaz Volkonsky his nephew, several aides-de-camp, and Thiemann the martinist, his secretary, followed him at some paces distance. Every time he turned about to utter a word, his attendants halted and took off their hats. His political mission,

cious avarice which has always distinguished them. On the contrary, he is compassionate and generous; and Lithuania is under great obligations to him, as it was through him and prince Gallitzin that it was saved from total ruin.

A stranger, who has heard the name of Suvarof, wishes, on his arrival in Russia, to see this hero. He is shewn an old man of a weather-beaten and shrivelled figure, who traverses the apartments of the palace, hopping on one foot, or is seen running and gamboling in the streets, followed by a troop of boys, to whom he throws apples, to make them scramble and fight, crying himself, " I am " Suvarof! I am Suvarof!" If the stranger should fail to discover in this old madman the conqueror of the Turks and the Poles, he will at least, in his haggard and ferocious eyes, his foaming and horrid mouth, readily discern the butcher of the

---

however failed of success. This prince, a field-marshal, formerly ambassador triumphant at Constantinople, and omnipotent at Warsaw, neither frightened nor cajoled the young king of Prussia, whom Paul had ordered him to oblige to rejoin the coalition. Repnin, dismissed from Berlin, repaired to Vienna, where the success of his negotiation is visible. But one of his secretaries, said to be a Frenchman of the name of Aubert, stole off with part of the papers and secrets of his embassy. This enraged Paul, and he dismissed Repnin at his return, for not having succeeded at Berlin, and for having employed a Frenchman in his service: however, as a mark of singular clemency, he is allowed to wear the uniform of armies which he has commanded with glory for forty years.

inhabitants of Praga. Suvarof would be considered as the most ridiculous buffoon, if he had not shewn himself the most barbarous warrior. He is a monster, with the body of an ape and the soul of a bull-dog. Attila, his countryman, and from whom he is perhaps descended, had neither his good fortune nor his ferocity. His gross and ridiculous manners have inspired his soldiers with the blindest confidence, which serves him instead of military talents, and has been the real cause of all his successes. He is accounted a brave and successful warrior; that, educated in camps, is unacquainted with the court, and could give no offence to the favourites. After having distinguished himself as a subaltern, he advanced step by step to the rank of commander in chief. He is endowed with a natural ferocity, which serves him for bravery, and spills blood, like a tiger, by instinct. When at the army he lives in the camp like a simple Kozak: he arrives at court like an ancient Scythian; and, during his stay, will accept no other lodging than the carriage which brought him. To relate the details of his life would be to record a series of extravagancies; and certainly if he be not mad, the ability to counterfeit madness is among the first of his qualifications, but his folly is that of a barbarian, which has nothing amusing in it.

He has not, however, been always successful.

At the siege of Otchakof, the Turks having made a feigned sortie, he chose, contrary to the orders of Potemkin, to pursue them, hoping to enter the city with the fugitives. A battery of mortars was opened upon him, and his whole column destroyed. He proceeded to the assault of Ismaïl without having reconnoitred the place *, and his exploits in Poland are those of a brigand. He hastened his march thither to satisfy the vengeance of Catharine, and to massacre the remains of an army already defeated by Fersen, and deprived of the brave Koschiusko, its principal strength. Suvarof, embracing the inhabitants of Warsaw, and granting them pardon on the bodies of twenty thousand citizens of every age and sex, resembles a satiated tiger that plays with his prey on the bones of his charnel-house.

The singularity of his manners is as striking as the eccentricity of his mind. He retires to rest

* He usually announced his successes in two or three words, and frequently in a couple of bad burlesque russian verses. Cæsar wrote to the senate, *Veni, vidi, vici.* Suvarof might with propriety be more concise by one-third than Cæsar, for he always conquered without seeing. He said himself: " Kamenskoi knows war, but war knows nothing of " him: I know her not, but she knows me: as to Ivan Soltikof, " he neither knows her nor is known by her." A few such traits, and some happy quotations from ancient history, have given Suvarof reputation. His partisans reported that he frequently shut himself up to study the dead languages, and even hebrew. French and german he speaks tolerably.

at six in the evening, and rises at two in the morning, when he bathes himself in cold water, or causes some pails of it to be thrown over his naked body. He dines at eight, and his dinner, like his breakfast, consists of the coarsest and commonest food of the soldiers, and brandy: to be invited to such a repast would make a man shudder. Often, in the middle of the entertainment, one of his *aides-de-camp* rises; and approaching him, forbids him to eat any more. " By whose order am I forbidden?" demands Suvarof.—" By order of marshal Suvarof himself," answers the aide-de-camp. Suvarof, rising, then says, " He must be obeyed." In the same manner he causes himself to be commanded in his own name to go and take a walk, or the like.

During his stay at Warsaw, a crowd of austrian or prussian officers pressed to see this original. Before he made his appearance, he inquired of which of these officers there was the greatest number; if Austrians, he decorated himself with a portrait of Joseph II. entered his antichamber, leaping into the middle of the circle, and offered to each of them the picture to kiss, repeating, " Your emperor knows me, and loves " me too." If Prussians composed the majority, he wore the order of the Black Eagle, and made the same grimaces. At court, he was sometimes seen running from lady to lady, and kissing the portrait of Catharine which they wear at the breast, crossing himself, and bowing. Catharine told him one day to behave himself more decently.

He is a devotee, and superstitious. He obliges his captains to pray aloud before their companies; and abuses such of the foreign officers or Livonians as are unacquainted with the russian prayers.

Sometimes he visits the hospitals of the camp, calling himself a physician. Those whom he finds extremely ill he obliges to take rhubarb or salts, and on those who are but slightly indisposed, he bestows blows. He sometimes drives all the sick from the hospital, saying, " It is not permit-" ted to the soldiers of Suvarof to be sick." In his armies, all those manœuvres are prohibited which relate to a retreat, as he shall never, he says, have occasion to adopt them. He exercises his soldiers himself, and makes them charge with the bayonet in three different ways. When he says, " March against the Poles," the soldier plunges his bayonet once; " March against the " Prussians," the soldier strikes twice; " March " against the execrable French," the soldier then makes two thrusts forward, and a third in the ground, and there sticks and turns his bayonet round. His hatred against the French was extreme. His letter to Charette has been seen in various newspapers. He wrote to Catharine from Warsaw, and frequently in these words: " Mo-" ther, permit me to march against the French." When the death of Catharine happened, he had already advanced for that purpose into Gallicia at the head of forty thousand men.

He frequently rides through his camp, stript to his shirt, on the bare back of a kozak horse; and at day-break, instead of causing the drums to beat the *reveille* he comes out of his tent, and crows three times like a cock, which is the signal for the army to rise, sometimes to march, or even advance to battle.

In the multiplicity of extravagances which he commits, or of insipid things which he says, if any singular or striking joke falls from him, every one repeats and admires it as a burst of genius. This man has nevertheless some virtues: he has shewn occasionally an uncommon disinterestedness, and even generosity, as well in refusing the gifts of Catharine as in distributing them about him. He will slaughter the wretch who begs his life, but will give money to him who begs for charity: because he sets no more value on money than on human blood. Almost at the same moment he gnashes his teeth in rage like a madman, laughs and grins like an ape, or weeps piteously like an old woman.

Such is the too famous Suvarof. He quarrelled

with his wife, and would not acknowledge a son whom he had by her; preferring his nephews, the princes Gortschakof: but the empress having made this son an officer in the guards, he said, " As the empress chuses I shall have a son, be it " so; but for myself, I know nothing of the mat-" ter." He had also a daughter, maid of honour to Catharine, who was distinguished at court for idiotism. Her father, after an absence of several years, appointed a meeting with her at the house of a third person. " Ah, father," cried she, " how big you are grown since I saw you last." In french, this would have passed for a happy play upon words, but in russ it was a blunder that excited universal laughter.

After the capture of Warsaw, he repaired to Petersburg to enjoy the fruits of his triumphs; and this Scythian, who had never before any other lodging than his carriage, accepted apartments in the Tauridan palace, and wore a superb marshal's uniform, which was given him by Catharine. On his receiving this dress, he played a thousand antics, hugging it in his arms, kissing it, and making signs of the cross; and when he lifted it, he said, " I am not surprised they do not give such a dress " as this to little Nicholas Soltikof; it would be " too heavy for him to wear*."

* Nicholas Soltikof was one of those most hurt by the promotion of Suvarof.

PORTRAIT OF VALERIAN ZUBOF. 221

We have seen the manner in which Paul dismissed him on his accession, and the motives which instigated him. The murmurs of the army afterwards obliged the emperor to recal him. It was to make use of him as a scourge to chastise the French.

Valerian Zubof, brother to the favourite, commanded the army which acted in Persia. Mention has before been made of this young libertine, who is naturally of a frank, honest, and courageous disposition, but has been spoilt by indulgence. He had lost a leg in Poland, and it was on crutches that he went to conquer Asia*. One of his couriers arrived at the moment of the death of Catharine, with the account of a battle. Paul sent him ribands of the order of St. Anne to distribute among his officers, and to each of the colonels a private command to lead their regiments to the frontiers. The general remained behind in his camp, without knowing what he was to do. He afterwards followed his army, and on his arrival at Petersburg gave in his resignation. He resides at present in Courland, where he possesses almost the entire domains of the ancient dukes.

* At the news of his wound, Catharine sent him her own surgeon, the riband of the order of St. Andrew, the rank of general in chief, and 100,000 rubles (10,000*l.*) to defray the expense of his cure. He demanded 500,000 (50,000*l.*) more, to pay his debts.

From generals of such character, and armies at a distance from court, and ignorant of what was passing there, nothing could be apprehended. The only corps which Paul had really to fear was the guards: for a long time these four numerous regiments, commanded by the first nobility in the empire, had viewed with alarm the approaching reign of the grand-duke, and regarded his accession as the term of their existence. Paul did not even conceal his aversion for them; and the severest reproach which he could use to his officers, and even to his soldiers, at the reviews of Gatshina and Pavlofsky, was, " Thou art fit for nothing but " to serve in the guards." These troops repaid him in turn the contempt he affected; and, by way of ridicule, bestowed on his soldiers the epithet of " *Prussaki*, or Prussians." It is beyond a doubt, that with these dangerous successors of the strelitzes, a slighter cause than the tears of an Elizabeth or the caressing attentions of a Catharine, would have served to excite them to mutiny: and Paul did not think himself in security till he had distributed, as we have seen, his own battalions in these formidable regiments, caressed the soldiers, and deprived the old officers of their commissions. But it was to little purpose that he lavished on them rubles and brandy: these acts of generosity gained only those who were near his person, while the army complained and murmured*.

Paul, as grand-duke, hated and despised by his mother, mortified by the favourites, derided by the courtiers, living in solitude and almost forgotten under a brilliant reign, and preserving the most regular and austere manners in the midst of a corrupt and debauched court†, required few amiable qualities or virtues to make his situation pitied by men of understanding, and his reign wished for by the people. He might have been expected as a deliverer: he was, however, generally feared as a scourge: his domestics, his officers, his courtiers, his favourites, and even his children, dreadful to relate, participated more or less in these horrid sentiments. The suspicion he en-

---

* Peter I. had abolished the strelitzy (archers), but their spirit revived in the four regiments of guards, who supplied their place. The guards, consisting of picked men, whose officers were taken from the wealthiest families (1), formed an army of near ten thousand men around the throne. The influence of this body was sufficient to effect a revolution, and indeed alone accomplished all that have taken place since Peter I.

† This is a piece of justice that must not be denied him; and if his attachment to the Nelidof have made him neglect his wife, it has not made him offend against decency or decorum in public, hitherto at least. The Nelidof, however, is dismissed.

(1) To be an officer in the guards, a man must prove that he possesses at least a hundred peasants or slaves.

†

tertained, that he inspired these sentiments, doubtless exasperated him, and perhaps rendered him incapable of correcting them; but with this character, the traits of justice and goodness which sometimes appear in him, are more striking, and occasion a deeper regret for those qualities which might have been expected in him.

Prior to his accession, his favour was dreaded: besides that it often excited the resentment of the empress and the favourite, it was considered as the same sign of disgrace as fine weather is proverbially regarded as the constant forerunner of rain. Never did man shew more eccentricity and fickleness in the choice of his friends. He began by opening himself with unbounded confidence and entire familiarity to the person who appeared to enter into his views; then, repenting this frankness, he regarded his friend as a dangerous character, perhaps the creature of his mother or of the favourite, who had flattered him only to betray him. Beside those on whom the slightest attentions of his wife, or the kindnesses of Benkendorf, caused the storms of his anger to fall, the empire swarmed with his banished domestics, disgraced favourites, and cashiered officers: it invariably happened, that he who had been nearest his person had most reason to complain, and he who had received most favours found himself in the end most unfortunate.

Having given some account of the ministers of his mother, it will not be improper to speak a few words of the courtiers who were in favour with Paul on his accession, and who will certainly continue in favour for some time. It may be said with truth, in their praise and in his, that the majority of these ministers are more disinterested, and abler statesmen, than those of the old court.

The two princes Kurakin, who alternately have been in favour and disgrace with Paul*, are the two men, next to the valet-de-chambre above mentioned, who possess most influence, and per-

* Alexius Kurakin had frequently been in disgrace with Paul on account of the attention and regard he always paid the grand-duchess; but the ill-humour of Paul on this score must not be ascribed to jealousy, which his character and that of his wife did not allow. Paul's ill-humour arose from political suspicions, not from love. One day, observing his wife speak low by the fire-side to prince Kurakin, he fell into a passion, and said to her, " Madam, you want to make your- " self friends, and prepare to act the part of Catharine, but be " assured you shall not find in me a Peter III." These inconsiderate expressions, which escaped him in his rage, alarmed every one, and Kurakin withdrew from court. From that period the grand-duchess was more unhappy, and under still greater restraint. The least message could not be sent to her without permission of her husband. He named those who were to offer her their arm for a walk, to make her evening party, or even to converse with her in the course of the evening. At length he found it more commodious to give her a sort of cicisbeo, who was never to quit her. Prince Nesvitsky was the man whom he deemed insignificant enough for this office.

haps they are persons most deserving of it. Previous to the death of Catharine, though powerful and rich, their employments were insignificant: one of them led a retired life, amusing himself with the cultivation of the arts and sciences, or the education of his children, and was generally respected and esteemed. His manners and habits of life were very different from those of the greater part of the russian nobility, who dissipate their time and fortunes in vices of every kind, in gaming, in luxury, and other follies. In a word, he appeared worthy to be at the head of affairs, and he now holds that station with his brother; the one being vice-chancellor of the empire, and the other procureur-general: to them must be attributed whatever is right in the conduct of affairs.

Two young chamberlains, who fortunately were in the service of Paul when the couriers arrived with tidings of the death of Catharine, were suddenly metamorphosed into generals of the army, and became his first aides-de-camp. One is M. Rastaptschin, who owes his favour to a very ingenious letter, and who, to preserve it, must renounce three-fourths of his understanding, and one-half of himself*. The other is a young count Schuvalof, whom Paul had recently taken into favour, after having long neglected him; and to

---

* He has already been twice dismissed and recalled.

whom he presented one of his own dresses, to serve as a model for the horse-guards, of which he appointed him major. The young man appeared at court in this habit, as if in a sack; and doubtless found himself much at his ease in it. Nothing can be more singular than the equal favour of these young persons, since it would appear that the exaltation of the one were sufficient to cause the disgrace of the other. M. Rastaptschin, some years ago, was gentleman in waiting to the grandduke at Pavlofsky. His young associates, and, among others, count Schuvalof and prince Baratinsky, considering their employments as a difficult and hazardous service, because a word spoken to the grand-duchess, or a coat too fashionably cut, was sufficient to ruin them, absented themselves as often as possible, feigning sickness, or alleging some other excuse. Rastaptschin, tired in his turn with not being relieved, wrote a sharp letter to the marshal of the court, in which he rallied his associates on the true motives which detained them at Pavlofsky; adding, at the conclusion, " For my own part, who have no disease to cure, " nor a fair italian singer to maintain, I will cheer- " fully continue to perform their duty to the " grand-duke." These strokes of satire were aimed at Schuvalof as well as at Baratinsky, whom Paul, though his relation, could not bear. The marshal shewed this letter to the empress, who at first laughed at it; but Schuvalof and Baratinsky, thinking they had reason to be offended, required an explanation from Rastaptschin. The affair made a noise: Baratinsky was sent to the army, and Rastaptschin was banished from the court for a year. From that time the grand-duke regarded him as his champion, and obstinately refused to accept the attendance of the other gentlemen in waiting, unless he was recalled; and accordingly, for more than a year, though they regularly came to Pavlofsky or Gatshina to offer their services, they were as regularly dismissed.

Among the favourites of the emperor, M. Pleschtscheief is a real phenomenon: being the only one who has always kept himself at the same distance. It is true, he has never ranked in the first class of favourites; but it is also true, that he has always been exempt from storms. He is a respectable and well-informed man: speaks several languages, possesses some knowledge of geography and government, and cultivates literature. He might even be of service to Russia, if, among his good qualities, he could reckon that of courage, to speak the truth; but unfortunately his constant enjoyment of favour seems almost a moral proof of the contrary*.

* He also has at last been disgraced, and with circumstances of great cruelty.

M. Nieledinsky, who had been the companion of the studies and amusements of Paul, was distinguished at Petersburg for great extent of capacity, and had acquired reputation by some love sonnets not deficient in harmony and sentiment. The emperor has appointed him his private secretary, but on condition, no doubt, that he strangles his muse, who has served him, however, too well to deserve so cruel a death. It is at least to be wished, that Nieledinsky may exhibit and practise the sensibility which he displays in his verses. His office is to give an account of the letters and petitions that are addressed to the emperor: the fate of numerous oppressed individuals is accordingly in his hands.

M. Nicolai came into Russia as governor to the young counts Razumofsky, who afterwards were his patrons. On the recommendation of madame Pretorius, his relation, waiting-maid to the duchess of Wirtemburg, he was placed near the grand-duchess in quality of secretary: he was baronized in Germany during the travels of the grand-duke, and became, on his accession, counsellor of state, director of the emperor's cabinet*, knight of the order of St. Anne, and re-

* What is called the *cabinet* in Russia is not a council of state; it is the room which contains the treasures, jewels, and private curiosities of the sovereign.

ceived some hundreds of peasants*. He comes from Strasburg, and is known in Germany by some imitations of Ariosto, and other poems agreeable enough, though extremely verbose. He also has been obliged to sacrifice his muse on the altar of fortune; to which, ungrateful as he is, she had herself conducted him. I know not whether the political haughtinefs, which he thinks himself obliged to maintain, render him more happy, but it does not at least give him the appearance of it.

M. Danorof, late librarian to the prince of Wirtemburg, and since aide-de-camp to Paul, is also become an important personage: but I abstain from speaking in detail of those with whom I am not sufficiently acquainted to form an adequate judgment of their merits. I shall only remark, that in the list of preferments which the

---

* He had before an estate in Finland, a province ceded by Sweden, where the peasants are not completely reduced to the same mode of slavery as the Russians; and Nicolaï frequently complained of it, saying, " These wretches scarcely " bring me in anything, and pretend to have rights." Those, whom he has just received, are in Poland, where he may do with them as he pleases, separate them, sell them, or make them work, like domestic animals, to embellish his gardens. From this anecdote the reader may judge what this Strasburger is become in Russia, who passes in Germany for a philosopher, and whom so many scribblers flatter as a Mecænas. If he read this, no doubt he will admire the moderation with which he is mentioned.

emperor has since made, I observe a number of persons deserving no other portion than the contempt and vengeance of the public.

Meanwhile it is apparent, that the persons that surround Paul are morally better than those who were about his mother*. He is surrounded

---

* The following piece of pleasantry will shew the opinion entertained of most of the persons in place and in favour at the court of Catharine. It occurred in a company where twelfthday was kept in the french manner, and where the king of the night was desired to dispose of the courtiers according to their talents and capacity.

" Zubof has never rendered any service to the state, and is
" no longer of service to the empress, since the Sapphics,
" Branicka, and Protassof, execute the functions of his office.
" Let a few emetics be given to him, to make him bring up
" what he has swallowed; and then let him be sent to the
" baths of Baldona for the recovery of his health.

" Count Nicholas Soltikof, president of the college of war,
" and governor of the grand-dukes, is appointed president of
" the college of physicians and deacon of the imperial chapel.
" He may likewise retain the water-closet of the young
" princes, provided he shut up his wife in a convent, or send
" her to Bedlam.

" Count Besborodko, chief counsellor of state, &c. shall
" be appointed cook to the court; unless he had rather be di-
" rector to the Lock Hospital for females, in which he will
" find all his friends.

" Vice-chancellor Ostermann shall repair to St. Denis, to
" replace the sword of Charlemagne, which was as long and
" as flat as himself.

" Prince Baratinsky, marshal of the court, shall be ap-
" pointed Jack Ketch. A more gentle mode of putting to
" death, than that by the knoot, is intended to be introduced;

by men of information and even of merit. I say he *is*, when perhaps I ought to say he *was*; for

" and he shall have the office of smothering and strangling in
" secret those that are intended to be dispatched, whether it
" be an emperor or his son: it is expected, however, that he
" do not let them cry out, as he did about thirty years ago.

" Marshal Suvarof shall have a patent for dealing as a
" butcher in human flesh; and the army shall be allowed to
" feed on it in Poland, where nothing but carcases are left.

" A committee of *utshiteli* (tutors) shall be appointed to
" examine whether prince Yussupof be able to read; if he
" can, he shall be appointed prompter to the theatres, of
" which he is now manager.

" Markof shall be sent ambassador to Paris, where he has
" been already so successful. It is hoped, that he will be the
" proper man to effect a reconciliation between Russia and
" the french republic, since he has been the scourge of the
" russian and polish jacobins, against whom it also has de-
" clared war.

" Samoïlof, procureur-general, shall be made one of the
" chevalier guards, he being a tolerably handsome man, which
" is a sufficient qualification.

" Kutusof, director of the corps of cadets in the room of
" the worthy count Anhalt, shall erect a monument to his
" predecessor, whom he studies to ridicule, and whom he
" makes us regret every day. His conduct, however, is the
" best panegyric on the memory of the worthy Anhalt.

" The corps of artillery shall remain with the old general
" Melissino, because he is the only general in that body who
" understands his business: but on condition, that he shall
" not have the management of the chest, and do not expose
" his grey hair in the antichamber of the valets of the court.
" He is requested likewise to employ less artifice in his con-
" duct, and less smoke in his artifices.

" Madame von Lieven, governess to the princesses, shall
" retain her place, though she has somewhat the air of an

his versatility displays itself on everything about him, not permitting merit to remain a sufficient time at his court to be corrupted*.

The prince, whom Paul appears to have chosen for the prototype of his reign and his actions, is Frederic William, father of the great king of

"Amazon; but the time will come when it will not be amiss
"to give young princesses a little of a military air (1).

"Countess Shuvalof, grand-mistress to the grand-duchess
"Elizabeth, shall likewise be confirmed; but she shall be
"enjoined not to let beasts only have permission to speak at
"the table of that young princess, unless they speak with
"sense, as they did in Æsop's days.

"Prince Repnin, having opened the door one day when
"prince Potemkin called for a glass of water, that he might
"himself repeat this important order to the lackeys, shall re-
"ceive a patent for the place of first valet-de-chambre to the
"favourites; a post which to him would be worth that of
"field-marshal. However, the crown of laurel which covered
"his grey hair shall be taken from him, because he suffered a
"buffoon to trample on him without saying a word, and be-
"cause the gift of a small house appeared suited to him, and
"to console him for the insult.

"M. Zavadofsky, director and plunderer of the bank, shall
"be sent into Siberia to catch sables, to replenish her ma-
"jesty's stock of furs, which it will not long be in her power
"to keep up by any other means. She is already unable to
"furnish her family with them, and Zavadofsky is well known
"to be a better huntsman than financier," &c.

* This has taken place. The princes Kurakin, and most of those whom I have named, are in disgrace at the moment of my writing this.

(1) This time is arrived.

Prussia*. The same austerity of manners, and the same passion for soldiers, are found in the russian autocrate. For the rest, I have drawn, I conceive, the character of Paul in relating his actions; if not, the task, I confess, is beyond my ability. It is well known, that nothing is so difficult to paint as an infant, whose physiognomy is as yet unsettled; and it is the same with the character of an eccentric man. The most favourable plea we can make for him is, that the light of the french revolution has touched his brain and disordered his intellects. It had already disturbed the much stronger head of his mother. It is said, that the people of Paris, crouding to see Paul, then a youth, cried, " My God, how ugly he is!" and that he had the good sense to laugh at it†. He is certainly not improved in his looks since he is grown old, bald, and wrinkled. The empress ap-

---

* This he does not allow; for he said one day, " I will be " Frederic II. in the morning, and Louis XIV. at night." Well, well! that will be an easy matter to you.

† He is greatly changed; or rather, he now dares shew himself what perhaps he was already. A poor soldier, in the agony of his sufferings under the cane by Paul's orders for a trifling fault in his exercise, cried out in despair, " Cursed " baldhead! cursed baldhead!" The enraged autocrate gave orders that he should expire under the knoot; and issued a proclamation, prohibiting, under pain of the same punishment, for any one to make use of the term bald, in speaking of the head, or snubbed, in speaking of the nose.

pears by his side like one of those beautiful women who are painted with a little deformed blackamoor near them, as a contrast to their shape and beauty. The singularity which he affects in his dress, and the severity of his manners, add greatly to his deformity. Without excepting even the Kalmuks and the Kirghises, Paul is the ugliest man in his extensive dominions; and he himself considers his countenance as so shocking, that he does not presume to impress it on his coin*.

I shall here subjoin a few particulars, which will serve to complete the picture of Paul by his own actions; and will prove, that when grand-duke, he announced what we have seen of him since his accession.

Near his palace of Pavlofsky he had a terrace, from which he could see all the centinels, whom he amused himself in stationing about him where-

---

* The new coins have not his effigy, but his cypher merely, with the following words of scripture, which, in such a connexion, have no meaning: " Not unto us, not unto us, but to " thy name." Probably it is some device of martinism, or of *obscurantism*, which Paul patronises. It even appears, that he intends to establish this order with that of Malta, of which, to the astonishment of all Europe, he has just declared himself grand-master, at the very instant of forming an alliance with the Turks. O my friends, can you refrain from laughter? But, alas!

Quidquid delirant reges plectuntur Achivi.

ever there was room for a centry box. On this covered terrace he spent a part of each day, in observing with a spying-glass all that was passing about him. He frequently sent a servant to a centinel, to order him to button or unbutton a little more of his coat, to keep his musket higher or lower, to walk at a greater or less distance from his centry box. Sometimes he would go himself nearly half a mile to give these important orders, and would cane the soldier, or put a ruble into his pocket, according as he was angry or pleased with him.

Pavlofsky was an open village, yet guards were appointed, who wrote down the names of all who entered it or went out of it, and who were obliged to tell whence they came, whither they were going, and what they wanted. Every evening each house was visited, to learn if there were any strangers there. Every man who wore a round hat, or had a dog with him, was arrested. The village, which had been much frequented on account of its beautiful situation, soon became a desert; persons turned out of their way to avoid it: and when Paul was perceived at a distance, he was studiously shunned. These circumstances increased his displeasure and suspicions, and he often caused the persons, who thus sought to avoid him, to be pursued and questioned.

One day he put all the officers of his battalion

under arrest, because they had saluted him aukwardly with the spontoon in filing off after their drill, and he ordered them to be called out for eight days successively to fiie off and salute before him, sending them regularly back to the guardhouse till they were able to salute him according to his fancy.

Exercising one day his regiment of cuirassiers, the horse of an officer threw him. Paul ran furiously towards him, crying, " Get up, rascal."— " Your highness, I cannot, I have broken my leg." Paul spat upon him, and retired swearing.

Passing at another time unexpectedly and secretly by one of his guard-houses, the officer, not knowing him, did not order out his men: upon which he instantly turned back, boxed the ears of the officer, and ordered him to be disarmed, and put under arrest.

One day, travelling from Tzarsko-selo to Gatshina, where the road runs through a marshy forest, he suddenly recollected something, and ordered the coachman to return. " Presently, your " highness," said the coachman; " the road is " here too narrow."—" How, rascal," cried Paul, " turn immediately!" The coachman, instead of answering, hastened to a spot where it was possible to comply: Paul, however, putting out his head, called to his equerry, and ordered him to arrest and punish the rebellious coachman. The

†

equerry assured him, that he would turn in a moment. Paul flew into a passion with the equerry also: "You are a pitiful scoundrel like himself," said he. "Let him overturn the carriage, let him "break my neck, but let him obey me, and turn "the instant I command him." During the dispute the coachman succeeded in turning, but Paul had him chastised on the spot.

Riding out, one day, his horse stumbled; on which he dismounted and ordered Markof, his equerry, to shut the poor animal up in a stable, and let him die of hunger. On the eighth day after, Markof told him the horse was dead; whereupon Paul answered: C'est bon! "That's well!" Since his accession, another of his horses stumbled with him in one of the streets of Petersburg: he alighted immediately, held a sort of council with his attendants, and the horse was condemned to receive fifty lashes with a whip. Paul caused them to be given on the spot, before the populace, counting himself the strokes, saying, "There, sir, that "is for having stumbled under the emperor."

One day, when only grand-duke, he met in the gardens a man with a round hat, who endeavoured to avoid him. Paul caused the man to be brought before him, and found that he was the clockmaker, coming to wind up the clocks of the palace. After preaching a long sermon to him on the indecency of round hats, he asked his wife for some pins, and raising the flaps of the hat, cocked it himself, and then replaced it upon the head of its owner.

Amidst this mass of absurdities, traces of humanity often appear: the pensions which he has bestowed on the unfortunate, the hospitals which he has founded for his soldiers, the provisions which he distributes among his poor officers, and other acts of benevolence and justice, attest that he deserves the character rather of a capricious than a bad man.

CHAP. VI.

WHAT REVOLUTIONS MAY BE EXPECTED TO TAKE PLACE IN RUSSIA.

Attitude and strength of the sovereign power in that country—Two ukases of Paul favourable to a revolution—Debasement of the people—Other local obstacles—The sovereign power becoming more absolute—The nobility offended—These alone can change the government—How, and why—Probability of a dismemberment of that vast territory, and of a change in the manners of the people and form of government.

IF, as some pretend, the french revolution be destined to spread over the globe, Russia will assuredly be the last place it will reach: it is on the frontiers of this vast empire that the french Hercules will erect his two pillars, and that liberty will long read, *Ne plus ultra:* it is there that a new world is still hidden from her. Despotism, standing on the forehead of a slave, and holding to the sky by his guilty hand, insults and defies her—a contest may, however, ere long, take place in the plains of Germany, which may decide the fate of the world. He has already seized unhappy Poland, and the principles which at present prevail in the east and north, are decidedly contrary to those which have of late distinguished the south and the west. Already the continent seems to be wholly divided between two preponderating empires, France and Russia, the views and interests of which are diametrically opposite: they seek an opportunity of jostling each other, and will crush in the shock the secondary powers by which they are still separated. It will be the combat of Day against Night, the last conflict of Philosophy and Reason against Barbarism and Ignorance. The famous wall raised by the Chinese against the incursions of the Tartars, that masterpiece of labour and cowardice, is neither so inaccessible nor so thick as the dark atmosphere that secures Russia from the approach of reason, and separates her from other nations. Muscovitism, trembling at sight of the danger, is incessantly occupied in fortifying this wall, and repairing the breaches made in it by reason. That political monster is like the salamander, which stifles the fire that surrounds it under the filthy foam it emits from its impure throat, and converts the flame into thick clouds of smoke.

Not that light and truth may not be found in Russia; but they who possess them, still more prudent than Fontenelle*, are so far from daring to open their hands to spread them abroad, that

* He says somewhere, "If I had my hand full of truths, I would take care not to open it."

they strive only to stifle them; for they who have knowledge are the only persons interested in maintaining ignorance and reducing bondage and tyranny to a rational system. Till there shall be found in Russia a numerous body of enlightened men, suffering by that state of servitude under which the people groan, a spontaneous revolution must not be expected in that country.

If anything at present could hasten the moment of attack, it is an ukase that Paul in his wisdom has just published; which, by abolishing the degrees of nobility attached to the possession of military rank and civil offices, has created a true *third estate,* never before known in Russia; a few emancipated vassals that have become tradesmen, or foreign mechanics, not deserving that name: there was scarcely any distinction of persons except slaves and nobles. All who held rank, civil or military, that is to say, all who had a little money or education, acquired nobility or its privileges, and eagerly affected its prejudices and spirit: but as soon as this enlightened part of the nation shall lose its claim to a participation in the honours and advantages of tyranny, and profit by the abuses of government and the degradation of the people, it will turn to the side of liberty. Thanks to the madness of despotism, it has created enemies to itself, and dug its own grave. The void heretofore caused by absolute power between the slave or peasant, and the free man or noble, is at last filled up. The third estate will rise up as a giant; with one powerful hand it will exalt the slave, with the other it will strike the noble; and perhaps before a century shall pass away, it may have reduced them to a level more happy for both than their present state.

Another proceeding of the emperor, as muscovitic in its principles, and as fortunate in the contrary effects it will produce, is the ordinance proscribing printing-houses in his dominions. He has permitted only three to subsist, for the purpose of printing his ukases, and church books, or such as can stand the triple ordeal of government, the schools, and the holy orthodox greek church*. In thus attempting to suppress learning and knowledge, he has rendered them the greatest service of which he was capable. The moment liberty and philosophy possess one free press, the greatest benefit that can be done them, is to destroy all others. All the books that have produced the revolution which the present age has witnessed, are to be found in Russia in great

* He has since carried the proscription of books to great perfection: he has even prohibited the importation of foreign catalogues, and ordered the booksellers to put on such books as can go through the triple examination, *by imperial permission*, instead of *imperial liberty*, which were the words used before.

numbers: such as may still be introduced into that country from foreign parts, even from Vienna itself, will be better than any that could be printed there with permission*: I maintain, therefore, that Paul has done great service to liberty and letters. Let his intention be pardoned for the sake of the effect.

Russia, however, is still very far from enjoying this benefit in its full extent. The Russian degraded by ages of slavery, resembles those degenerate animals to whom the domestic state is become a second nature. It must be gradually, and by long and difficult paths, that he returns to liberty: he is yet a stranger to the import of the

---

* If the reader wish for a specimen of the scrupulosity of the russian censor, I will give him one or two prior to Paul's tripling the office. In the reign of Catharine, one Legendre was the censor for french books printed at Petersburg. From a poem, in which the god of love was introduced, he struck out the words *ce dieu malin*, observing, that it was indecent to give the epithet of *malicious* to a deity. He allowed the author, however, to substitute the word *badin*, " wanton," for it. Another time he struck out of an ode in praise of Catharine a verse, in which were the following lines:

Partout la foudre gronde et le glaive s'aiguise;
Un roi tombe du trône, et son sceptre se brise.

" Each sword is sharpen'd, heav'n with thunder shakes,
" A monarch falls, his pow'rless sceptre breaks."

This was an allusion to the preparations for war in 1790, and the commencement of the revolution. At that time it was a political heresy to dare surmise that Lewis XVI. would fall from the throne.

word: to him, to be free signifies to be able to quit the glebe to which he is chained, and lead an idle vagabond life. Work he detests, because he has never worked for himself: he has not even an idea of property; his fields, his goods, his wife, his children, himself, belong to a master who can dispose of them, and who does dispose of them at pleasure. He is interested in nothing, because he possesses nothing: his attachment to his village is that of an ox to the crib to which he is accustomed. He is without country, without laws, without religion. Christianity, as taught and practised among the Russians, no more deserves the name of religion, than the sound which the carman uses to direct his horses, deserves the name of language; as will be evinced in a subsequent chapter.

The despair of some of these wretched peasants may occasionally, as heretofore, produce local rebellion against their lords: but to expect a general revolution in Russia would be chimerical. Russia is too extensive, and too thinly inhabited, for the people to rise in a mass; and a body so scattered and spread abroad would soon be subdued. Paltry towns, containing a few thousands of inhabitants, are commonly at a distance of more than a hundred miles from each other, without any seeming connection but hamlets dispersed in the woods every twelve or fifteen miles, and almost every one of which has its particular petty tyrant. How can a people so scattered ever combine? A single regiment of Phanagoria, under the command of a Suvarof, would be sufficient to exterminate the population of a government.

The natural obstacles, which muscovitism will long oppose to all innovations, even the most salutary, are every day reinforced by auxiliaries arriving in Russia from foreign countries. Russia is now the common asylum of the ignorance, the barbarism, the superstitions, and the prejudices that are persecuted in Europe. Nowhere do men, imbued with such principles, meet with so friendly a reception as in that empire. There they find the infancy of their own country, the golden age of the feudal system. On their arrival, they are astonished at finding themselves already too enlightened, too far advanced, for this happy land: afraid of appearing dangerous, they with joy replunge into the thick night of barbarism in which they were born. Thus the sluggard closes his eyes, and sinks again into that slumber from which the sun-beams had roused him in spite of himself. The man who carries into those climes something of knowledge and sentiment, finds it gradually obscured and extinguished in his heart; and if the despot makes him a grant of a few hundred souls as the price of his own, he thinks it very just and very fortunate that there should be slaves, and that he is one himself*. Autocrats of Muscovy! why do ye not oftener employ this infallible method, which has even something generous in it? Have you a foreigner in your empire, whose talents may be useful while his probity may be dangerous to you, give him an hundred peasants: had he the soul of a Frenchman, he will take that of a Russian. But have a care; these auxiliaries will at last betray you, if not by the lucid seeds they bring, it will be by their very corruption. As the trunk of the beech, stripped of its foliage and deprived of life, still shines as it rots.

Yet even in the court of Russia, and among the nobility, there are some lofty and generous spirits; who, without being the dupes of a system of perfect equality, are indignant at the degrading self-denial required of them: for absolute power suits none but barbarians, and this the russian gentry are no longer. Despotism, far

---

* Nothing is so fatal to humanity as men who have knowledge without principles, or who abjure those of which their conscience reminds them. They resemble those worm-eaten fruits, which are tempting to the eye, but prove nauseous to the taste. These men are particularly dangerous, when they have art enough to conceal errors, shocking in themselves, under specious sophisms.

from softening, and assuming a less disgusting mien in proportion as men's manners grow civilised, becomes more and more stiff, and renders its yoke more ridiculous and more odious; it endeavours to return to barbarism, as the people advance towards civilisation. In other european countries power has descended a few steps from its throne, in deference to reason and public opinion *; but in Russia it mounts still higher, and tramples even on common sense. Till the eighteenth century, it is true, the progress of the human mind in Russia was so far from running parallel with it in the rest of Europe, that the date of the complete enslavement of the Russians, is that of the establishment of commons and emancipation of vassals everywhere else. It is somewhat remarkable, that the tzar who drove the Tatars out of Russia, was the same that imposed

* The conduct of the young king of Prussia exhibits a striking contrast to that of Paul: one endeavours to exalt himself to heaven; the other, to descend to the level of his people, and appear only the first servant of the state. In the same paper, I read a russian proclamation, which condemns a dozen unfortunate Poles to have their noses and ears cut off, and to be sent to Siberia, for having been *wanting in the respect and fidelity* sworn to his muscovite majesty (it is not said in what); and a letter from the king of Prussia to a little town, in which an insurrection had taken place, and in which Frederic William speaks like a father to his children — like a good king, who is proud to be a man.

on the Russians the servitude of the feudal system, before unknown in that country *: so true it is, that tyrants never work but for themselves.

This stubborn conduct must in the end prove fatal to that pride and folly which it is meant to protect: the present race of mankind requires management. Autocracy, exhibiting itself in the form of a graceful woman crowned with glory, with ease received a homage, that had nothing humiliating in it: the character of the warrior had something in it of chivalry, and that of the courtier of gallantry, which seemed to ennoble it; but to require personal adoration, without any of the qualities that might justify it, must be revolting to every reflecting mind. Can a young man of generous sentiments be every moment bowing the knee and kissing the hand of a man who is neither his father nor his benefactor, who inspires him with neither love, nor esteem, nor gratitude, and whom perhaps he despises at the bottom of his heart, without feeling himself deeply degraded? and when this homage, by an effrontery altogether incredible, is rendered more disgusting by ridiculous affectation and ceremony, must it not become yet more insupportable?

Reason can never become extinct in minds

---

* This was the tzar Ivan Vasilievitch I. The russian history notwithstanding styles him the deliverer; and prince Sch. has written a tolerable epic poem in honour of him.

which it has once inhabited: like the lion in the desert, it retires slowly at the sight of a numerous and cowardly troop; but if these have the audacity to pursue and harass him even in his lair, he bursts through their weapons, and conquers or dies. Governours should dread and avoid such actions as may drive reason, honour, and good sense to extremities: the exaction of unnecessary homage may accelerate some unexpected catastrophe*. There is no likelihood that a revolution, after the french model, should break out in Russia as yet; but there may be one, for which it is already ripe — that of a more enlightened aristocracy.

It must be confessed, that the friend of liberty and of Russia cannot wish for a change of any other sort at present; it is the only one of which this vast empire is yet susceptible. The people, in the deplorable state in which we have seen them, are unfit for liberty: they must be prepared for it, they must be brought to desire it, before it be offered them: they would abuse it; or, what is more horrible, they would reject it. It may be said with truth, however shocking as disgraceful to humanity, that the russian government is less inclined to tyranny than the people are prone to

---

* The french emigrants have proved, that the revolution in France would never have taken place, had not the queen been too negligent of etiquette, and the king too popular!

slavery: so low are they debased, so much is their nature changed by their tyrants! With them, therefore, nothing can be done at present *.

Though the nobles still continue the habit of bending before the despot, while they exact still greater submission in their turn from their slaves, yet are they becoming daily more and more enlightened. They have been corrupted rather than civilised; but they retain some virtues, which the last thousand years of bondage or tyranny have been unable to annihilate: worthy in future of a government less barbarous, they will require laws written elsewhere than in the crazy brains of their autocrats. They begin to feel the weight of their chains: some day they will burst them, and then lighten those of their vassals †: and perhaps that day is not very far distant. Many

---

* When I speak here of the russian people, I include not the tatarian hordes, or the kozak tribes, who still retain some remembrances of a sort of liberty; but it is the liberty of barbarians, who employ it only to make slaves.

† Let not the term of nobles startle the reader: those of Russia do not form, like those of France and Germany, that feudal and chivalrous body which literally conceived itself sprung from different blood from other mortals, and which remained separate from them by its morals and prejudices, as much as by its privileges. The word noble, both in french and german, marks this difference: denoting an innate quality of the mind: *dvorannoï*, the term in russ for a nobleman, implies only a *proprietor of land*, because land can be possessed by none but a freeman.

young minds are warmed with the examples of antiquity, and meditate in secret on modern events: many, after having forgotten themselves for a moment in the history of other nations, turn their eyes with dissatisfaction on their own, and on themselves. How in fact can such a government exist at the end of the eighteenth century, in a country not surrounded with a triple wall of brass, in a country where several can read, and some can think? Will Russians in future suffer themselves to be treated like the people of Morocco? In our age, and in Europe, justice, glory, virtues, or benefits, can alone sanction the possession of absolute power, and induce us to pardon the possessor. Reason cannot be compelled to silence, but by being dazzled with great actions. Despotism is an idol, having arms of iron, but feet of clay: its body is of gigantic size, but it is hollow: its head is concealed in a thick cloud, which slaves mistake for heaven: there are none but fools, however, who continue to worship it; none but cowards who pretend to pay it adoration.

When I point out the nobility, as the only body in Russia on which liberty can first rely on her setting foot in this empire, I mean not the contemptible herd that attends the court, as a flight of unclean ravens follows the camp, to devour the carcases. These are everywhere vile, and upstart valets still more so than those who were born courtiers. It is neither the throne, the altar, nor the sacred person of the despot that produces their attachment; it is the most sordid cowardice: the man in authority and power is always the god they adore. They are seen creeping from favourite to favourite, as a caterpillar crawls from leaf to leaf, leaving his excrement on the last he gnawed. There is not perhaps one of these wretches who now devoutly kneels to kiss the hand of Paul, that would not have cut off that hand a few months ago, at the command of a Potemkin. From such dastards nothing can be expected but court intrigues or court revolutions, already too frequent in Russia, as serving only to prolong the reign of barbarism or misery. But a few powerful families, in which knowledge has taken its seat as a stranger beneath some hospitable roof*; a few young men of courage and talents, desirous of a name, will perhaps avail themselves of some lucky circumstances, to qualify at least the oppressive forms of government, till something better can be done; to secure a

---

* Many of these families have not less than twenty thousand slaves, towns, cannons, immense wealth, and, above all, relations, who are generals and commanders of regiments. This is more than enough: one battle would decide the business in their favour.

sovereign worthy of power upon the throne, and give to a senate or council of some sort the influence now confined to unworthy favourites; to prescribe at least some bounds to abuses, which at present have not any. What a Dolgoruky could perform half a century ago, others may effect more permanently now*. This project, however, it must be confessed, can be conceived only by the noblest ambition, totally divested of petty interests: it can be executed only by great courage, great reputation, and still greater perseverance. What may accelerate the fermentation in some keen heads, is, that for a long time past merit is a reason for exclusion from the court of Russia. For arriving at posts and distinctions a man must be servile beyond all power of expression, and have such an impotent self-denial as falls not to the lot of every one. There is a great difference between the possession of talents to fill an important station with dignity, and having the little arts necessary to obtain or preserve it: hence they, who are discontented and in disgrace, are generally the choice of the nobility and of the inhabitants of Mosco: if these unite, and once

* The families of Dolgoruky, Galitzin, Soltikof, &c. have often deserved well of Russia. They were the principal persons concerned in shaking off the infamous tyranny of a Mentchikof and a Biren; and who would have established a less arbitrary government at the death of Peter II.

agree on a plan, the reign of blockheads is over. Of all dominations that of folly and ignorance over reason and knowledge is the most absurd, and most shameful to bear. In Russia every path to glory is blocked against the ambitious youth, who is conscious of the powers to reach it. Unfortunately for despots, but happily for the rest of mankind, not one autocrat, from their first existence, has ever been able to conceive, that the man who is least forward to obtain their favours by meannesses is always the most deserving of them by his talents or his virtues. In Russia every path to honour is shut against the ambitious youth who possesses the means for arriving at it. Would he find glory in vanquishing savages, or conquering *steppes* *, under the orders of a favourite, a fool, or a barbarian? Would he see it in the antichamber of the court? Would he place it in the pursuit of a servile routine, or in forwarding plans, the impolicy or absurdity of which he durst not blame, at some foreign court, or in some office at home? No: for him the only road to glory is in a new order of things, to which every thing invites him. The courtiers are the dregs of the nation; the favourites the dregs of the courtiers: the despots take such pains

---

* *Steppes* is the name given to the desert plains that surround Russia. It is the best a russian general can do.

to keep persons of real merit at a distance, that they are obliged to put up with the rabble.

But a nearer and more unfortunate catastrophe, which seems to threaten the tzars, is a dismemberment of their vast empire. For a century past, the empire of Russia, under the iron rod of despotism, like the paste under the rolling-pin of the cook, has grown thin in proportion as it has been extended. All the bulk of the centre has been squeezed towards the circumference, to form a border, deceptive in regard to its real strength: these thickened borders will separate from the centre, which will become unable to support them. If we cast our eyes on the map, we shall be surprised at the vast extent of this romantic empire, reaching from the banks of the Vistula to the farthest end of Asia, nay even to America, and from the shores of the Pacific ocean to Lapland. It comprises almost a fourth of the inhabited continents. This superficies reckons at most thirty millions of inhabitants; and these of twenty nations, differing in manners, language, and religion. And this immense territory is autocratically governed by the head of Paul, from the centre of Petersburg, from the midst of the court of his palace, where he has planted a piquet, from the middle of a battalion drawn up in a square, where five or six officers salute him with their spontoons! To me the russian empire appears like that spider, which with a very small body has long legs, that fall off at the least obstruction it meets in its gigantic march. Less than a Potemkin would suffice to occasion this dismemberment; but Russia will not gain much by it*.

The most flattering hope which Russia can entertain, is, that she may one day see on the throne an emperor sufficiently wise and great to give it laws, to which he himself will submit; a prince of such magnanimity, as to be ashamed to reign inglorious over a people destitute of rights, and who may be capable of forming from the summit of his throne a gentle and easy descent, to arrive at freedom without a fall. This is what a true friend of Russia and humanity should wish for; this alone can now immortalize an emperor. Peter I. himself lamented, that he was only the despot of a nation of slaves. At an interview he had with the king of Prussia at Marienwerder, he publicly congratulated him on the happiness of being the king of a nation which he could govern by laws, while he could rule his only with the knoot;

* From the turn affairs are taking, it is not hazarding too much to predict, that the first crack in this huge piece of paste will take place on that side towards which it seems inclined still to extend itself; I mean, towards Turkey; whether the Greeks, regenerate and emancipated, at length repel the barbarous Mussulmans and Russians; or the French make their way through the Hellespont.

and he promised to bestow on it a milder government, as soon as it should be sufficiently civilised to be susceptible of it *. This time is now arrived: the Russians are well worthy to be permitted by their sovereign to rise to the level of the least enslaved people in Europe. Reason and humanity would gain much, had they but a mild government; even were it still absolute, like that of Prussia, or mixed like that of England: under this new system the Russians might still figure a long time in history, and prepare themselves for that grand revolution of the human mind, of which some think them already susceptible. This can only be the last step of civilisation, and the return to simple and primitive ideas, after having revolved the immense circle of human errors and follies. Liberty and equality cannot constitute the happiness of mankind, till the people shall be prepossessed only in favour of sound principles of government: it is

* This circumstance was related by baron Pœllnitz, ear-witness of this conversation with the king. Another, which does no less honour to this great character, and which shews how much he was above the little imperial vanities of his pretended descendants, is, that, being surrounded by the turkish army, and despairing of escape, he wrote to the senate, like a second Alexander: "Choose for my successor him who "appears to you most worthy." The senate at that period was very different from that of the present day: in it was a Dolgoruky, who, like Sully, had the courage sometimes to tear the edicts of the tzar.

to be feared that Russia is yet ages from prepossessions of that nature.

Take heart, then, *staroïvertzi* Russians (Russians of the old stamp), who have trembled at the progress of the French revolution; take heart all you, who still dread its success, and who tremble at a truth, as the guilty at a flash of lightning: the time is not yet come. Before you arrive at that dreaded regeneration, you have still to pass through all the stages of civilisation. A nation must be polished before it can be informed; yours is yet in its infancy. Before it can come to a reasonable government, it must have had kings; you have yet had only autocrats: before it can dread democrats, demagogues, and jacobins*, it must

---

* I know not what is now understood in France and Germany by this term Jacobin, which is become so dreaded and odious: but it may gratify my reader's curiosity, to inform him what it implies in Russia, where it is as fatal to him to whom it is given, as that of Jew was formerly to an unfortunate Spaniard. The present political inquisition has even more expeditious modes of proceeding, than the religious ever had.

A man who can read and write, of whatever nation, is strongly suspected. If he be a Frenchman, he is undoubtedly a Jacobin.

Whoever reads the gazettes is a dangerous man: whoever talks of them, is a Jacobin.

He who seems to doubt that Suvarof, with fifty thousand kozaks will conquer France in one campaign—Jacobin.

He who dares say that the French are good soldiers, that they have any great generals, and that the Austrians have been sometimes beaten—Jacobin.

have had royalists, aristocrats, monarchists: you have yet only slaves. Augment their chains, spill their blood, drink their sweat in security; tear the

He who ventures to entertain any doubt whether Poland belongs to Russia, or whether it was allowable for the Poles to defend themselves against the Russians—Jacobin.

Every russian gentleman, who dares to say that a man may still continue for some time a loyal subject, though he ceases to be a vile slave—Jacobin.

Every captain in the guards, and every russian officer, who dares to murmur at his corporal's being made his commanding officer—Jacobin.

The man who imagines that the Russians should be treated like men, and no longer sold or bartered like cattle—Jacobin.

A young nobleman, whose dancing-master has not taught him to make a bow sufficiently low, and who, when he kisses the emperor's hand, and does it not as tenderly as if it were that of his mistress—Jacobin.

He whose coachman, not knowing his tzarian majesty (who to be sure is easy enough to be known), does not stop his carriage, in order to alight, and prostrate himself in the snow or in the mud—Jacobin.

In Catharine's days, he who wore a dark green coat, and large boots, was strongly suspected by the favourites. Now, the wearer of a light green coat, and half boots, is odious to Paul.

Whoever is followed by a dog, wears a round hat, and has a waistcoat without sleeves and flaps, is arrested, and treated as a Jacobin.

This enumeration of particulars, which might have been enlarged, may appear perhaps exaggerated: but it is too true, that any one of these charges might prove fatal to the man against whom it was brought, and that the ruin of several persons has been owing to causes equally ridiculous, and not more reasonable.

infant from its mother's breast, to compel her to suckle your puppies, that have lost theirs*: the day of retribution will not yet dawn on Russia.

Do you fear a constitution? you have not yet laws. Do you dread a national assembly? you have not yet a parliament, not even a divan; for your senate is far from meriting such a name. A mufti, with the koran in his hand, has sometimes repressed the tyrants of Byzantium;—but who can repress yours? Are your laws, your religion, contained anywhere, but in the emperor's head? Are not your souls his? is not his staff your sceptre? your meanness his greatness; and your nullity the cipher that marks his value? Take heart; your clock has not yet struck the hour of liberty.

Before that hour, terrible to you, the sun will long continue to rise on the same crimes. You will still change sovereigns before you change your government; you will still experience all the horrors of court revolutions, before you see popular ones.

At last, however, this memorable epoch must arrive, in Russia as elsewhere. The progress of liberty is like that of time; slow, but sure: and some day will reach the north. Much has been written on the influence of climate on man; and

* An atrocity of this nature actually took place in Livonia.

a political * philosopher maintains, that it has a great deal on their laws and governments. With regard to secondary circumstances, I believe it; but principles are everywhere the same. Climate cannot act on the morals of a people, but from the want of law and religion, which are their primary regulators, and which may be transplanted anywhere. I am well aware, that a desert and uncultivated plain in Russia will spontaneously produce some plants different from those of a field left untilled in France; but if one be ploughed up like the other, and the same seed sown in both, you will reap from them the same grain. Thus the influence of climates cannot perceptibly take place, except under the zones, where the human race has physically degenerated: and besides, does not Russia include at present all the climates of Europe? What, shall the Russian, the descendant of the free and valiant Slavi, be condemned to perpetual thraldom, while the Swede, still farther north, boasts his liberty? Shall Mosco, under the same latitude with London, be for ever a barbarian city, a stranger to arts and laws? Under what climate then did the great Novgorod flourish so early as the eighth century,—that powerful, free, and commercial city, at a time when the people, who now boast most proudly

* Montesquieu.

of their liberty, still crouched in ignorance beneath the feudal system*? The Slavi †, who founded that republic, seem, like the Franks, to bear their destiny and character imprinted on their immortal names. A thousand years of bondage and tyranny have not been sufficient to efface the noble impression. All the Russians have not yet forgotten, that their fathers were more happy.

---

* Alexander Nefsky, whom the russian monks have canonised as a saint and a hero, completed the destruction of this illustrious city by a general massacre of all its inhabitants. Far from uniting himself to the Novgorodians, who courageously threw off the yoke of the Tatars, he took upon himself the office of executioner of his own subjects to please these robbers, and destroyed the cities that refused to pay tribute to foreigners. Such was *saint* Alexander!

† *Slava*, in russ, signifies glory. The word *slavoï*, or *slavnoï*, which means *the glorious*, whereof foreigners have made *slavi, slaves*, and *Sclavonians*, is strangely disfigured. Other etymologists maintain, however, that all the Slavian or Sclavonian nations being known in Europe as subjugated, the appellation of *slave* was given in the west to the unfortunate beings who had lost their liberty like them, and that from these regions every species of servitude came into Europe.

CHAP. VII.

NATIONAL CHARACTER.

Of the nobleman, the courtier, the peasant, the artificer, and the soldier of Russia.

THE character of the Russian, it has been said, is to have no character at all, but to possess a wonderful capacity of assuming that of other nations. If this be understood of the higher class of Russians, there is much truth in the observation: but the same will equally apply to all people, who are but half polished; and even to the inhabitants of all great cities, whose physiognomies are confounded together as well as their manners, because they derive their institutions and food from the same sources, because their blood is mixed, and their way of life is the same.

The noble Russian, the only one to be seen in foreign countries, or well understood in his own, has in fact a great aptitude for adopting the opinions, manners, customs, and languages of other nations. He can be as frivolous as a quondam french *petit maitre*, as musically mad as an

Italian, as reasonable as a German, as singular as an Englishman, as mean as a slave, and as haughty as a republican. He will change his taste and character as easily as the fashion of his dress: surely, therefore, this suppleness of mind and senses is a distinguishing feature.

This great pliability will not appear astonishing, if it be remembered, that the Russians are a new people, on whom all nations have had more or less influence. From foreigners they have received arts, sciences, vices, and a few virtues. The genius of the government, and the particular character of the emperor, are imprinted on all the nation, as on one single individual; and the greek religion, the absurdest of all christian sects, has completed the alteration of its nature. It may be said of the Russian, that his government debases him, that his religion depraves him, and that his pretended civilisation has corrupted him.

Thus the primitive character of this great nation can be traced only through all these vicious institutions. A thousand years under the dominion of the *Varags*, the *Tatars*, and its own tzars, have not been able to efface it: what then must this people have been, which even now display so many excellent qualities! The russian peasant, without property, without religion, without morals, without honour, is hospitable, humane, obliging, gay, faithful, and brave: the farther you penetrate into the country remote from cities, the better you find him; the most savage is always the best, the farthest from the tyrant is the nearest to virtue: in a word, he has all those innate qualities, which remind us of patriarchal manners; his vices are only those of the slave. The remains of barbarism, still exhibited by the most enlightened part of the nation, presents a disgusting contrast. This barbarism is displayed in vulgarity of manners, an insulting contempt of mankind in general, disdain of inferiors, and servile fear of superiors, indifference for everything tending to improvement, ignorance of the forms of society, insolent pride, baseness, immodesty, want of patriotism and public spirit, but above all, the want of that honour which sometimes answers the end of probity, and even of virtue. The half enlightened Russian is the most abject of men; he crawls like the worm, which invites the foot of the oppressor to crush him; he is more servile than his government is despotic: it is impossible for his master not to be his tyrant.

This semi-barbarian is peculiarly fit for the trade of a courtier; being equally cruel, covetous, cowardly, and artful: but, when speaking of a Russian, we must not affix to the word courtier those ideas of urbanity, elegance of manners, and delicacy of mind, with which the courtier is embellished in other countries. In Russia, he who makes his way at court, particularly with the great, is frequently the most impudent and infamous of men, who is ready to offer his back to the king of the frogs, not lying in a marsh, but swayed by an arm as vigorous as that of Peter I. No man of sound judgment, no young man of a noble mind or cultivated understanding, will please at court; and if his birth or circumstances lead him thither, he will be in disgrace the moment he is found out.

In general the Russians are fond of acquiring knowledge, and have a respect for strangers: such only as are totally destitute of education hate foreigners, or are jealous of them, when they come into competition with them. One thing, less to their honour, likewise distinguishes the Russians: this is a base and servile kind of politeness, which evaporates in foolish flattering compliments. Their cringing gestures, and humble and submissive countenance before their superiors, remind one of their oriental slavery. They know not how to be polite without meanness, or to flatter without falsehood: but at this we cannot wonder; for, to be truly polite, a man must be truly honest, and not do, from constraint or interest, what ought to proceed from right feeling and a proper sense of decorum.

In Russia the higher classes may be divided into two *casts*, absolutely differing in manners and opinions. They appear like beings of different centuries; and you would scarcely suppose them to be of the same nation, though they are frequently of the same family. The one are those who reprobate all reform, instruction, and improvement,: they would carry the nation back to a state of barbarism, and keep it apart from all the rest of Europe: they consider all civilisation as perversion, and deem Peter I. the corrupter, not the legislator, of his empire; they are made up of superstition, ignorance, and prejudice. The political *raskolnikis* detest foreigners more than the Turks or Chinese*: but they frequently possess native morals and virtues, and the excesses of the french revolution gave a triumph to their system. The others, adopting the manners and customs of Europe, endeavour to keep pace with their contemporaries, and too

* Nothing can equal the stupidity and rudeness with which they sometimes apostrophise foreigners. We have *bread*, they say, and you are forced to come to us, otherwise you would be starved. Wretches, too barbarous to blush at the causes of that abundance of bread, which they boast. Yes, a few thousand of their fellows eat wheaten bread, because thirty millions of slaves browze on herbs, and gnaw birch bark, on which they feed like the beavers, who surpass them in understanding. A few cities enjoy the pleasures of life, and exhibit palaces, because whole provinces lie desolate, or contain only wretched hovels, in which you would expect to find bears rather than men. In the caves of robbers, too, you may find abundance, and the benighted traveller has often found hospitality in them.

often outdo them in corruption and absurdity. They glory in despising, or being ignorant of the ancient customs of their own country: they have sense, are sociable, and possess knowledge and talents. Among these you will find amiable men and of great merit; but for the most part they have more politeness than honesty, more depravity than information, more vanity than pride. They are persecuted under the gloomy reign of Paul, who is employing every effort to restore the age of Ivan Vasilievitch; and the gleams of the french revolution have terrified several, who return with docility to the confines of barbarism.

Amid all these defects, the Russian nation has remained exempt from three fatal errors, which have tainted the rest of Europe with crimes and abuses. The Russians have never established among them the false point of honour, of avenging the lie by a murder*: their history mentions no war, no massacre, occasioned by reli-

* The Russians, as well as the Greeks and Romans, have shewn that a warrior may be brave without the madness of cutting his comrade's throat in a duel. The officer, who returns with his cane a blow you have given him with your hand, mounts to the assault the next instant like a hero. At the same time it is true, that, in a society, where the affront of a box on the ear may be wiped out by knocking a man down, and where you may spit in the face of him who insults you with his tongue, that politeness and ceremonious respect, which polished nations practise, are not to be expected: accordingly, the russian officers in general resemble a band of

gious fanaticism*; and they have never considered birth as superior to merit†. Hitherto in Russia the nobles have not been esteemed in the inverse ratio of their factitious value, I mean, their antiquity: but what is there called nobility has an origin truly valuable and noble, that of liberty; a noble signifying only a man who is free and possesses land, as already observed.

Next to drunkenness, the most prominent and common vice of the Russians is theft. I doubt whether any people upon earth be more inclined naturally to appropriate to themselves the property of others: from the first minister to the general officer, from the lacquey to the soldier, all are thieves, plunderers, and cheats. In Russia theft does not inspire that degrading contempt which stigmatizes a man with infamy, even among the lowest of the populace. What the

---

footmen in uniform. A russian prince affirming something to me " on the word of a man of honour," I said to him: " How " can you pledge me the word of another?" This repartee might have been addressed with propriety to most of them: but those who have education are inferior to none in point of honour and politeness.

* The persecution of the *raskolnikis* by the liturgist Nicon is scarcely an exception. This national toleration has moreover been guaranteed by the happy ignorance of the popes, who, at all times, have been more addicted to drunkenness and sleep than to dogmatizing.

† Paul is endeavouring to establish a gothic nobility, to make out genealogical trees, and to introduce heraldry, the only science he allows to be cultivated.

thief dreads most is the being obliged to restore his booty, as he reckons a cudgeling for nothing; and if detected in the fact, he cries with a grin: *Vinavat, gospodin! vinavat:* "I have done wrong, "Sir:" returning what he had stolen, as if that were a sufficient amends. This shameful vice, pervading all classes, scarcely incurs blame. It sometimes happens, that in apartments at court, to which none but persons of quality and superior officers are admitted, your pocket-book is carried off as if you were in a fair *. A stranger, who lodges with a Russian, even a kniaz, will find to his cost, that he must leave nothing on his dressing table or his writing desk: it is even a russian maxim, that what is not locked up belongs to any one who has a mind to take it. The same quality has been falsely ascribed to the Spartans: but an Englishman, who has published a book on the resemblance between the Russians and Greeks, after having proved, that they eat, sing, and sleep like them, has forgotten to add, that in stealing they are still more expert.

Whence is it then that the Russians are more addicted to theft than other half polished na-

---

* The king of Sweden, after the battle of the 9th of July 1790, invited a party of russian officers, who had been made prisoners, to dine with him. One of them stole a plate; upon which the offended king ordered them all to be distributed among the small towns, where they never again ate off silver.

tions? Is it because stealing is less severely punished in Russia than elsewhere? No, it is owing to the immorality of the greek religion *,

* One proof, that it is their religion particularly, which leaves, or rather gives them this quality, is, that it is not common among the people of other religions living under the russian government. The mussulman Tatars are of tried fidelity; even the pagan Siberians are of exemplary good faith; and the Livonians, Esthonians, and Fins, who are lutherans, are neither knaves nor thieves. The worship of images, however, has introduced one happy prejudice among the Russians. He who would force open a strong box without scruple, dares not break a seal. The following is a fact: Having one day given a young soldier, my servant, two rubles, to pay for two letters, which I bade him carry to the post-office, I went out. On my return I discovered that my trunk had been broke open, and robbed of ten rubles in copper, which were in it: and I learned, that my soldier had been gaming with the couriers of the chancery, to whom he had lost a good sum of money. He was sought after by my orders, but in vain; and I denounced him as a deserter. Three days after he appeared, fell at my feet, and begged forgiveness, confessing, that he had stolen the ten rubles, and concealed himself in the depth of a wood, but hunger and repentance had brought him back. Instead of delivering him up as a thief and deserter, I satisfied myself with ordering a non-commissioned officer to give him twenty blows with a rattan. At this order, he fell at my feet again, and begged me with tears to punish him more severely, that nothing might lie on his conscience, he said, for having robbed his master; that he deserved a hundred blows at least, and that he should have more if I sent him to the regiment. He persisted in his entreaties to obtain this singular favour. Surprised at such a request, and moved by his penitence, I would by no means consent to it, but said to him, " Now you have " confessed the whole, tell me what you did with the letters,

the want of laws and police, and more especially the bad education of the nobles, who, from the very cradle being surrounded by slaves, imbibe from them the baseness of their sentiments.

If you are more exposed to pilfering in Russia than in other countries, you are in less danger of being assassinated than even in England. I traversed the vacant spaces of Petersburg, and the deserts of Russia, with more security than the crowded streets of London, or the well-frequented roads of France. Wherever I found a hut, I was sure of meeting hospitality at the threshold; and, if I wore a cockade in my hat, I was respected and even feared by the ill-disposed *.

If stealing and drunkenness be the most prominent vices of the Russians, hospitality and courage are the most striking qualities.

" as they were of importance."—" I carried them to the post-
" office."—" What! would you make me believe that you
" did not begin with gaming away the two rubles I gave
" you, before you broke open my trunk?"—" Yes, Sir, God
" forbid that I should touch money belonging to anything
" sealed." In fact, after having lost ruble after ruble of the money he had stolen, he had carried the letters and the money for them to the post-office, and I received the answers in due course.

* A traveller, on entering the cottage of a peasant, first salutes the image in the corner, by making the sign of the cross, then his host, saying, " Bread and salt;" this done, he sits down on the bench and eats with the family, as if he were a member of it.

From the extreme of wretchedness some good arises, as germs from the bosom of corruption. The countries where men are slaves or savages, are thinly peopled, even if they be fertile: hence in such countries men are strangers to want, and, if allowed ever so little of their time and strength, can procure the necessaries of life in abundance. Having few wants, and their property being insecure, they live from hand to mouth, and freely bestow what they have. A vassal readily shares his bread, his salt, and his hut with the traveller; and the noble is equally prompt to admit the stranger to partake of his table and his pleasures*. Every year the russian and the livonian slave may set fire to a forest, and sow the virgin earth, which will return him ten or fifteen fold: this slave employs for his own use only so much of his time and produce as is absolutely necessary to prevent his dying with hunger or sinking under fatigue; all the rest is destined to augment the superfluities of his lord †. Now in Russia,

* In Russia parasites are not yet despised. The general, the wealthy merchant, every man in tolerably easy circumstances, keeps a sort of open house, so that his friends and acquaintance, officers in the army, and the crowd of young men and foreigners who have no house or home, daily find admission to his table.

† Many russian and livonian lords make their slaves work five days in the week: some even leave these poor creatures only the *day of rest* to cultivate the ground that must feed their family. But I leave the task of exhibiting at large the

where there are thirty thousand slaves, there are not a hundred thousand lords, who fatten on their sweat and blood; and these alone compose the *consuming* class of an immense and fertile empire. It is not surprising therefore, to see the russian lords display a luxury and profusion, which impose upon the people, and which you would seek in vain where good and ill are more equally distributed. Many of these great lords, it must be avowed, possess laudable qualities. They are in general more inclined to enjoy what they have, than to accumulate wealth: their riches are constantly renewing, like the race of men whence they flow, and frequently cost them nothing to acquire. The munificence of their tzar, and peculation of every kind, are commonly their impure sources: but they know that they may lose them as easily as they were procured;

inconceivable evils which the Russians, and more especially the wretched Livonians, suffer, to one of my friends, who is treating this subject and several others more minutely. Merkel (1) has lately roused the indignation even of Germany, by drawing a picture of their condition. Never did the feudal system, or the black code, present such atrocities. Paul, by destroying at the commencement of his reign all that his mother had done in favour of the slaves, has replaced them at the mercy of their private owners, as so many domestic bipeds. And Livonians, Germans, dare thus to treat human beings in the present century and in the face of Europe!

(1) Author of a german work, intitled The Lettonians.

and therefore they enjoy them while it is in their power. This some of them do so nobly, that they gain credit for having virtue, or at least for feeling remorse.

The genius of the russian people turns eagerly to commerce, for which it appears to be particularly calculated. When a peasant can obtain a passport from his master*, he hastens to quit his ungrateful furrows, and apply to some trade, in hope of accumulating money enough to purchase his liberty: but in this he is frequently deceived †. The russian traders, for the most part slaves, and fettered besides by the regulations of government, can seldom rise to great speculations, in spite of all their industry: they confine themselves to inland traffic; and instead of being

---

* For five and twenty rubles a year, a peasant sometimes obtains a passport, or licence, from his master, in virtue whereof he can exercise his ingenuity in the towns and cities; but this tribute is increased in proportion to his industry.

† The russian slave, when he has contrived to make a little purse, cannot always offer it for his ransom; since his master sometimes appropriates his treasure to his own use and increases his burdens. Many of these slaves become very rich; but their master refuses to sell them their liberty, considering their capitals and their industry as his property, and as a last resource for himself. There are masters, who, after they have ruined themselves by gambling, have searched the houses of their slaves, to seize on all they could find in them. This plundering is one of the reasons why the peasants frequently bury their money, and die before they have been able to discover it to their children.

merchants in their own country, are merely factors to the English, and find themselves obliged to be content like the Jews in other countries, with the petty trade of retail dealers and pedlars.

It is truly astonishing, to see how strenuously russian politics tend to ruin the subjects of that empire. These cannot carry on trade to advantage, but in proportion to the rivalry between foreign nations, that are in want of the natural productions of their country: yet the cabinet of Petersburg has shut all its ports to the rivals of England. The English are the sole purveyors of Russia, and the arbiters of the price of its produce, as well as of the value of its rubles, since they alone fix the course of exchange. In short, they carry on this trade to the same advantage as is done with all barbarous nations, the government of which, more barbarous still, sells exclusive privileges to some particular company*.

* Whatever the people in Russia may say, the balance of trade is always against them; the natural productions of that immense empire not being sufficient to pay for the foreign articles of luxury imported into the two capitals. One ship, laden with english hardware, is equal in value to thirty laden with iron, hemp, or timber. The English carry away leather and bring back shoes; grain, for which they return beer, &c. The only nation with which Russia could carry on an immediate exchange of produce, is France, from which it might receive oil and wine; but these Russia chooses to purchase at the third or fourth hand, and pay double the price for them. —The Russians, seeing their coin disappear, and nothing

Mirabeau has said, that the Russians are the most malleable of all people. A young peasant, rough, savage, timid, torn from his hamlet, is metamorphosed into an elegant and agile footman, or a spruce and courageous soldier, in less than a month. His master makes him in a short time his tailor, his musician, or even his surgeon, or counsellor at law.

I had been told a hundred times, that the best way to teach them any thing was by blows. I could not believe it; but I saw it was so. When a few hundred recruits are delivered to an officer to form a new battalion, the cloth and leather necessary for equipping them are given him at the same time. Having drawn the poor fellows up in a rank, he says to one, " You shall be " tailor to the company;" to another, " You

---

but paper left, notwithstanding the great quantity of gold and silver they draw from Siberia, suppose it is carried away by the foreigners who come to their country to seek their fortunes, follow arts or trades, or serve in the army. This, however, is a great mistake. Soldiers, or men of letters, seldom grow rich; and in Russia less than anywhere: the artist and the mechanic, too, more frequently meet poverty than wealth; and most of these strangers die or settle in the country. All who arrive bring at least a few ducats with them; and there is not one in twenty who goes away with any property: if a calculation were made, the balance with respect to these would be in favour of Russia. For a long time none but musicians, milliners, pawnbrokers, and Englishmen, have enriched themselves in Russia. [*With leave of the french author, the fortunes made by the English there have been extremely few indeed.—Tr.*]

" shall be shoemaker;" to a third, " You shall
" be musician." If they grumble, they receive
some strokes of the cudgel, and a few bad implements are given them, to go and practise at
their respective employments. The drubbing is
repeated occasionally, till they produce a boot or
garment tolerably well made, and can play the
march of the regiment. " But," said I to a colonel, who boasted of having thus formed the
Mosco grenadiers, " among those men there
" must have been several who had exercised in
" their own villages the trades you wanted: why,
" instead of choosing them yourself, did you not
" interrogate them on this head? he who could
" play on the *balaleika** would have made a good
" fifer; and he would have been the best shoe-
" maker, who had learned of himself to make
" *lapkis* †."—" O," replied he, " you are a
" stranger; you know nothing of our Russians:
" among all those fellows, there was not one
" who would have confessed what he could do."
Strange and melancholy truth! but it is not so
with the Russian alone; it is the same with the
slave of every country; and always will be,
where a man is obliged to exert his corporal and
mental faculties by compulsion.

* A sort of lute with two strings, on which the Russian peasants play.
† Shoes of linden bark, which the Russians wear.

This spirit of mechanical submission imposed on the Russians, has an unfortunate influence on all their imitative arts. They have a national music of their own invention, which is extraordinary, and bears the characteristic stamp of their enslaved genius: it appears formed to be executed by a machine, rather than by men. About half a hundred musicians, as they are called, have each a horn, differing in size in regular gradation, like the pipes of an organ: each of these horns gives but one tone, and each of the players has before him only one note, the greater or less length of which, and the longer or shorter intervals between its repetitions, form all the variation. Thus these musicians, each repeating his own note, perform by common accord the simplest and even the most complicated airs. The bulk of these horns, and the purity and depth of their tones, render their concert sublime; and its effect is particularly grand by night, and in the open fields. I doubt the possibility, however, of forming a band of this strange music anywhere but in Russia; as it would not be easy to muster fifty men, who would consent to devote their lives to the sole purpose of sounding one note on a horn, and wait whole hours measuring rests, in expectation of the moment for sounding this note, incapable of being moved by the air they are employed in playing, or by the art they profess. Nothing but an automaton, an organ-pipe, or a slave, can be brought to this exactness. The Greeks and Romans had slaves likewise, but they had liberal arts: in Russia there are none; all the arts there are servile or foreign, and can be naturalized only with freedom.

Whether he exercise arts, guide the life-supporting plough, or handle the destructive musket, the Russian is fettered, and trembles under the lash of a master: all the qualities of his mind are withered, and the tenderest feelings of his heart are outraged*. How astonishing is it, that, with these debased beings, torn by force from their families as sheep from the fold, and of whom the greater part die of grief and terrors before they reach the army, to which they are driven by the

---

* What has disgusted me is, to see men with grey hair, and patriarchal beards, lying on their faces, with their trowzers down, and flogged like children. Still more horrible! I blush to write it, there are masters, who sometimes force the son to inflict this punishment on his father: and, most abominable of all, there are sons who comply with such an indignity. These and many other horrid acts are committed especially in the country, where the lords, in their castles, exercise the same authority over men as over animals. Even women are subjected to the most indelicate insults. These barbarities, however, become more rare, and inspire the better kind of Russians with as much horror as they do my readers: but they are still committed, and attest to what a pitch of degradation the human species may be reduced.

switch, Russia should have gained so many victories over her neighbours? Reasons for such apparent contradictions, however, may be assigned. The Russian, who can support the wretched life necessary to complete the education of a soldier, may be considered as an invulnerable, or at least an insensible being, immersed in the waters of the Styx. Scarcely one in three endures the trial, but he who does remains indefatigable, and hard as the iron that has repeatedly passed under the hammer. From the proud russian prince, who devours a raw turnip or cucumber, after having gormandized on the most exquisite dishes at a sumptuous table*, to the filthy Siberian, who feeds on stinking fish, all the Russians seem to have iron constitutions, capable of supporting equally the extremes of heat and cold, of gluttony and abstinence. The veteran soldiers are the hardest of men. Reeking from the vapour bath, they roll themselves naked in the snow, and sleep on a bed of ice. From the severest toil they pass to the most indolent repose; after the longest and most rigid abstinence they gorge themselves with food with impunity; and having a *sukaré* (biscuit) and an onion in their

---

* Potemkin has often been seen to present himself in the midst of his courtiers with his legs bare, and his hair about his ears, eating, like an Oran-outang, a raw carrot or turnip, when just come from the empress's table.

pocket, they will travel sixty versts a day, to follow Suvarof.

> Lassant la faim, la soif, et la fatigue,
> Le soldat russe affronte les revers,
> Brave la mort, et franchit les deserts.
> Fier et soumis, de soi-même prodigue,
> Guidez son bras, il détruit l'univers.

> "The Russian—hunger, thirst, fatigue subdues,
> "His foe across each desert wild pursues,
> "Dares adverse fortune, dares impending fate,
> "And prodigal of life is bravely great.
> "Humble, yet proud, his banners wide unfurl'd,
> "Guide but his arm, he'll subjugate the world."

In short, if, as it has long been imagined, to be a good soldier require nothing more than to be a very exact machine, the Russian must certainly be the best in the world. His valour is so mechanical and so docile *, that he dreads the cane

---

* The russian soldier sometimes gives very laughable proofs of this mechanical exactness. Peter I. had issued orders, that every man who went through the streets without a a lantern after ten o'clock at night, should be stopped. A physician, returning from a visit to a patient, was preceded by his servant with a lantern. The servant was suffered to pass, but the physician, notwithstanding all he could say, was conducted by the sentry to the guard-house. In a battle with the Swedes, a galley was sunk, on board of which were several officers of the guards. The commander of the next galley cried out to his men: "Save the officers of the guards." One poor fellow sinking held up his arm for assistance, and a soldier caught hold of it; but before he would pull him out, asked, "Are you an officer of the guards?" The poor fellow being unable to answer, the soldier let him go, and he perished.

of his officer more than the cannon of the enemy: it may be said of him, that he is brave from cowardice. Contrary to what is seen in many other nations, the russian soldier is more intrepid than his officer. His powerful incentives are, his ferocious disposition, the thirst of plunder, and his desperate condition. The officer has not the same stimulants, and is often destitute of that sense of honour which supplies the place of courage and patriotism. Catharine substituted for these a lure of recompenses of all kinds, of which she was prodigal on every occasion. The officer who had been present at an engagement * was promoted a step: such as were mentioned with honour by the general in his report, received crosses, or gold-hilted swords; and they who were wounded, peasants or pensions. I have seen officers, who, in one campaign had received two crosses, a gold-hilted sword, and two degrees of promotion. There is a wide difference, however, between the

---

* The soldiers received a silver medal, and I have seen whole regiments, where none but the recruits just arrived were without them. The medal distributed to those who were present at the expedition against Tschesme, or Clazomene, where the Turkish fleet was burned, has great sublimity in the inscription: *Bouil,* " I was there." Paul recompenses his soldiers by giving permission to a regiment, with whose services he is satisfied, to play *the grenadier's march:* being sure at the same time that the musicians get a shower of blows to make them learn it: This is Paul's Marseilloise.

†

valour of these soldiers and that of those warriors, whose heroic exploits were rewarded by a branch of oak, or the simple approbation of their country.

The russian soldier has retained some virtues, of which he frequently exhibits proofs amid the excesses in which he too often indulges; for, notwithstanding the dread and horror which the peasant feels for the life of a soldier, young men have been seen to cast themselves at the feet of the recruiting officers, and beg that they might be taken instead of a brother, about to be torn from his family *. The greatness of such a sacrifice can only be properly estimated when we recollect that a russian soldier is inlisted not for a certain number of years, but for his whole life. Once dragged from his hut, and all that are dear to

---

* I was much interested for a young man, who had come five hundred miles, to beg that he might be received into the regiment instead of his brother, who had a large family; and I spoke of it to the minister at war, relating the particulars of a sacrifice, which in my opinion deserved to be rewarded by setting the soldier at liberty, without detaining his generous brother. A relation of the minister, who was present, said, " We must dismiss all our soldiers, then; for I have seen a thousand times such things as these which seem to astonish " you." This silenced me, not knowing which to admire most, the general good nature of the russian slaves, or the hard-heartedness of their lords. This man had been taken by Pugatshef, tied up in a bag, and was on the point of being thrown into the river, when a russian party came up to his rescue.

him, he must grow old under the severest discipline, if he do not fall by the sword of the enemy. If he be married, scarcely will he have quitted his wife before his master may give her to another*; and if he have children, he will never behold them again †. He is lost, dead to his family for ever: becomes a warrior, and at length is pleased with the business of slaughter.

You then see him giving proofs of courage and confidence in his generals, which serve him instead of patriotism ‡: so the well-trained dog

---

* This is forbidden; but it is frequently done, that the master's income may suffer no diminution: as he would be obliged to support the wife and children; but by marrying her again, the same fields are cultivated by the husband's successor, who pays the same tribute. Frequently a lord marries a stout girl of twenty to a boy of ten or twelve, in order to establish a fresh houshold. Sometimes a father of a numerous young family, finding his task too severe, solicits a stout wife for one of his boys, and supplies the place of a husband to his daughter-in-law, till the child is grown up. Such disorderly conduct is very common in the country.

† The soldier never obtains a furlough.

‡ At the siege of Otchakof, a piquet guard, going to an advanced post, met an officer in the trenches, who said to them: "The Turks have made a sally; the post, to which "you are going, is already in their hands; turn back, or you "will be cut to pieces."—"What is that to us?" replied one of the soldiers; "prince Dolgoruky is answerable for us." Notwithstanding the officer's representations, they went on, and returned no more.—At the attack which the Turks made upon Kinburn, Suvarof went out drunk, at the head of his garrison, to repulse the enemy. The Russians gave way at

displays from obedience the same courage, as the generous lion defending his life or liberty. In his bravery, native hilarity, gait, and cleanliness, the russian soldier is admirable. There are regiments, which, for these sixty years, have been almost always in sight of the enemy. These continual combats have rendered the Russians warlike; but the scenes at Otchakof, Ismaïl, and Praga, and the devastations in unhappy Poland, have stamped their valour with the most ferocious barbarity. This, however, was the character of the generals that commanded them, of Catharine who excited them, rather than their own. Yet amid that horde of savages which were let loose upon that wretched nation, by the side of the Suvarofs, Denisofs, Kakofskies, and Kretschetnikofs, whose names are even less barbarous than their characters, were seen the Repnins, Gallitzins, Buchshefdens, Fersens, the young Tolstoï, and several superior officers, whose humanity and even urbanity formed a complete contrast to the

---

the first charge, and several took to their heels. A soldier, enraged, stopped the fugitives with his bayonet, obliged them to turn back, and charged at their head, as if he had been their officer. Catharine, being informed of this action, which was the cause of the first victory in the last war, would have given him a commission: but this he refused, saying that he could neither read nor write, and would rather be a good soldier than a bad officer. The empress then sent him a gold medal, and conferred on him a pension of three hundred rubles [30*l.*].

barbarity of their companions. The Russians, who became so ferocious under the reign of Catharine, were much less so under that of the mild Elizabeth. Their memory is still respected in Prussia: the conduct and discipline which they observed there during two years, were acknowledged with gratitude by the inhabitants. The irregular Kozaks, the Bashkirs, the Kirghises, and the Calmucs, who compose their light troops, are the only barbarians without discipline.

The genius of Catharine required a nation so new, so malleable, and of which she might say, as the statuary in La Fontaine says of his block of marble: "Shall I make of it a god, a table, or a "trough?" Of the Russian she could not make a god, but she might have made a man: her greatest crime is in not having made it her glory to do so*. By submitting to the reign of Catha-

* Catharine, the disciple and idol of our philosophers, the legislatrix of the north, has rivetted the chains of the unhappy Russians. By what fatality was it, that she, who in her youth was not afraid to have the question discussed, whether it would not be proper to emancipate the peasants, should finish by reducing to similar slavery those provinces which had retained some franchises? Væsemsky, whom Momonof punningly called *Volterre* (the land-stealer), with a single stroke of the pen reduced the Kozaks, Tatars, and Fins to the state of slaves, in order to augment the capitation; notwithstanding Catharine had acknowledged and guaranteed their rights! This Væsemky, whose knavery was equal to the stupidity of his successor, was procureur-general and treasurer of the

rine and her twelve favourites, Russia proved herself the most degraded of nations.

Peter I. having employed a monk to translate Puffendorff's Political History of Europe into russ, the monk, from a sentiment of mean and false delicacy, softened all the expressions he found relating to slavery and Russia: he even took the liberty to omit altogether the chapter where that author treats of the national character of the Muscovites. Peter, turning over the book, presently discovered the omission, gave the monk a severe reprimand, and ordered him immediately to correct the whole of the translation, and render it perfectly faithful. This noble frankness demands our esteem: but what will the reader say, when he is informed, that, under the reign of Catharine, a new translation of Puffendorff appeared, with all those omissions which the monk had formerly made?

Russia, brave, powerful, amiable, and hospitable nation! where I found friends and protectors, forgive the frankness of a stranger, who ventures to depict you as you appeared to him; and who, if he had been speaking of his own country-

---

empire; and, according to the russian expression, was *the sovereign's eye*. Count Panin, speaking of him, said to Catharine: " You have a purblind eye there:" to which she answered: " For that reason I will have the senate obey
" it."

men, could not always have spoken of them with praise. In painting your good qualities, I have displayed your heart: in painting your vices, I have shewn only the marks of your chains. May freedom efface them at some future day!

CHAP. VIII.

RELIGION.

The Greek Church—Priests—Festivals—Fasts—Images.

IT has often been made matter of reproach to religion, that her most zealous defenders are not always the best of men in their own characters—Russia in particular affords matter in support of this sarcasm. It is there that the most illiterate or most degenerate sect of christianity, still substitutes dogmas in the place of morals, miracles instead of reason, the performance of ceremonies instead of the practice of virtue, and expiations of guilt instead of repentance or punishment. There, the devotee is assuredly a knave, and the hypocrite a villain*. I have already asserted, that the principal cause of the vices of the people is the immorality of their religion; and he who considers, that in the russo-greek

---

* A foreign officer having picked out a servant from his soldiers, was taking him home; when, passing opposite to a church, the soldier stopped, bowed, and crossed himself. Oh! my friend, said the officer, thou art a rogue, I will have nothing to do with thee. The last man I had did the same; and he robbed me. Accordingly, he sent back the devotee, and changed his choice till he found a man that went by the church without stopping. Him he kept, and he proved an honest fellow.

church there are neither sermons, nor exhortations, nor catechism, will at once be of my opinion. A sort of auricular confession, but very different from that of the catholics, is the only act which reminds the Russian of a few of his duties: but all that the confessor enjoins him consists in fasting, in repeating litanies and making the sign of the cross. It is true, the archbishop or metropolitan, sometimes preaches a sermon in the chapel of the palace: but this sermon used to be nothing more than a flattering oration to Catharine, who heard it with downcast eyes, and kissed the hand of the preacher by way of acknowledgment. It is true, likewise, that Plato, archbishop of Mosco, who is really a man of merit, has composed some very sensible and eloquent homilies; and that he has enjoined the parish priests to make similar ones, or at least to read his on Sundays and festivals. But the country popes are not always capable even of performing the latter injunction; the rest are still less equal to the former; and they who are able never mind it.

Beside the fifty-two Sundays in the year, the Russians celebrate sixty-three festivals, twenty-five of which were dedicated to Catharine and her family*. At court these were days of Te

---

* Five of these festivals were exclusively in honour of Catharine: 1st, her birth-day; the 21st of April, old style; 2dly,

Deum, or rather *Te Deam*, pomp, balls, distribution of favours, and feasting: in the towns, of drunkenness and disorder. In the country they might have been days of rest for the wretched; but if their masters did not send them to their usual tasks after mass, they dedicated those moments to the hasty gathering in of their own harvest: in this respect, therefore, the festivals were a benefit to them.

The most despicable and most despised of all persons in Russia are the priests. Many of them cannot even read; yet they are more despicable for their drunkenness and intemperance than for their gross ignorance. There are seminaries for their tuition, indeed; but it is not always necessary for a man to have been educated in them, in order to become a priest. A father bequeaths to his son his living, his church, and his flock: for this he wants nothing but the consent of his lord, who easily obtains that of the bishop. If the son be able, as his father was before him, to read a little in the slavonian language, say mass,

her accession to the throne, the 28th of June; 3dly, her coronation, the 22d of September; 4thly, her inoculation for the small-pox, the 21st of November; and 5thly, her name-day, the 24th of the same month. For these solemn days each of her generals were anxious to send her the news of some important victory, which she preferred to any other homage. It was necessary for the enemies of the Russians to be particularly on their guard some days preceding these festivals, for they were sure to be attacked.

and chaunt vespers, he is master of his trade, and follows it. He often gets drunk, and fights with his parishioners; who notwithstanding kiss his hand, and ask his blessing, after they have given him a drubbing*. It is not uncommon in the streets of Mosco and Petersburg, to meet drunken priests and monks, reeling along, swearing, singing, and insulting the passengers, male and female. One of the chief causes of the vices and ignorance of the russian priests, however, is to be ascribed to the greek religion itself, by prohibiting them to read any book except their breviary, to employ themselves in any occupation, to do any work, or to play on any instrument of music.

The indecency with which these priests officiate, renders extremely ridiculous the ceremonies, which would be much less so in themselves †.

---

* On certain days in the year these popes make the tour of their parishes, demanding from hut to hut eggs, butter, flax, fowls, &c. On their return they are seen either lying dead drunk in a cart among these provisions, or merrily singing from this moving pulpit.

† A russian general, having a child of one of his domestics baptized in his antichamber, conducted thither the company who had dined with him to amuse them with the sight. The priest having officiated with an ease and dignity which were not expected, the general applauded his performance by clapping, and crying " Bravo! Bravo!" These russian baptisms by immersion are always extremely indelicate when the

Many lords keep private chaplains to say mass, in their own houses: but they commonly live with the footmen, and are not admitted to their master's table. The condition of these priests, however, is free *.

The superior clergy are more respectable, and certainly much more respected. Nothing can be more pompous than a solemn mass celebrated by an archbishop, who is arrayed in his robes by his clergy in the midst of the temple, as the high priest formerly was †. Plato and Gabriel, arch-

---

person is a Turk or a Calmuc of five and twenty. Their marriages, too, have many ridiculous ceremonies. I saw a lady, at the marriage of her waiting woman in her own private chapel, smartly scold her chaplain for not knowing the proper ceremonies, and take the direction and ordering of them upon herself. The bride on this occasion was an English woman, and the clergyman of her own nation gave her away. His grave deportment formed a singular contrast to that of the officiating pope, and shewed that it is not always the beard that gives a respectable air.

* During the war with Sweden, as there was a pressing want of men, several thousands of priests' sons were notwithstanding taken away, and some battalions of artillery formed of them. Several of them had already commenced their sacerdotal functions: yet they were dragged, like slaves, from their altars and their wives, to go and handle the cannons of general Melissino's camp.

† Count d'Artois, during his stay at Petersburg, happened to be at such a ceremony, when Catharine sent an officer to him with the news that Dumouriez had been defeated at Nerwinden. The Russians, imagining that it was his devotion to their St. Alexander which had procured him such

bishops of Mosco and Petersburg, are men venerable for their character and conduct, and particularly for the pains they have taken to reform the manners of their brethren. M. Samborsky, chaplain to the grand-dukes, is a man who does honour to his cloth and country. He is the only russian priest to be seen without a beard While in London, he obtained permission, though with difficulty, to shave himself; and he has had the courage to persevere in the practice since his return. But if he left his beard in England, he brought thence taste and knowledge, from which his country may reap advantage. He applies himself to the improvement of agriculture in the environs of Tzarskoselo, where he has cleared deserts and drained marshes, to form ferfile fields or english gardens*. This is the only revenge he

a happy message, the prince was willing to pay the archbishop a compliment on the occasion; but he very unpolitely answered, that he had prayed only for true believers. Perhaps the reader will be surprised to hear that Catharine, who so much ridiculed the consecrated sword which the pope sent to the austrian general Daun, herself ordered a sword to be blessed by the metropolitan of St. Alexander Nefsky, which she designed as a present to count d'Artois. Its hilt was of gold, ornamented with brilliants, and on the guard were these words: " God and the king:" it has not performed more miracles, however, than marshal Daun's.

* Those of the grand-duke Alexander, of which he formed the plan, and was not unfrequently its executor, were founded on a very ingenious idea. Catharine had written a

takes on his bigoted brethren, for their contempt of one whom they consider as a heretic. He has obtained another dispensation equally extraordinary. His wife being dead, he is permitted to continue in the exercise of his clerical functions as a widower, which is contrary to the canons of the greek hierarchy. According to these, a man cannot act as a parish priest without being married: and, as a priest can marry but once, if he lose his wife he must shut himself up in a convent. For this reason the wives of the popes are the most tenderly treated, and the happiest women in Russia.

The ignorance and sottishness which characterise the russian clergy, are perhaps, as I have observed, the chief causes of the happy exception their church affords in the annals of christianity. Their disputes and mistaken zeal have not, as elsewhere, occasioned wars, massacres, and per-

---

tale for her grand-children, intitled, The Tzarevitch Chlore. The little Chlore undertakes a journey, to reach the top of a mountain, where blooms a rose without a thorn, and gathers it after a thousand dangers and a thousand toils. M. Samborsky has exhibited all the scenes and adventures of this tale in the field of nature. The centre of the garden is a mountain, on the summit of which stands the temple of the thornless rose, and the path leading to it presents all the instructive allegories that Catharine had invented for the young princes. An adopted son of the worthy Samborsky has written a description of these gardens in verse, which the author of the present work has translated into french.

secutions. If we except the violent acts of Peter I. in reforming their beards and long garments; and those of Nicon, in establishing his new liturgy; the russian history exhibits none of those religious contests which have deluged the earth with blood. Archbishop Nicon was no doubt right in endeavouring to render the form of worship more pure and simple; but he was wrong in exhorting the tzar Alexius to employ violence. They who would not make the sign of the cross with three fingers, had their hand cut off: hence arose a schism. These schismatics refused to admit either the translation of the sacred books by Nicon, or his new litanies; and even now they would rather lose their hand than not make the sign of the cross with two fingers, as a symbol that the Holy Ghost proceeds from the Father alone. These are called by others *raskolniki**, but they style themselves *staroï-vertsi* (of the old faith). They were prohibited from celebrating worship in public, but they held private meetings, and under prince Potemkin they obtained permission to build themselves several churches. His plan was, to support himself on this powerful and fanatic sect at some future period. There are some wealthy merchants and great lords who are attached to it, and it is

* Schismatics.

widely diffused among the peasants. However, the *raskolniki* are no longer persecuted, and the Russians in general display the greatest indifference about the faith of others.

The common people observe with the most scrupulous exactitude the four grand lents which are enjoined them: at which times their superstition carries them so far, that they abstain even from their wives and their snuff-boxes. The conscience of a Russian would not be so much affected by a theft or a murder, from which he might obtain absolution, as by having eaten meat, milk, or an egg, during lent. Linseed oil, fish, herbs, roots, and mushrooms, are then his sole nourishment; and such an abstinence for six weeks reduces him to a skeleton. The rich have sumptuous tables, well provided with fish and exquisite fruits; and on some of them even flesh is served for strangers or the sick: but I have seen a devotee refuse to touch his fish-soup, because he was helped with a spoon that had been in soup-gras. These rigid fasts made some one say, that the Russians knew not how to take heaven but by famine.

Every Russian, beside the consecrated amulet he wears about his neck, which he receives at his baptism, and which he never after lays aside, commonly carries in his pocket a figure of St. Nicholas, or some other patron saint, stamped on brass. This he carries with him everywhere as devoutly as Æneas did his lares and penates. It is frequently the only thing that a peasant, or a soldier on his march, has about him: nothing can be more common than to see him occasionally take this figure out of his pocket, spit upon it, and rub it with his hand to clean it; then place it opposite to him, and on a sudden prostrate himself, making the sign of the cross a thousand times, fetch a thousand sighs, and recite his * forty *gospodi pomiloï!* " Lord have mercy upon " me!" Having finished his prayer, he shuts his box, and returns the figure into his pocket. The Ægyptians had their gods in their gardens or in their stables; the Africans carry them in their arms, and the Russians frequently in their trousers.

A russian nobleman is a little more ceremonious. His god likewise accompanies him on his journies; but he is dressed in gold or silver: and, on his arrival at a place where he means to put up, the first business of his servant is to take him from his case, and place him in his master's room, who immediately honours him with his prostrations.

I knew a russian princess who had always a

---

* The number forty has something sacred in it among the russian clergy.

large silver crucifix following her in a separate carriage, and which she usually placed in her bedchamber. When anything fortunate had happened to her in the course of the day, and she was satisfied with her admirers, she had lighted candles placed about the crucifix, and said to it, in a familiar style: " See, now, as you have " been very good to-day, you shall be treated " well; you shall have candles all night; I will " love you, I will pray to you." If, on the contrary, any thing occurred to vex the lady, she had the candles put out, forbad her servants to pay any homage to the poor image, and loaded it with reproaches and revilings.

Even Catharine affected to have great devotion towards images. She was frequently seen to prostrate herself before the door of her chapel, take up the dust from the ground, and scatter it over the diamond crown on her head. Once an image of the virgin, covered with diamonds, of which the empress Elizabeth had made her a present at her confirmation, and which she had placed in this chapel, was stolen away. All the officers of the police were set in motion to discover the perpetrator of so daring a theft, but in vain. " Alas!" said Catharine, " it is not the " loss of the diamonds, but of the holy image, I " regret: I would give double its value to reco- " ver it." Her prayers were heard: after great search had been made, and several persons had been imprisoned, the image was found in the course of a few days, stripped of all its valuable ornaments, in the snow near the admiralty. Catharine, delighted at her good fortune, rewarded him who brought it, directed the image to be arrayed more richly than before, and replaced with great ceremony on her altar.

The girls of the town, too, in Russia, are very devout to the saints. When they have a visitor, before they grant him any favours, they always veil their images, and extinguish the candles placed before them.

I shall not particularise all the superstitions with which such a religion, if it deserves that name, must necessarily inspire an ignorant and enslaved people. It is the coarse policy of the present tzar to thicken the cloud of errors and follies which the genius of Peter, the humanity of Elizabeth, and the philosophy of Catharine sought in some degree to attenuate*. A toad

---

* It may be amusing to see how saints are still made in Russia; an edifying article, translated from the imperial gazette of Petersburg, will shew the process. I translate it verbally:

"*Petersburg, 17 December, 1798.*

"In 1796 a coffin was found at the convent of Sumorin, in
" the city of Trotma, in the eparchy of Vologda, containing
" a corpse in the habit of a monk. It had been interred in
" 1568, yet was in a state of perfect preservation, as were

ever keeps raising the mud of his slough in order to conceal himself the better. While we pity

" also the garments. From the letters embroidered on these,
" it was found to be the body of the most venerable Feodose
" Sumorin, founder and superior of the convent, and who
" had been acknowledged as a saint during his life for the
" miracles he had performed."

It is then stated, that the directing synod had made a very humble report on this occasion to his imperial majesty: after which follows this sublime ukase of Paul.

" We Paul, &c. having been certified, by a special report
" of the most holy synod, of the discovery that has been made
" in the convent of Spasso Sumorin, of the miraculous re-
" mains of the most venerable Feodose; which miraculous
" remains distinguish themselves by the happy cure of all
" those who have recourse to them with entire confidence;
" we take the discovery of these holy remains as a visible
" sign that the Lord has cast his most gracious eye, in the
" most distinguished manner, on our reign. For this reason
" we offer our fervent prayers, and our gratitude, to the su-
" preme disposer of all things, and charge our most holy sy-
" nod to proclaim this memorable discovery throughout all
" our empire, according to the forms prescribed by the holy
" church, and by the holy fathers, &c. The 28th of Sep-
" tember 1798."

Whatever I might add to a fact of this nature, could only tend to enervate the ridicule and indignation that it provokes. —Paul has enriched the russian calendar with a few festivals, in addition to those already mentioned: among others, those of this saint lately dug up, and of the Madonna of Kazan, which he has ordered to be kept holy. Every child, too, that he has, gives rise to two new festivals, his birth-day and his name-day: and Paul has nine children already!—He has also very lately added the commemoration of the transmission of the picture of the virgin Mary, painted by St. Luke, and

the state of degradation under which a great people crouches, we should do justice to the enlightened Russians, by whom it is lamented: but they are enchained by prejudices, as the giant Gulliver was by the Lilliputians; his bonds were weak and imperceptible, like his enemies; but each of his hairs being separately fastened to the ground, he was unable to raise his head.

three fingers of St. John the baptist, from Malta to St. Petersburg, as may be seen in the Almanac of that city for the year 1801.

CHAP. IX.

GYNECOCRACY, OR FEMALE GOVERNMENT.

Its influence on the women of Russia. Their character—immodesty—manners—baths—talents—charms—Princess Dashkof.

RUSSIA presents an example truly singular in the annals of history. The same century has seen five or six women reign * despotically over an empire, where the women were before slaves to men who were themselves enslaved; where Peter I. was obliged to employ † force to raise them out of this barbarous state of debasement, and give them a place in society; where even now the code of slavery does not allow them a soul ‡, or count them among human creatures.

* Sophia, sister to Peter I. Catharine I. Anne I. the regent Anne, Elizabeth, and Catharine II.

† Before Peter I. women never appeared at court or in company, or even at their husband's tables. Peter issued an ukase directing their husbands to let their wives appear in public, very wisely deeming the society of women necessary to civilise the nation: but he was often obliged to employ the officers of the police to conduct the ladies to the balls.

‡ In the russian language the word *soul* is employed to designate male slaves. Instead of asking how much such an one has a year, the question is, how many souls he has: and a man has frequently ten or twenty thousand, without reckoning those of the women or his own, which certainly some may think least deserves to be taken into the account.

x

The reigns of these females afford a strong argument in favour of those nations, who have never suffered the sceptre to be placed in hands that were formed for the distaff; since it would be difficult to find six reigns more prolific in wars, revolutions, crimes, disorders, and calamities of every kind. That the manners of the court were softened, I am ready to admit: but then they were corrupted; and wretchedness increased in equal pace with luxury and disorder. Abuses of every kind, tyranny and licentiousness, became the very essence of government.

The old proverb, " when women reign, men " rule," is false, or unmeaning. When women reign, their lovers tyrannize over the people, and all in power plunder them. But, without entering into the political effects of petticoat government, which may well be considered as the extreme of baseness or extravagance in mankind *, I shall notice only the influence it has had on society and the female sex in Russia.

* From what inconsistency have the offices of empress, and of queen, which require vigour both of mind and body, and knowledge or talents of every kind, been so frequently given to women? An army of five hundred thousand men was at the disposal of Catharine, yet she would not entrust another woman with a single company! She directed the politics of Europe, and gave it peace or war; though a woman could not enjoy the most trifling office in it! Is there not great inconsistency in this conduct?

The existence of the Amazons appeared to me no longer a fable, after I had beheld the russian women. Had the succession of empresses continued, we might perhaps have seen that nation of female warriors locally reproduced, and in the same clime where they formerly flourished*. Great energy is still observable in the women of the slavonian nations, of which their history furnishes many proofs. That feminine activity, which love, tenderness, and domestic cares absorb in other countries, the women of the north, who are born with more cold and robust constitutions, employ in the lust of dominion and political intrigue. They frequently experience a physical necessity of inspiring love, but their hearts seldom feel the necessity of loving.

Under the reign of Catharine the women had assumed a pre-eminence at court, which they carried with them into company, and displayed at home. Princess Dashkof, that " Tomyris talk-" ing French," as she was called by Voltaire;

* It is singular enough, that in the same countries which were said to have been inhabited by a society of women, who proscribed all men, a society of Zaporogian kozaks has since dwelt, who would not suffer a single woman among them, recruiting their force solely by carrying away youths from the neighbouring territories. This barbarous republic was destroyed by Potemkin, and they who composed it distributed in the different armies, or among the other kozaks.

masculine in her tastes, her gait and her exploits, was still more so in her titles and functions of *director* of the academy of sciences, and *president* of the russian academy. It is well known that she long solicited Catharine to appoint her colonel of the guards; a post in which she would undoubtedly have acquitted herself better than most of those by whom it was held. Catharine, however, had too much distrust of one who boasted that she had seated her on the throne, to confide such a place in her hands. One more female reign, and we might have seen a woman general of an army, or minister of state.

Many russian generals, of some reputation abroad, were at that period governed by their wives. Count Poushkin, who commanded in Finland, durst not make a movement till he had dispatched a courier to his, to consult her. Count Ivan Soltikof was as inferior to his wife in moral qualifications as in physical strength, and the minister at war trembled before the wrath of his better half. The reader must not suppose that this submission, which became almost general, was that gallant and chivalrous deference which has sometimes been paid to the ladies; as those whom I have cited as examples were old, ugly, and ill tempered: it was literally the submission of weaknefs to strength, of cowardice to courage, of imbecility to understanding. All the sex seemed to participate in the respect and fear which were paid to Catharine by her courtiers.

The same effects were frequently perceived at a distance from the court. The wives of several colonels received the reports of the regiment, gave orders to the officers, employed them in particular services, dismissed them, and sometimes appointed them. Madame Mellin, *coloneless* of the regiment of Tobolsk, commanded it with a truly martial dignity, received the reports at her toilette, and regulated the mounting of the guard at Narva, while her good-natured husband was employed elsewhere. In an attempt made by the Swedes to surprise the place, she came out of the tent in regimentals, and marched against the enemy at the head of a battalion. Several women accompanied the army against the Turks. Potemkin's seraglio was always composed of handsome Amazons, who delighted in visiting the fields of battle, and admiring the handsome corpses of the Turks, as they lay stretched on their backs, their scymetars in their hands, and with an air of defiance even in death, as the Argante of Tasso appeared to the gentle Herminia *.

* After the storming of Otchakof, heaps of dead bodies were piled up on the Liman, then frozen over, and remained

The manliness of the women is still more observable in the country. Something of this character no doubt may be remarked in all countries, where the men are slaves: for here widows, or daughters come of age, are often obliged to take on themselves the government of their estates, the people whereof are their wealth, their property, like beasts of the field; and are thus engaged in businesses by no means suitable to their sex. To buy, sell, and exchange slaves, assign them their tasks, and order them to be stripped and flogged in their presence, would be as repugnant to the feelings as to the modesty of a woman in a country where men are not degraded to the level of domestic animals, and treated with the same indifference*; but these are offices to which the russian women are often obliged to submit, and they not unfrequently perform them with pleasure.

The habit of treating men thus, and that which both sexes have of mixing together in

there till the thaw. Round these pyramids the russian ladies used to take the air in their sledges, to make their observations.

* A french woman from St. Domingo informed me, that some creolian ladies are not more scrupulous than those of Russia. Some of them go themselves on board the slave ships, to select and purchase slaves, who are exhibited to them quite naked. A well-made negro of twenty-five is called *un negre toutes pièces*, " a negro at all points."

their public baths, deaden, at a very early age, that modesty which is natural to women, and I have seen some as bold as the most shameless of our sex*.

That effrontery conspicuous in some russian women must not be ascribed to libertinism, or gross voluptuousness. They live from their childhood in the greatest familiarity with their herd of vassals: a thousand private and even secret services are performed for them by male slaves, whom they scarcely consider as men. Their domestic manners afford them daily opportunities of satisfying, and even anticipating, their curiosity respecting all the mysteries of nature, and stifling in the birth the irritability of their nerves. Only an equal can put them to the blush; to them a slave is not a being of the same species.

I have already mentioned the shocking manner in which men are treated in Russia. Sensibility must be deadened, and the heart already hardened by spectacles of cruelty, ere a man can behold, for a single moment, without indignation and horror, the punishments sometimes in-

* Being once at the house of a lady in the country, she was desirous of amusing herself with fishing. She sent for nets, and ordered some of her servants to strip and go into the water. They immediately stripped themselves in the presence of their mistress, and she gave them directions in their fishing with all the unconcern imaginable.

flicted on slaves. But, it must be confessed, it is still more revolting, to see women present, and even presiding at them, or sometimes inflicting the punishments themselves. I have been at tables, where, for some trifling fault, the master has coolly ordered a footman a hundred blows with a stick, as a mere matter of course; on which he has been immediately conducted into the court, or into the antichamber only, in presence of the ladies, married and unmarried, who continued to eat and laugh while they heard the cries of the poor fellow undergoing the cudgel *.

* The little reflection with which a man is ordered to be bastinadoed produced a strange blunder a few years ago. Count Bruce, governor-general of Petersburg, had a slave for his cook, who ran away. At court he saw Kleïef, the master of the police, and gave him orders to make the necessary search in order to recover his cook. This was done, but in vain. Just at this period a french cook arrived from Warsaw, who was come to seek employment in Russia, and had been recommended to Kleïef by one of his friends in Poland. Kleïef, thinking to provide the man a place at once, sent him immediately to count Bruce, telling the Frenchman, that he need only say he came from him. Accordingly count Bruce was informed by his servant, that a cook was come, sent by the master of the police. " O," said he, " my fellow is " come, is he? Let him have two hundred stripes immedi- " ately, and then conduct him to the kitchen." The servants of the governour immediately seized the poor devil, and conducted him to the riding-house. There, in spite of his cries and protestations, he received the punishment ordered. His surprise and terror may easily be conceived. He was left half dead, and scarcely able to crawl to the ambassador, to whom

I am not the first person by whom it has been observed, that in Russia the women are usually more malicious, more cruel, and more barbarous than the men: it is because they are still far more ignorant and more superstitious. They scarcely ever travel, are taught very little, and do nothing. Constantly surrounded by slaves, to gratify or prevent their wishes, the russian ladies spend their time either lolling on a sofa, or sitting at a card table. They are very seldom seen with a book in their hands, still seldomer with any kind of work, or attending to their domestic affairs. They, who have not been humanised by a foreign education, are still actual barbarians. Among them you may find such women as that mentioned by Juvenal, who, to a person that entreated her to spare a slave she had ordered to be punished, conjuring her to take pity on the man, answered: " Blockhead! is a slave a man*?" and another, that said to her friends, frightened at the screams they heard while she was shewing them her jewels and trinkets, " It is nothing at all, it is only a man I " have ordered to be flogged."

If there were such women at Rome, what

he made his complaint. Bruce, informed of his mistake, hushed up the affair for a few hundred rubles, which he gave the unlucky french cook.

* O demens, ita servus homo est!

may be expected at Petersburg and Mosco? Some horrible instances might be mentioned, were they not too dreadful and too indelicate to detail—they proceeded from monsters in their kind; and ought not even to be alluded to, but to shew how far the ferociousness of a woman can carry her, when she seems authorized by the government, the religion, the laws, and the customs of the country. Are we to be surprised, if slavery and tyranny pervert the hearts of men, when they can transform the gentler and more susceptible sex into furious beasts. One who bears the title of princess, though she deserves not that of woman, by name K......ky, exhibits a picture of such crimes, such excesses, and so great turpitude, that the reader would shudder at the bare recital of particulars.

The outrages which she perpetrated on her slaves at Mosco, obliged the brother of this Tisiphone to send her to Petersburg, to save her from the vengeance of the people. He was at length compelled to forbid her to employ her own slaves as domestics, and she was fain to hire free persons, who never staid more than a day with her; till at last she was attended wholly by soldiers, who were sent to her house as to task service.

This monster of cruelty is forty years of age, immensely tall, and of huge bulk; resembling one of those sphinxes found among the gigantic monuments of Ægypt. She is still living; and I would give her address to any that were desirous of seeing her.

I knew another lady of the court, who had in her bedchamber a sort of dark cage, in which she kept a slave, who dressed her hair. She took him out herself every day, as you would take a comb out of its case, in order to dress her head, and immediately shut him up again, though seldom without his having had his ears boxed while she was at her toilette. The poor fellow had a bit of bread, a pitcher of water, a little stool, and a chamberpot in his box. He never saw daylight but while he was dressing the perriwig on the bald pate of his antiquated jailor. This portable prison was kept close at her bed's head, and carried with her into the country. And her husband permitted this abomination! How he could sleep undisturbed at the sighs of the poor wretch, lying thus shut up by his side, is inconceivable. He spent three whole years in this *gehenna*; and on making his re-appearance he was frightful to look at, pale, bent double, and withered like an old man. The chief motive of this strange barbarity was the wish of the old baggage to conceal from the world that she wore false hair: and for this she sequestered a man of eighteen from all human society, that he might renovate in secret her faded charms. The fasting and ill treatment which she made him endure besides, were to punish him for having attempted to escape, and because in spite of all his art and care, she grew every day more old and ugly.

Again I repeat it, that these infamous acts, not more incredible than they are true, are not mentioned here as general and characteristic of the russian ladies: they are the crimes of individuals; but these crimes could not have been committed, except in Russia. In any other country, the relations, the friends, the acquaintance of the furies by whom they were perpetrated, would not have looked upon them as singularities of their humour; and the relations of the young man would have had a right to prefer a complaint against his mistress, and to demand justice*.

It is not at court and in domestic affairs only, that the women assume a superiority over the men. Nowhere do so many women arrogate to themselves the right of making the first advances, and being the active party, in affairs of love. The example of Catharine was but too well calculated to give them those bold and masculine tastes

---

* During the reign of Elizabeth, a grandmother of these furies had already distinguished herself by similar atrocities, and her relations were obliged to confine her.

and manners. More than one Maria Pavlovna are well-known instances of female licentiousness.

Almost all the ladies of the court kept men with the title and office of favourites: I say not lovers, as that would imply sentiment; while theirs was merely gross sensuality, or frequently a wish to follow the fashion. This taste was become as common as eating and drinking, or dancing and music. No tender intrigues, and much less any strong passions*. Debauchery and ambition had banished love. Marriage was merely an association, in which convenience alone was considered: it was fortunate if friendship sometimes came unsought, to lighten the chains which

---

* The young princess Shakofsky, who was married to count Aremberg, lately furnished a very tragical exception. At the period of the revolution in Brabant, in which her husband took an active part, Catharine ordered her to leave the seditious count, and return to Russia, under pain of confiscation of all her property. She returned, under the care of her old mother, and Catharine declared her marriage null. One of her cousins ran away with her to Mosco, to marry her there, that he might the more easily obtain a dispensation afterwards. However, he possessed not the heart of his young wife, or at least not entirely. She loved an officer in the guards, of the name of Kamasofsky. The jealousy of her husband hvaing traced her assignations, and complained of them, the princess poisoned herself, and died in dreadful convulsions. Her husband, a man of a melancholy cast, lost his reason for a time, and his happiness for ever.

the interest of parents, or vanity alone, had formed.

The discovery of a society, called the Physical Club, made a few years ago at Mosco, completely proves the depravity of tastes and manners under the reign of Catharine. This was a kind of order surpassing in turpitude every thing related of the most immodest institutions and mysteries. The men and women, who were initiated, assembled on certain days, to indulge promiscuously in the most infamous debaucheries. Husbands introduced their wives; and brothers, their sisters. The novices were not admitted, till they had been examined, and gone through their probations: the women being admitted by the men; the men, by the women. After a sumptuous feast the company were paired by lot. When the french revolution took place, the russian police was directed to examine and dissolve all kinds of orders and assemblies; and on this occasion the Physical Club was examined, and its members were obliged to disclose its mysteries. As the members of both sexes were of the most wealthy and powerful families, and their assemblies had no concern with politics, nothing more was done than to shut up and prohibit this scandalous lodge.

Accounts of the russian baths have been given by various travellers; but, as they have a great influence on the character and manners of the women of the lower class in particular, it may not be amiss to speak of them here in that regard. At my arrival in Russia, one of my first objects was to examine them. I figured in my mind the voluptuous baths of Diana, and thought of nothing less than surprising the nymphs like another Actæon. Accordingly one day I descended the banks of the Neva with a friend, towards a public bath; but I had no occasion to go far, to be convinced that the russian belles were accustomed to expose their charms to the eye of the passenger. A party of women of all ages, tempted by the heat of the month of June, had not thought it necessary to go so far as the precincts of the baths. They had stripped themselves, and were swimming and sporting near the banks of the river. This spectacle, to which I was not accustomed, making a strong impression on me, I stopped and leaned over the quay, and my presence proved no interruption at all to the sports of the bathers.

I afterwards went several times into the baths, and I have seen similar sights on the banks of the islands of the Neva*: but, after what I have

---

* On one of these occasions, an old woman seeing some men of her acquaintance bathing a little way off, swam up to them, and began a conflict with one of them. The young man not being a swimmer, his antagonist had the advantage, and seiz-

said, more ample accounts are quite unnecessary. It is true, there exists an ukase of Catharine, which enjoins the proprietors of public baths in the cities to construct separate rooms for the two sexes; and not to allow any men to enter into that of the women, except the necessary attendants, or painters and physicians, who should come to prosecute their studies. Accordingly an amateur assumes one or other of these titles to obtain admission. At Petersburg both sexes now have their rooms and enclosures separated by a partition; but many old women still prefer mixing with the men: and moreover, both men and women, after having taken the vapour bath, run out perfectly naked to plunge together into the river that runs behind it. In the country, the baths are still on the old footing; that is to say, persons of all ages and both sexes use them promiscuously, and a family consisting of a father of forty, a mother of thirty-five, a son of twenty, and a daughter of fifteen, appear together in a state of innocence, and mutually rub each other down.

These customs, which appear to us so shocking, and which are so to all people who wear

---

ing him by the beard, ducked him repeatedly, to the great amusement of both parties, as well as the spectators, who laughed heartily at the scene. This transaction took place near a part of the shore, where persons of all ages and sexes were walking, and the young ladies in the neighbouring houses might enjoy it from their windows.

clothes and are no longer savage, are yet by no means either the effect of corrupt hearts, or indications of libertinism. It is not even these baths, so conducive to the health of the Russians, that dispose them to debauchery. On the contrary, these free interviews becoming habitual from an early age, deaden the senses and cools the imagination. A russian youth will never feel his blood boil, and his heart palpitate, at the idea of a rising bosom. He never sighs after secret charms, at which he scarcely dares to guess; since from his infancy he has seen and examined every thing. The russian maiden will never have her cheek suffused with an involuntary blush at an indiscrete idea or curiosity, and her husband will have nothing new to communicate to her, nor will marriage have any novelty for her. Love is here a stranger to those delicate and exquisite approaches which constitute its real charms, and to those preludes to pleasure more delightful than pleasure itself. Where poignant sentiments do not ennoble the happiest of human passions, it becomes a mere momentary impulse, too easily gratified to be highly prized.

I am at a loss to conceive how Rousseau came to give his Wolmar such a country. The land of slavery is not that of the generous passions; it would be difficult to find in it the materials for a romance. Yet the Russian is sensible, gay, sings and dances willingly, and the collection of popular ballads bears witness that he formerly felt the inspiration of love. In these an exquisite sensibility and affecting melancholy frequently appear, which interest and delight the reader *.

What I have said of the russian ladies, among whom there are so many amiable and charming †, will tend, I fear, to excite too unfavourable an idea of them. Almost all of them are naturally witty, and by no means destitute of grace; their eyes, feet, and hands, are every thing that could be wished; and there is an ease in their manners, a taste in their dress, and a charm in their conversation, which are peculiarly agreeable.

These sprightly and amiable russian ladies have a taste for the arts. They laugh at the representation of a good comedy, readily perceive a satirical stroke, perfectly understand an equivoque, and applaud a brilliant line: but expressions of

---

* If a change of circumstances should take place, and I can revive my acquaintance with some of the men of letters in Russia, I shall some day give a few pieces of this kind to the public.

† Perhaps the unfortunate chance which gave me a close view of the most malignant and contemptible of the sex, has mixed some gall with my ink in spite of myself. It must be confessed, likewise, that the girls appear as reserved and modest as the women are impudent. They are born susceptible of the most profound and gentle sentiments: it is with difficulty, that examples and the general corruption render them depraved.

sensibility appear lost on them, and I never saw one weep at a tragedy. Mothers, daughters, and lovers behold with dry eyes the moving scenes of Merope, Antigone and Zaire, though exhibited at the french theatre of Petersburg by those excellent performers, Floridor, Aufréne and la Hus.

The domestic virtues, and that spirit of order and economy so necessary to a moderate fortune, are rarely to be found among the russian women. They aim at being the delight of society, rather than careful managers of their family affairs; and are more calculated to give pleasure to many, than to confer happiness on one. But all the charms that luxury sets off, all the enchanting talents that ease of circumstances affords opportunity for cultivating, commonly heighten the beauty of the young russian ladies. They particularly excel in speaking foreign languages, and numbers of them converse in three or four with equal elegance and perfection*.

Those who have had a good education, whom the manners of their families, and the care of a prudent governess, or a respectable mother, have

* A livonian lady, who has received a tolerable education, speaks german, which is her native language; russian, with which she cannot dispense; and french, which is the language of fashion: to these several add italian, on account of music; and some, english. They speak, besides, the livonian, or the esthonian, which are the peculiar and original languages of their provinces. The livonian women, however, are of a different character from the Russians.

formed to the graces, without moulding to vice; those in particular, whom reading, or some travelling, has improved; deserve a foremost place among the amiable women of Europe*. But these are flowers thinly sown, and blooming in obscurity. Superstition, envy, and calumny are in arms against them; and if they cannot support the tortures of the gossiping conversation of the place, they are obliged to form a circle of select females, and especially foreigners†, which redoublest he hatred and persecution raised against them.

It will not be amiss to finish this delineation of the russian women with some particulars of the princess Dashkof, who of all the women of Russia next to Catharine, has been most the subject of conversation, and whose portrait would form a proper companion for that of Potemkin, were it drawn by the hand of the same master ‡.

---

* I could easily mention some of these respectable women, as I have the despicable; but I shall not be blamed for sparing the modesty of those, more than the impudence of these.

† M. Kapief has written a tolerable comedy, in which he has endeavoured to display the ridiculousness of these gossips. The gaiety and mask of Thalia herself were requisite, to render what is most stupid and insipid in life entertaining; but he dared not copy the originals with fidelity.

‡ It may be found in a book entitled *Vie de Catharine II.* The author or compiler of this history, however, has been led into mistakes respecting a number of facts and persons. The princess Dashkof was already in disgrace, and had left

I shall neither refute nor repeat what has been said a hundred times in print of this virago, the real heroine of the revolution of 1762. For some years the friendship between her and her royal mistress had singularly altered, and the following is the true cause of the last quarrel, which was never made up.

In hopes of gaining a few rubles, in 1794, the princess directed a posthumous tragedy of the poet Knæginin* to be printed at the expense of the academy. At any other period no notice would have been taken of this piece, the merit of which was trifling. But from the time of the french revolution, and particularly after the death of Potemkin, Catharine had become fearful and suspicious: surrounded by weak and timid beings, their characters had infected hers. This tragedy was mentioned to her as a seditious piece. It was prohibited; all the copies were seized, and search actually made for those that had been already sold. As the work had been printed by the express orders of madame le president Dashkoff†, she was sent for by the empress. " Good

Petersburg, when he speaks of her as still there; and the outlines of the work are as false as they are improbable.

* A Russian author of considerable repute.

† The reader will pardon me this solecism, which is employed in the russ. She was appointed by an ukase president and director, in the masculine gender, and she was addressed by the title of *madame le president*.

" heaven, what have I done to you, that you
" should print such an infamous and dangerous
" work?" said Catharine, with great emotion:
" if it be so great a crime to reign, was it not
" you who made me commit it?" The princess, surprised at this pointed attack, said in excuse, that she had no ill design, and had not even read the piece, but relied entirely on the censor. To this Catharine sharply replied, that in such critical times people should rely on no person, but do their duty themselves. Madame Dashkof, mortified at this reprimand, procured her nephew, Bakunin, to be vice-president, to supply her place, and asked permission to retire to Mosco; which was granted her. The censor was punished; and it was happy for the author that he was dead *.

The princess had long rendered herself odious and contemptible by her sordid avarice. This celebrated conspirator, who boasted of having

* The scene of this piece, intitled *Vadime*, is laid at Novgorod the Great, at that time a republic, but oppressed by the princes of Moscovy, from whose yoke it was attempting emancipation. This Vadime is the hero of the story; and the following passages which are all that I preserved, are, I believe, the most alarming in the work. Vadime, conspiring to restore liberty to his country, says:

" A king unites the weaknesses of a man with the power
" of a God."

" To wear a crown is sufficient soon to render a man cor-
" rupt and wicked."

conferred a crown, sent to all the officers or aidesde-camp of her acquaintance, to beg tarnished epaulettes and old lace. To untwist and sell these was become her chief employment; and persons, who were interested in obtaining her favour, began by sending her old gold or silver lace. She made no fires in winter in the apartments of the academy, and yet expected that the academicians should regularly attend the meetings. Many chose rather to expose themselves to her vulgar abuse, and lose their medals, than shiver in an ice-house: but the princess never failed to be there, muffled up in rich furs; and it was a singular spectacle to see this lady only, seated in the midst of bearded popes and russian professors, trembling and submissive before her; for she treated these academicians with a haughtiness and even brutality worthy of Peter I. She took men of letters for soldiers, and the sciences for slaves.

Her adventure with count Gregory Razumofsky made all Petersburg laugh, and rendered her contemptible in the eyes of every man of sense. She had sent him an academician's diploma unsolicited. Some time after she consigned to him a bale of russian books, to the value of about 600 rubles (60*l.*). Razumofsky refused to take them, saying that he had the originals of these russian translations already in his library*. The princess replied, that she had created him an academician only on condition of his purchasing these books; and in consequence Razumofsky sent back his diploma. The princess wished to persuade the world, that he was not in his senses; but the ridicule fell upon herself. Thus she prostituted her academy: as to herself, it was what no longer remained to be done †.

What rendered her completely ridiculous, both at court and in the city, was her lawsuit with Alexander Narishkin, who had a country seat in the neighbourhood of Petersburg, adjoining to hers. One day Narishkin's pigs got into the grounds of the princess, and devoured some of her cabbages. The heroine ordered them all to be massacred. Narishkin, seeing her at court, said " There she is, still red with the blood " of——‡ my pigs."

* When I began to understand a little of the russian language, I wished to read some of their original works: but I was astonished to find, that what were given me for such was frequently a translation of some well known work, but which was never mentioned in the title page.

† One day having lost thirty rubles at cards to S——, she sent him the next morning thirty of the academy's almanacs by way of payment. I speak here only of her ridiculous meanness: the turpitude of her manners would carry me too far.

‡ This marked pause brought to the hearer's mind Peter III. and the crimson face of the princess was singularly suited to the expression used.

Such was this celebrated woman, who prided herself on the share that she had in the revolution of 1762, who went to fisty-cuffs with her landlady in Holland, who at Paris wanted to blow out the brains of poor abbé Chappe, whom Voltaire pretended to admire, whom german authors, on whom she never bestowed a farthing, treated in vain as a genius, and who at last became a laughing-stock to all Russia.

CHAP. X.

EDUCATION.

Anecdotes of the education of the grand-dukes—their governors and preceptors—Education of the Russians in general—Of the utshiteli, or tutors, their influence—Of the young Russians—Proceedings of the present emperor unfriendly to civilisation—The Gazettes—Radischef—Fable of the owl and the glowworm.

CATHARINE drew up a plan of education for her grand children*, as she had composed instructions for the legislation of her people. This plan, compiled from Locke and Rousseau, as the instructions had been from Montesquieu, Mably, and Beccaria, does honour to the empress's head; and had she possessed no other merit than that of adopting the ideas and maxims contained in those performances, it would not have been small. If this plan had been followed, Alexander and Constantine Pavlovitch would certainly have been the best educated princes in Europe. But it happened to Catharine's plan of

---

* This has never been printed. Catharine sent copies of it to the chief preceptors as a rule to go by. It is in the form of instructions, and addressed to count Nicholas Soltikof.

education, as it did to the instructions for her code. The compiling of the laws ended, as has been observed, with being abandoned to the management of a committee of dunces, bigots, and buffoons, which happily never assembled; and the education of the young princes was entrusted to people, scarcely capable of reading the plan, whereof they were to follow the letter, and to study the spirit*. The only rule they seemed to comprehend was the following, probably because it was negative. " The grand-" dukes are not to be taught either poetry or " music; because it would occupy too much of " their time to become expert in either." This rule they carefully extended to all the sciences †.

* This bad choice of Catharine is somewhat similar to that of Peter I. That illustrious instructor of his people was a very bad one for his only son. After having allowed him to spend his infancy with monks, priests, and servants, he gave him for a governor Mentchikof, who, it is notorious, was never able to read. It is true, that he appointed for his subgovernor a Dutchman, a man of knowledge, but who soon experienced the same fate as l'Harpe, under a similar chief.

† This has certainly the least merit of any rule in the instructions. Not that a prince should be made a fidler, or a poet; but it is impossible to give them too much taste for those arts which inspire and cherish sensibility of mind. The accurate sciences, which are said to render the judgment more exact, deaden the feelings. History is the proper study of princes and rulers. Without the belles lettres, the great Frederic would have been nothing but a tyrant: with them Peter I would have ceased to be a ferocious barbarian.

It was the intention of Catharine, however, that her grandchildren should be instructed in every science capable of enlightening their reason or adorning their minds. Luckily for the young princes, a man of superior talents, l'Harpe, was chosen for their first preceptor. He had incessantly to contend against the interested flattery and base adulation which surrounded them from the cradle. The ill will and ineptitude of the principal persons concerned in their education were a still greater restraint upon him. But the esteem and confidence with which he was honoured by Catharine, encouraged him; and the idea, that he was rendering an important service to mankind, by instilling useful truths into the minds of princes called to decide the fate of so many millions, supported him in the arduous task. Inflexible in his course, he rendered himself beloved by one of his pupils, feared by the other, respected by those under him, and esteemed by his superiors: insomuch that he effected almost as much good as the corrupt persons about the princes did harm. He was seconded by some of the persons of honour that

---

God preserve all monarchies from having geometricians or mathematicians for their kings: they measure men by the yard, and reckon them as they would their money. The most important matter is, to be humane, good, and just; but with that justice, which arises from a sense of truth, not that which is proved by $a+b$.

were appointed them*: and hereafter, perhaps, Russia will be more indebted to l'Harpe, than to his countryman le Fort; for, if Peter I. reformed and civilised his people, Alexander gives hopes of rendering them some day more free and more happy.

The frankness with which l'Harpe professed republican sentiments in Russia exposed him to the shafts of the envious. The Bernese, having seised his letters to his cousin, general l'Harpe, sent them to Catharine. The Prince of Nassau, and Estherhazy, whose wife is a native of Berne, were his accusers, and endeavoured to represent him as a very dangerous man in the confidential post he occupied. Catharine one day sent for him into her closet; and the following particulars of the interview will shew at once the esteem with which the preceptor was honoured and the magnanimity of Catharine.

Catharine. Come, sit down, Mr. Jacobin; I have something to say to you.

L'Harpe. I must protest against the title which your majesty thinks proper to give me, not knowing how I have deserved it.

The empress then shewed him the letters she

---

* Particularly the two Moraviefs, who cultivated literature, and possessed considerable merit and talents, and Tutulmin, a man of sense and good breeding.

had received, and informed him of the charges brought against him.

To this l'Harpe replied nearly in the following words: Your majesty knew, before you entrusted me with the education of the grand-dukes, that I was a Swiss, and consequently a republican. I have not altered my sentiments; and you are too equitable, madam, to consider that as a crime in me now, which did not appear so then. My countrymen are oppressed by the Bernese; I exhort them to claim, by lawful means, our antient rights: this is not being factious. For the rest, madam, I admire your great qualities, I respect your administration, and I faithfully discharge the duties devolving on me, when I devoted myself to the education of the grand-dukes. I shall always endeavour to render myself worthy of the confidence with which you have honoured me, by inspiring them with sentiments suitable to their birth and station, and by endeavouring to render them capable of imitating hereafter the example you set before them. This, madam, is my defence: it remains with your majesty to pass judgment on me, after examining into my conduct in the post with which you have deigned to entrust me.

Catharine, struck with this open behaviour replied: " Sir, be a jacobin, a republican, or

" what you please: I believe you to be an honest
" man, and that is sufficient for me. Stay with
" my grandchildren, retain my entire confidence,
" and instruct them with your wonted zeal*."

Such was Catharine. Her conduct as well as that of l'Harpe will be better appreciated, when it is considered, that this happened at the very period when the Austrians were flying before Dumouriez, soon after the death of Lewis XVI. when Gustavus was dying from the wound inflicted by the assassin Ankerstrœm, when Leopold was said to have been taken off by poison, and when every king in Europe was trembling on his throne. His accusers, however, though rebuffed, were not silenced; but the marriage of the grand-duke Alexander, putting a period to the term of his education, l'Harpe took his leave, and thus preserved himself from the dire catastrophe he had reason to dread on the accession of the successor of his generous mistress.

Nicholas Soltikof I have mentioned in another place. Being chief governor of the young princes, his principal occupations were to preserve

* It was in a similar conversation, that l'Harpe one day made Catharine sensible of the danger of sending a russian army against the French. The open language of a man that she esteemed made more impression on her than all the arguments of Mr. Pitt and the importunities of the coalition.

them from currents of air, and to keep their bodies open. Protassof, the governor of the elder would have been more in his place had he been appointed his apothecary. He came every day to make a circumstantial report to Soltikof of the most insipid particulars, carefully specifying the number of stools the prince had had. Though a narrow-minded-man, bigotted, and pusillanimous, he had not a bad heart; but he rendered himself ridiculous in the eyes of every one, except his pupil; who saw in him nothing but his attachment to himself, for which he expressed his gratitude.

Baron Sacken had the misfortune of being governor to the younger prince, after having been preceptor to Paul. He was superior in every respect to his colleague; but his easy and complying character rendered him the sport of his pupil*, whose petulance and want of application, as well as his unconquerable obstinacy, required constantly about him a man resolute as l'Harpe, the only one who was able to keep him in any

---

* Sacken was incessantly preaching to the prince, and exhorting him to read. " I won't read," said Constantine to him one day, " for I see you always reading, and you only " prove the greater blockhead for it." This sarcasm produced a laugh. He would strike and bite his governors, his chevaliers, and his masters. L'Harpe was the only person who had the spirit to complain, and to require him to be corrected.

degree of awe, and might have softened his natural ferocity, had he been properly seconded.

Among the masters of the grand-dukes, professor Kraft, who gave them lessons in experimental philosophy, was distinguished for his good-nature, perspicuity, and immoveable formality. Alexander Pavlovitch made some progress under him; being attentive, and desirous of learning, as he was in all his studies. Kraft, speaking one day of the hypotheses of some philosophers on the nature of light, said, that Newton supposed it to be a constant emanation from the sun. Alexander, then twelve years of age, answered: " I " do not believe it: for if it were, the sun must " grow less every day." This objection, made with equal simplicity and acuteness, is in fact the strongest that has been brought against the immortal Newton, and proves the early sagacity of the young grand-duke.

The celebrated Pallas was giving the princes a short course of botany in their garden near Pavlofsky: but the explanation of Linnæus's system of the sexes gave them the first ideas of those of human nature, and led them to put a number of very laughable questions with great simplicity. This highly alarmed their governors; Pallas was requested to avoid entering into further particulars concerning pistils and staminas; and the course of botany was even broken off. Catharine had particularly enjoined, that her pupils should be kept in the most perfect ignorance as to what related to the intercourse of the sexes. Her great modesty in this respect appears strikingly contrasted with other parts of her character. But it is well known, that the regent of France, who was the most debauched of men, caused Lewis XV. to be brought up in such complete ignorance of things, which he afterwards so extensively practised, that on the eve of his marriage, he was obliged to be taught his part, by being shewn prints in which it was displayed. Catharine thought it better, that her grandchildren should receive their first lessons in nature. At least, a lady of the name of T.....kof was chosen to initiate the grand-duke Constantine; from which she reaped the pleasure, as her husband did honour and promotion.

One of Catharine's most ardent wishes was, like Lewis XIV, to see her great grandchildren. That a moment might not be lost, she ordered the instant of their puberty to be watched; but her hope was frustrated by the very impatience with which she sought its accomplishment. These premature marriages appear only to have ruined their constitutions. Neither of the young princes have as yet had any children, and it is to be feared they never will*.

* Their marriages have been mentioned in the first chapter.

The birth of the two grand-dukes had filled the empress with joy. Her vast projects and hopes now took a wider range, of which the very names of the princes gave intimation. In their behalf she resolved to partition the world into two empires: she had the children every where painted, one cutting the gordian knot, the other bearing the cross of Constantine. Their education seemed at first to be merely the developement of these grand ideas. Constantine had grecian nurses, and was surrounded by Greeks: in his infancy he spoke no other language; but he forgot it, as soon as masters were appointed to teach it him more fully. The persons about Alexander were Englishmen, and endeavours were made to inspire him with a predilection for that nation, which he may, perhaps, some day discard, as his brother became disgusted with Greece.

I have already observed, that Paul had neither authority nor influence over the education of his children. He was obliged to solicit Soltikof's permission to see them; or to gain their valets-de-chambre, to know what was doing with respect to them. During the summer they had permission to spend an hour or two with their parents once or twice a week; and the fantastical Paul deprived himself of this pleasure for one whole year, because he would not see the countess Shuvalof by whom they were latterly attended.

To conclude, the following is one of the humane lessons which this tender parent was heard to give his sons. News had just been received of some of the bloody scenes in the french revolution: you see, children, said Paul on this occasion, mankind must be treated like dogs. He seems hitherto to have been faithful to his maxim.

The Russians in general, following the example of their latter sovereigns, had for some time endeavoured to emerge from barbarism, by carefully attending to the education of their children. To bestow on them knowledge and talents, was formerly the happy means of bringing them into notice, and procuring them advancement. Neither pains nor expense were spared to cultivate the arts and sciences in a country where they were exotic, as fruits are forced to ripen in their winter gardens and hot-houses. Elizabeth and Catharine founded several institutions in favour of youth, some of which, as the normal schools, and particularly the three different corps of cadets, presented the interesting sight of several thousand young men educated at the expense of the state, and taught morality, languages, sciences, and arts. Paul has abolished the schools, and the corps de cadets are now nothing more than barracks and houses of military exercise.

The convent of young ladies, though the sentiments from which it was founded were worthy of the generosity of a great princess, has completely failed of its end, like most of the other institutions. Two or three hundred young women of no fortune receive here an excellent education; but, as soon as they reach the age of eighteen, they are turned out of doors. They enter into a world from which they have lived secluded since their infancy: seldom find either relations, or acquaintances; and are ignorant what course of life to chuse. Accordingly they generally fall victims to the officers of the guards, whose barracks surround the convent, and who watch every term of dismission to ensnare the prettiest. Some part of the immense cost of their education might be spared for portioning them out, or at least to maintain them till they gained an establishment.

The education of young Russians, who have some fortune, is commonly entrusted to private governors, known and decried in Russia by the name of *utshiteli*, " teachers." Most of them are foreigners, chiefly French or Swiss. The Germans, notwithstanding their good qualities and pedagogical erudition, are too incompatible with the character of the Russians, to rival them; and the trials which some have wished to make of their own countrymen from the university of Mosco, or from the schools of Petersburg, have not given satisfaction. The famous answer of the grecian philosopher is applicable in this place,

To a man, who said to him: "With what you ask for the education of my son I could purchase a good slave, who would educate him in my own house;" he replied: "Purchase a slave: he and your son will make two."

The *utshiteli*, whom coxcombs endeavour to ridicule, and the old ladies consider as dangerous, have contributed more than any others to polish Russia; as they have given instruction in detail, man by man. They are the only people whose office has been to preach philosophy, virtue, and morals, while diffusing knowledge: for we have seen that the orthodox greek religion is far above meddling with such matters; and a colonel, the only preceptor the young Russians afterwards have, is not more addicted to them. From the celebrated le Fort, who inspired Peter I. with the desire of gaining knowledge, to the petty clerk of some french attorney, who teaches his pupils to conjugate a few verbs in his own tongue, the *utshiteli* have been the persons who have communicated to the Russians that taste, those acquirements, and those talents, for which many of them are admired in foreign countries. No doubt it is to be lamented, that among the number of those who devote themselves to private tuition, and make it their trade to form men, there are so many unworthy of the employment, whose ignorance and immorality bring ridicule and odium on their colleagues. But such tutors begin to find it difficult to obtain situations, except in remote country places, where some honest Russians of the old stamp fancy they have bestowed a good education on their children, when they hear them speak a foreign language. At Petersburg people were become more difficult in the choice of tutors, and among them were to be found persons of real merit. They were the only class of men in Russia, without excepting the academicians, who cultivated in some degree literature and the sciences. A Bruckner, at prince Kurakin's; a Granmont, at princess Dolgoruka's; a Lindquist, an abbé Nicole, and several others, without having places equally advantageous *, were worthy of the profession to which they devoted themselves, and were distinguished for their success as much as for their merit.

The great men of Russia, who have much wealth and high posts, are too ignorant, or too much engaged in gaming and intrigue, to interfere with the education of their children; and as colleges and universities are wanting in that country, they pursue a very prudent plan. As soon

* Mr. Bruckner received thirty-five thousand rubles (3500*l.*) for the fourteen years he engaged to devote to the education of the young princes Kurakin; and Granmont received twenty-five thousand (2500*l.*) for the education of the princes Dolgoruky.

as they have made choice of the man as their substitute in the duties of a father, they give him great confidence and authority: the most intelligent could not do better, were they but discreet in their choice. It is seldom that a governor is so destitute of sense, erudition, and honour, as to abuse his functions; he feels himself most happily disposed towards his pupil: to instruct him, form him, acquire his attachment, and gain his love, are the wishes of his heart. If he be in a worthy, opulent family, he has no occasion to regret the sacrifice of ten or twelve years to gain a provision for life*. In his pupil he often finds a real friend, and always a patron. His own interest prompts him to inspire his pupil with just and noble sentiments, and to give him a taste for the sciences; which is far more important, and far more difficult, than to teach him the elements of them. Thus, most of the young Russians pass their early days with a foreigner, who becomes their second father, and for whom they retain a due sense of gratitude, at least if they are naturally of good dispositions.

* The great french lords sometimes gave rich abbeys to their tutors: the wealthy English act still more generously. The Russians frequently follow their example: their governours receiving annuities at their departure, or places and rank if they settle in Russia. Thus at least those act who consider the tutors of their children as something more than their head servants.

This education by means of foreigners has one inconvenience; but it is by no means injurious to the Russians. Almost all of them, being educated by Frenchmen, contract from their infancy a decided predilection for France. With its language and history they are better acquainted than with their own; and as, in fact, they have no country, France becomes that of their heart and imagination. Such was the scythian Anacharsis educated by the grecian Theagenes: such were the Romans formed by the Greeks; but the Romans had virtues to lose, which is scarcely the case with the Russians. Besides, they get a knowledge of France only on the fair side, as it appears at a distance, and to such as regret it. They consider it as the native soil of taste, politeness, arts, delicate pleasures, and amiable people: as the asylum of liberty, as the hearth of that sacred fire at which the torch may one day be kindled to illumine their benighted country. The french emigrants, driven to the territories of the modern Cimmerians, were astonished to find men better acquainted than themselves with the affairs of their own country: since there are young Russians who reflect with Rousseau and study the harangues of Mirabeau; whereas the emigrants have read nothing, and bring nothing with them but their prejudices. They found many young

Russians better acquainted with Paris, than those who had been tramping the pavement of it all their lives*. It has in general been remarked, that the Russians have the most happy dispositions, and a surprising facility of conception; whence they make a very rapid progress in whatever is taught them. No children are more amiable or more interesting: many, on completing their domestic education, have acquired more select and extensive knowledge, than other young men who have frequented the german universities; and they have particularly a wonderful readiness at displaying their knowledge on all fit occasions. Too frequently however, these blossoms are premature, and produce no fruit: they seldom travel like an Anacharsis; and their return to their own country usually puts an end to their studies, and even to their taste for science and literature.

> Telle on voit s'élever l'alouette légère;
> Elle charme un instant par son chant matinal,
> Puis retombe et se tait sur le gazon natal †.

---

* Count Butturlin had carried this local knowledge so far that he could converse with a Parisian on the most minute details of the theatres, streets, hotels, and public buildings of Paris. The Frenchman was struck dumb with astonishment when the Russian confessed at last that he had never been in France.

† From an epistle to a young Russian.

" So the gay lark, with light ascending wing,
" Soars high in air to charm the meads around,
" Till ceasing thus in strain sublime to sing,
" Silent he sinks upon his natal ground."

In like manner a Swiss, after having spent his youth in the service of France, and contracted splendid vices, leaves them on returning to his own country, to resume the simplicity of his ancestors. He returns to virtue, but the Russian returns to barbarism. Strong minds alone, completely taken with the charms of philosophy or the attractions of true glory, are able to resist the torrent: for those talents, which the autocrats pretended to encourage, became at length a motive for exclusion from the posts and honours of the court. Thus the manners of Europe, and even the character of Catharine, were in perpetual contradiction with the barbarous forms and impulse once given to the russian government, which destroyed by its re-action all that humanity and philosophy strove to establish. Despotism exacts a continued self-denial, and that even of the improvements it once encouraged. The influence of foreign preceptors over the character and morality of the Russians is therefore combated by prejudices and obstacles almost invincible: but this influence is constant and continual: it operates in secret on the mind; and its progress, slow as the foot of time, is but the more certain.

Perhaps the young russian nobility are the best informed and most philosophical in Europe, but a complete counter-revolution has just taken place in their education: since the progress of the french revolution, especially since the commencement of the gloomy reign of Paul and the arrival of the emigrants, the human mind has taken a retrograde course in Russia. Most of the *utshiteli* at present are chevaliers, counts, marquises, or priests; for the same thing has taken place with the emigrants as did formerly with the colonists whom Catharine imported to cultivate her deserts; all who could read and write left their fields to become tutors. But the effects of this will be transient: the new trade adopted by these gentlemen will teach them to think, or they will not pursue it long. It is almost impossible to be an *utshitel*, without becoming in some degree rational: what is heard, seen, and felt, every day, in these territories, operates more in favour of liberty than all the victories and the eloquence of the French. A Montmorenci in the office of *utshitel* infallibly becomes a democrat.

In the *Voyage de deux Français en Russie*, "Tour of two Frenchmen in Russia," are some strange reflections on these *utshiteli*. The travellers are astonished that they are almost all democrats, though enjoying an easy and agreeable life in the house of some great lord; and rally them for not quitting it, to devote their lives to the cause which they espouse. You say that they are acting properly in France; why, then, do you not go thither? this is the dilemma proposed by these gentlemen. But, were any one to praise the custom in China for the emperor to plough a field himself, would they in the same manner say to him, Why do you not repair thither and hold the plough? Such is the inconsistency of people! May not a man acknowledge the truth of a principle, all the consequences of which he cannot carry into practice? May not a Frenchman in Petersburg rejoice at the victories of his countrymen, because he could contribute nothing to them but his secret prayers? May he not rejoice to see liberty, order, and happiness reestablished in his country, though he cannot return thither? Such is the language of little minds, who dare not avow a truth when they are in a place where it is dangerous not to abjure it.

The progress of the human mind in Russia, however, has lately been stopped, or at least fettered, by the ridiculous and arbitrary measures, though consistent enough, adopted by his muscovite majesty to break off all communication between the rest of Europe and his blessed dominions. Peter I. never took such pains and care to reform and polish his empire as Paul now takes precautions to prevent light from penetrating among his Cimmerians.

A more completely ridiculous code of laws could not be exhibited to Europe than a collection of the ukases promulgated by Paul since he came to the throne. He has lately forbidden all his subjects, the Livonians and Courlanders in particular, to send their children to study in Germany, because corrupt principles prevail there. He recals, under penalty of confiscation of their property, all who are at present at any foreign university *: but he promises to permit the establishment of an university in his german provinces, where young men may be instructed in such sciences as are more immediately necessary. Till this university is founded under his auspices, and the disciples of Kant quit Germany, to visit it in quest of a more luminous philosophy, the Finlanders and Courlanders, Esthonians and Livonians, must remain without any means of instruction; since there are not even any public schools throughout their vast provinces. Paul, as the utmost effort of his wisdom, has also forbidden the employment of foreigners in their courts of justice, and the giving them ecclesi-

* There were thirty-six students at Leipsic, and sixty-five at Jena, subjects of the tzar, who hastily returned home in pursuance of this ukase.

astical benefices. He has even outgone himself: by another ukase he prohibits all foreigners from entering his dominions without a special permission from his muscovito-chinese majesty; and, as the ultimate proof of barbarism, this *imniennoi-ukase* * has not been published. Merchants, foreigners who have possessions in Russia, and young men who have been invited thither, are stopped at the frontiers, or on board the vessels in which they arrive, and sent back, after the expense they have been at, and the dangers they have incurred by a tedious voyage.

Another ukase prohibits the reading of french newspapers. No paper can enter Russia, without having been examined and stamped by a committee of censure; and every man who receives by the post, by a courier, or from a traveller, any newspaper, or printed book of any kind, is enjoined to carry them immediately to the committee, under penalty of being punished as a rebel!

The people of Germany are more happy, as the Russian newspapers are admitted into that country; and the following advertisements extracted from them, must be highly edifying to readers of sensibility.

" Any person wanting to purchase a whole

---

* An ukase under the sign-manual.

"family, or a young man and a girl separately, may apply to the silk-scourer, facing the Kazanskoi church. The young man, named Ivan, is one and twenty years of age; healthy, robust, and knows how to dress ladies' hair. The girl, well made, and in good health, named Marpha, aged fifteen, understands sewing and embroidery. They may be examined and had at a reasonable price*.

"At the same house a stallion from Holstein to be sold. For viewing him apply to the coachman."

"At the printing office of the academy, the few remaining copies of the Instruction for the Code of Laws, by Catharine II. are selling off †, &c."

And these advertisements appear in Europe! in a christian country; in an empire that Peter civilized, where Elizabeth, where Catharine reigned and excited admiration! Surely, if Paul had any sense of decorum, he would much rather prohibit the exportation of russian gazettes than the entrance of foreigners.

---

* The ordinary price for a girl or woman is from fifty to two hundred rubles: varying according to age, comeliness, or talents. That of a man likewise varies from three hundred to five hundred, or even a thousand rubles. Sometimes a slave is bartered against a dog or a horse, and occasionally sported away on a card at the gaming table.

† Anhang zu der Petersburger Zeitung, No. 56, 1798.

It is to be observed, that, under the reign of Catharine, Russia was for a time the only country in Europe in which french papers were not prohibited. The Moniteur having spoken several times of the empress, and particularly of Paul and his court, Catharine gave orders that the Moniteur should not be distributed till she had looked it over. A few weeks after she found a paragraph, in which she was styled the Messalina of the north, &c. Having read it, she said: "As "this concerns only myself, let it be distributed." At a time when french gazettes, cockades, and songs were proscribed in nations farthest from barbarism: when at Turin, they who sung *ça ira* were imprisoned, when birds that repeated those words had their necks wrung in England, and at Vienna french was not allowed to be spoken, the russian government appeared to be above these little inquisitorial acts, and the pupils of colonel l'Harpe were allowed to chaunt french revolutionary airs in the palace of the tzars. One of them carried a national cockade in his pocket, which he displayed with an air of triumph and defiance to the most timid courtiers. It was not till after the death of Lewis XVI. and the assassination of Gustavus III. that Catharine, struck with consternation, began to yield to the suggestions of her base favourites, and the emigrants by whom she was beset: it was only then that she began to take precautions which betrayed her fear*.

Still there was always more to be apprehended from the zeal of the subordinate tools of government, than from the disposition of Catharine. With abler ministers, more honest courtiers and less pusillanimous favourites, she would not have finished like the syrens of Virgil, who are fine women terminating in fish-tails. Among the numerous victims of the political inquisition Radischef deserves particularly to be regretted by the friends of reason. It is well known that Catharine frequently sent young Russians to travel and improve themselves at her expense. Several of these were happily chosen, became men of merit, and brought back to their country a store of knowledge, with notions of philosophy and humanity. The most distinguished and most unfortunate of these pupils of Catharine was Radischef. On his return he was made director of the customs;

---

* One fact will farther prove the dignified security of Catharine. A brother of the famous Marat was at Petersburg, as tutor in the house of Soltikof the chamberlain. This Marat, while he condemned the excesses of his brother, did not conceal from his friends his own republican sentiments, yet he lived in peace, and sometimes attended his pupil to court. However, as his name might have exposed him to some danger, at the time of the king's death he requested Catharine's permission to change it, and called himself Boudri, from the place of his birth.

and in this office of a publican, his probity, the amenity of his manners, and his agreeable company, rendered him esteemed and courted. He cultivated literature, and had already published a work, intitled *Potshta Dukof*, " the Post of " Wits;" a periodical work the most philosophical and poignant that ever ventured to appear in Russia. Yet he was not molested on account of it: but after the revolution, he had the courage to print a little pamphlet, in which he scrupled not to avow his hatred of despotism, his indignation against the favourites, and his esteem for the French. It was singular, that several copies of it are with the approbation of the police. Kleïef, master of the police, as famous in Russia for his blunders, as a d'Argenson, a la Noir, and a Sartine were in France for their address, was cited to answer for this approbation. He knew not what to say, not having read the work; which indeed would have been above his comprehension. But Radischef, who was also cited, honestly confessed, that the boldest passages were not in the manuscript, when he submitted it to the censure, but that he had printed them at his own house *. To have pardoned him would

---

* Radischef's work is intitled a Journey to Mosco. Russian merchants have been known to give five and twenty rubles (2*l*. 10*s*.) to have it for a single hour to read in private. I have read only a few fragments of it, among which

have been worthy of the character which Catharine displayed on other occasions: but Radischef was sent off to Siberia. He begged permission to embrace his wife and children once more; and on being taken out of prison to be sent off, he was allowed to wait for them a moment on the bank of the Neva: but it was night; the drawbridge had just been raised to let a vessel through, and at this instant his unfortunate wife arrived on the opposite bank. Radischef entreated that his departure might be deferred till the vessel had passed, or his wife could get a boat; but in vain: his pitiless guard made him remount, and shut him into his tumbrel again in sight of his distracted wife, who stretched out her arms to him across the river with loud cries of distress. Thus he departed, his heart torn by despair. If he be still living in the vast deserts to which he is confined, or if he draw breath in the mines of Kolhivan, may his virtue be his comforter! his courage has not been useless to his country: in spite of the domiciliary scrutinies of

---

was an allegory, in which he exposes the pride and foolish grandeur of a despot surrounded by dastardly flatterers. The following words particularly enraged Catharine, as being directly pointed: "I enter the palace of Tzarsko-selo: I am "struck with the awful silence that reigns: every one holds "his peace, every one trembles: it is the abode of despo-"tism." These words procured Radischef a residence in Siberia.

despotism, his work subsists in the hands of several of his countrymen, and his memory is dear to all men of honour and sensibility.

The proscription of every one who dared to think, suggested the following apologue. It was written when the present emperor was grandduke; and it will not be amiss to conclude this chapter with it, as it is but too well justified by his conduct since.

LE GRAND-DUC *

ET

LE VER LUISANT,

FABLE.

Dans une sombre nuit d'été
Un ver luisant caché sous l'herbe
Jetoit une douce clarté.
Ce n'etoit point un phare éclatant et superbe,
Il n'éclairoit qu'un pas à l'environ;
C'étoit là son horison:
Mais pourtant l'insecte lucide
Servoit de guide
Aux petits hôtes du gazon.

* A nocturnal bird, found particularly in Russia. See Buffon.
Duc, in French, signifies both a duke and a horned owl: *le grand-duc* is the great horned-owl in natural history.

A sa lueur douce et tranquille,
La fourmi retardée atteignoit son azile,
Le papillon léger s'égayoit à l'entour :
 En un mot, cet astre reptile
Embellissoit les nuits de son humble séjour.

Non loin de là, dans une vieille tour,
 Prison de sa triste famille,
 Un vieux hibou tenoit sa cour.
Un hibou hait les *vers* qui lui montrent le jour.
" Audacieux !" dit il à l'insecte qui brille,
" Qui t'a fait si hardi que d'approcher de nous ?
" Tu mourras."—" Monseigneur," lui répond
 " l'humble insecte,
" Je suis indigne, hélas ! d'un si noble courroux,
 " Je vous honore, vous respecte ;
 " Je tremble d'approcher de vous :
" A sucer la rosée ici je me délecte ;
" Mais d'aucun bruit pourtant je ne trouble vos
 " nuits.
" Comment un animal foible comme je suis
 " Peut-il offenser Votre Altesse ?"—
 " Insecte dangereux ! *tu luis* ;
 " Péris, la lumière me blesse."
 Cela dit, le nocturne oiseau,
En écrasant le ver, éteignit son flambeau
 Sans rendre la nuit plus épaisse.

THE OWL AND THE GLOW-WORM.

A FABLE.

'Twas on a sombre summer night,
  A glow-worm, shelter'd by a flow'r,
Spread round its mildly glimm'ring light,
  To decorate the silent hour:
No brilliant beam, no gaudy glare,
  Diffus'd afar its lustrous ray,
But thro' the softly breathing air
  The insect shed its mimic day.

  While pleas'd its harmless life to pass
  On hillock green of dewy grass,
Attracted by its azure gleam;
  The butterfly, with sportive wing,
  Would form the gay fantastic ring,
(As in the burning noontide beam,)
Where, 'mid the gloom, this insect star display'd
Its cheerful lamp,—spangling the realms of shade!

Near, on a mould'ring antique tow'r,
  The prison of its moping race,
An owl had chose its murky bow'r,
  And hating day's effulgent light,
  Its joy the sullen frown of night,
  Its blank domain the silent space!
  There, prompt to spread its shad'wy wings
  Imperious, o'er less daring things,
  Soon on the glow-worm's peaceful state
  Fix'd his dull eyes, in envious hate.

"Bold worm!" exclaim'd the tyrant vain,
"Thou, who with sparkling light art seen
"Peering the lonely shades between,
"How dar'st thou mock my gloomy reign?
"Thou shalt expire!" The glow-worm meek,
(Its trembling light more faint and pale,)
In humble accents, low and weak,
Thus told its true, but artless tale:
"I own that, of the insect race,
"I boast no gaudy splendid grace;
"I light with feeble lamp the way
"Where prouder, loftier beings stray;
"I sip the balmy dews around—
"But ne'er am heard with busy sound;—
"Ne'er on your calm repose obtrude
"With counsel vain, or clamour rude;
"Can *I* offend superior things,
"Or cope with birds of pow'rful wings?".

The owl, indignant, bold, and base,
Exulting o'er the insect race,
Replied—"*You shine!* detested thing!
"To me, offensive *light* you bring—"
Then, pouncing on his humble prey,
Darken'd, in death, its little ray;
But found, tho' quench'd the quiv'ring flame,
His sombre hour was still *the same!*

CHAP. XI.

SUPPLEMENT*.

French and Swiss in Russia—Persecutions they undergo—Proscription of some—Oath required of them—Billet of absolution—Additional traits of the present emperor—Reflexions.

UNFORTUNATE young men, whom false accounts and fallacious hopes attract from various countries to the stormy banks of the frigid Neva, may you be at length undeceived by the sketches I have drawn, and those I am about to trace†. Of a thousand, who quit their country to seek wealth and happiness at a distance from it, few find the former in Russia; the latter, none. The rest sigh out their lives in penury and regret, or vegetate under the rigours of an

---

* This article is partly compiled by the editor from fragments and notes left by the author, and oral but indisputable information.—*(Note of the french editor)*.

† It is no longer possible for a Frenchman or Swiss to enter Russia. An artist, and two demoiselles de Montbéliard, having been sent for to fill particular places, could not obtain leave to disembark, notwithstanding the strongest recommendations, and were ordered to depart immediately. Russia is now shut up from Europe, like Japan. The Paul of that country requires foreigners to trample on the cross; he of Russia insists on their giving up their understanding.

inclement sky. The remembrance of their youthful sports, and the manners of their country, is the only pure pleasure which the most worthy taste. Amid the abundance and dissipation in which many pass their monotonous days, they experience a vague anxiety, that keeps them in perpetual alarm: the oppressive air of Russia seems a weight on their brows, that bends them towards the earth: they rapidly decline into a premature old age; their blood grows thick and grumous; and their soul becomes mere matter. As Ovid depicts the gradual metamorphosis of Daphne: the rude, unyielding bark envelopes her heart, which, though it still beats, has no longer any feeling. She loses the faculty of thought before she loses existence; and ceasing to live begins to vegetate.

Happy, however, he, who attains this animal vegetation! He is at least insensible to the shocking scenes that pass around him, and to his own degradation; while the man, who retains his sensibility, is incessantly tormented by the indignation which bare-faced despotism, vile servitude, and degraded humanity inspire. O you, whose spirits are exhausted by contemplating the storms of liberty, who perceive its sacred fire expiring in your hearts; go to the courts of tyrants to recreate the temper of your minds! There you will see despotism trampling with his muddy foot on every spark of reason that falls around him. Woe to him who suffers a single ray of light to escape him. The frightful deserts of Siberia, the subterranean regions of Kolhivan, and the bastilles of the north, keep pace with the deportations and other enormities committed in the name of liberty.

Of all the foreigners who happened to be in Russia during the revolution, the French and Swiss were most exposed to inquisitorial vexations. The very name of Frenchman was an affront; and the russian populace, who were in themselves peaceful, tolerant, and hospitable, were stirred up against them—Men who had before rendered themselves distinguished by their capacity, knowledge, and talents; many of whom held important posts at court or in the army, or confidential situations in private families; courtiers, officers, tutors, artists, players, chamberlains, cooks*, &c. instantly became objects of hatred, distrust, and proscription. Catharine, who had herself accustomed the Russians to some

---

* One le Bœuf, french cook to the late king of Prussia, having been sent for by Catharine, did not arrive till after her death. Paul, thinking he was sent to poison him, clapped him into prison. There he remained six months before he obtained his liberty, and then was ordered to depart immediately, without the slightest indemnification.

liberal opinions, on a sudden adopted the opposite principles. The death of Lewis XVI. and the arrival of the emigrants, were the signals of proscription. The emigrants particularly sought to accuse and supplant such of their countrymen as did not participate their opinions; and the ancient French, who beheld the light of the revolution from afar, without seeing the firebrand whence it issued, who embraced its principles with the more candour, because men of worth and letters had long borne them in their hearts, were the first attacked: cowards, knaves, hypocrites, and valets, who began loudly to exclaim against innovation alone were spared.

One of the first victims was Cuinet d'Orbeil, who was known to all Petersburg, and even in other parts, by his poetical pieces in the *Almanachs des Muses*. He was a Frenchman of a warm heart and lively expression; a poet in the common acceptation of the word, but incapable of undertaking anything, or plotting anything, at which the government could have reason to be alarmed. The court was at Peterhof, celebrating the festival of St. Peter and St. Paul. The fountains played, a ball was given, and the palace and gardens were illuminated. These rejoicings attracted the more company, because the empress had not visited Peterhof for several years, having an aversion for that palace, which must have inspired her with gloomy thoughts*. In the midst of the festivity a courier arrived with the news of the escape of Lewis XVI. The rumour was great, the joy loud, and the dance interrupted, while the news passed triumphantly from ear to ear. Count T, who knew d'Orbeil, met him coming out of the empress's saloon. "Well, Mr. Democrat," said he to him, "have "you heard the great news?"—"Yes," answered d'Orbeil, who was just come from Petersburg, "I have heard some great news."—"Do "you know that the king has escaped from "Paris?"—"Yes, count:—but do you know "the still greater news, that he is re-taken?"— These words were a clap of thunder to the hearers. The fact was, two couriers had arrived at Petersburg nearly at the same time; but he who announced the fortunate escape of the king having been dispatched immediately to the empress, to heighten the festivity of the day, no haste was made to send off the second to disturb it. The conversation of d'Orbeil with the count, however, having formed a sort of smart and striking scene, he was from that time observed and

* Peterhof was the palace she inhabited at the period of the revolution in 1762. Peter III. was arrested there, and strangled in a small country seat at Ropsha, not many miles distant.

watched. A short time after, a few expressions in favour of the revolution escaped him at la Hus's, an actress kept by Markof, secretary of state: in consequence of which he was taken in the night, from the house of count Chernichef, conveyed to a vessel in the harbour, and put down into the hold. The surprise and affright made him desperate; he contrived to get on deck, and threw himself into the sea: this state trick was played off by that cadaverous reptile Markof.

Such events occurred towards the end of Catharine's reign, when insipid courtiers and emigrants were besieging her with fears and suspicions; yet she was frequently seen to resume her wonted equity, and even her natural generosity, whenever truth could force its way to her. At the time this happened, Mioche, another Frenchman, having been denounced as a patriot by the emigrants, was likewise thrown into prison: but Catharine soon ordered him to be set at liberty, and indemnified him for his sufferings by some particular exemptions which she granted him in the wine trade.

Paul, very different from his mother, makes the principles of justice consist in his infallibility. He cannot mistake; nobody can deceive him. In consequence of this well known opinion of his, they who wish to establish themselves in his good graces begin by confessing themselves guilty of some fault, even if they invent one for the purpose. Woe to him who endeavours to prove his innocence! it is not the fact that constitutes guilt, but the opinion of Paul.

One of the most flagrant acts of injustice, which excited most indignation in honest men of all parties, was the proscription of colonel and major Masson, which signalized the commencement of his reign.

These two brothers, who were either Swiss or Wirtembergers, had served in the russian army from their youth, where they had acquired some reputation. One of them, who had been aide-de-camp to Potemkin, having made the campaigns against the Turks with him, had obtained as military rewards the cross and gold-hilted sword which Catharine bestowed on such officers as had displayed their courage in them. He had married a niece of the celebrated general Melissino, who died not long since as grand master of the ordnance. The other, after having been some time in the artillery, and then aide-de-camp to count Soltikof, minister at war*, had been placed about the person of the grand-duke Alexander, after the departure of colonel l'Harpe.

* He likewise finished the education of two other young noblemen, whose merit does great honour to him.

He also married a russian lady, of a livonian family of distinction. Both of them, having a turn for science and literature, led retired and tranquil lives with their families; beloved for the amenity of their manners, and esteemed for their wit and understanding. These two superior officers, who had been in the service twelve years, both married to russian women, allied to respectable families, and possessing lands and slaves, were torn from their wives and children by a private order of the emperor, and carried away separately, in covered sledges, under a strong guard, without even knowing of what crime they were accused. The wife of the younger, but just recovered from a lying-in, hurried on by despair, went the next day to wait for the emperor under the arches of the winter palace, and loudly demanded justice for her husband. " Your hus-
" band is guilty," answered Paul: " get out of
" the way, or you will be trampled on by my
" horse." The unfortunate lady fainted on the ground, and the emperor's horse luckily passed on one side. These acts and the indignation excited by such despotic obduracy were even recorded in a citation, which the friends and relations of those oppressed persons ventured to publish; and of which the following is a literal translation.

FRENCH AND SWISS IN RUSSIA.

"*Earnest citation and petition to Messrs. de Masson,*
"*late officers in the russian service*.*"

" These two brothers have served for several
" years the russian empire, and have acquired
" the reputation of being men of courage and
" understanding. The elder was colonel, che-
" valier, &c. the younger, major. Both were
" married; the former to the daughter of general
" Yhrmann, a brave and respectable soldier,
" lately dead, after having long and faithfully
" served the state†; the latter, to a baroness
" Rosen of a livonian family, well known and
" esteemed‡. Both had lovely children, and

* See the journal intitled *La Minerve, par M. d'Archen-holz,* May 1797, p. 366. " Ernstliche aufforderung und
" bitte, an die, in russischen diensten gestandenen, Herren
" von Masson."

† The brave general Yhrmann was governor general of Siberia, and director of the mines of Kolhyvan, for twenty years. The sums he drew from them were greater than they ever yielded before or since, as the registers attest. He augmented the civilisation, population, commerce, and welfare of those vast provinces; and retired poor, after having long superintended the working of the richest gold and silver mines on the continent. As a reward for his probity, the crown did not even pay him 10,000 rubles (1000l.) which are still owing to him; and his only daughter, proscribed with her husband, wanders far from the tomb of her worthy father. She is likewise niece to the celebrated general Melissino, who has rendered Russia such great services; and related to the Dolgorukies and the Soltikofs.—*(Note of the French Editor.)*

‡ Catharine II. wishing to reduce Livonia to the same

" lived with their families as good husbands and
" fathers. The elder even possessed estates in
" Esthonia.

" One day last December [1796], the two bro-
" thers were summoned before general Arkarof,
" director-general of the police. With him they
" found a certain count de Plaisance, an officer

form of slavery as the other provinces, required, according to her custom, that the Livonians themselves should come to implore these new chains as a favour. The deputies were accordingly sent for with those of the other nations: but general Rosen, father of the person here mentioned, who was at the head of the deputies, so far from subscribing what was required of them, made some remonstrances to Catharine, who said angrily: " Who gave you the audacity thus to op-
" pose my will?"—" The name of Peter the Great, who
" signed our franchises; and that of Catharine the Great,
" who has sworn to maintain them:" said the old man. Catharine the Great, however, displaced him, and ordered other deputies to be appointed. Count Stackelberg was found more complying; and, proud of what Rosen considered as a disgrace, sold his country (1). He was rewarded by immense tracts of land, surrounding those of the old general, which were taken from the states of the province. Such was the origin of the fortune and influence of Stackelberg, who so long ruled Poland, embroiled Sweden, and afterwards acted the buffoon in the antichambers of Zubof. Beside her relations in Livonia, the wife of the younger Masson is related to several russian families of considerable weight, as the Sievers, Besborodkos, Tamaras, &c. who, far from employing their influence in obtaining the restoration of her property; deserted her in her distress as soon as her husband was proscribed.—*(Note of the french editor)*.

(1) The words country, liberties, &c. when used of Russia or Livonia, relate to the nobility only; for the people are mere property.

"in the corps of cadets of the artillery, a man whose very existence seems to accuse nature of an illiberal joke. This man had written a letter to Mosco, in which he said to his friends, among other things, 'Many jacobins* are sent to the frontiers, and I am much afraid Messrs. Masson will be served in the same manner.' This letter was opened at the post-office, no doubt by order from the sovereign, and gave occasion to this disagreeable rendez-vous. The count de Plaisance defended his expression by the terrible accusation, that Messrs. Masson, when they read the newspapers, had always taken the part of the French. Messrs. de Masson avowed the charge; but begged to know what inference could be drawn from it derogatory to their character, their honour, or even their duty as Russian officers. The result of this business, divulged to the public, was, that the two brothers, without any farther information, were thrown into a *kibitka*†, and conveyed to the frontiers under a strong guard.

"The wife of the younger Mr. de Masson fell at the feet of the emperor in the public street, and loudly exclaimed: 'Justice! jus-

---

* What the term jacobin signifies in Russia has been mentioned in a preceding chapter.

† A covered sledge used in Russia.

"tice! and no favour!' The emperor answered: ' They are guilty; I love order in my country:' and would have passed on; but the lady in a fit of despair seized the horse by the bridle; on which the emperor told her to take care she was not trampled under foot.

" ' I had rather die,' answered this courageous lady, 'than be the wife of a man who has forfeited his honour.'——It was in vain: the emperor spurred his horse, and went forward*.

" All Petersburg has just witnessed the transaction. The emperor is just, and we presume, either that he has been deceived, or that Messrs de Masson have actually committed some crime, which at the time escaped notice†.

---

* The wives of the two brothers left their country to follow them, and their property was confiscated.

† As, to the great astonishment of their friends, Messrs. de Masson have not yet answered this citation, they give room for suspicion, that their proscription might have arisen from more serious causes than those mentioned above. Brought up on the heights of Mount Terrible, they there perhaps imbibed some liberal ideas which Russia could not stifle. The elder had been in the suite of Potemkin, and that of Zubof: the younger was at court, about the grand duke Alexander, and under the protection of the empress:—had they not some concern in the project formed of placing that prince on the throne instead of his father? a project which Catharine entertained, and which occasioned many others to fall into disgrace at her death. Even Alexander was watched, and all the officers in his suite dismissed. They who know Russia, and remember, that a few officers of the

"It is true the mystery in which the affair is in-
"volved cannot be unravelled: for if they be
"guilty, why are they spared? if they be inno-
"cent why are they punished? In the former
"case, we venture to observe, that his majesty
"the emperor owes it in some degree to his
"people to make known their crime; his people,

guards, with Lestocq, a french surgeon, were sufficient to effect the revolution that placed Elizabeth on the throne, will not think this supposition improbable. It is known likewise, that the two Massons were among the principal members of a society named the Philadelphic, founded by their uncle, general in chief Melissino, and into which several other generals or courtiers were admitted. This society, which was much talked of at Petersburg, appeared, it is true, to be rather a convivial meeting than a political assembly; and Catharine, to whom it was denounced, laughed at it: but the present emperor may have considered it in a different light; for at the same period the son of Melissino, commander of a regiment of grenadiers, and the chamberlain Mettlef, a member of the same society, were also disgraced and exiled. Be it as it may, no doubt it might appear astonishing to one, unacquainted with the character of Paul, that two superior officers should be thus taken away from their families, without trial, and without cause. But he is known to have treated the agent of Sardinia with less ceremony, because Besborodko said of him, that he advised his court to remain an ally of France. Paul exclaimed in a fury: "What! a "jacobin at my court! let him depart instantly." The bavarian minister, Reglin, was likewise treated as a jacobin, put into a covered sledge, and conveyed to the frontiers as a criminal; and this because his master would not immediately acknowledge Paul as grand-master of the order of Malta.

" who adore him*, who repose all their confi-
" dence in his justice, and who would be
" wretched if they had to dread every secret in-
" former.

" The undersigned, all of them relations or
" friends of Messrs. de Masson, to whom it is
" consequently of importance to develope this
" fatal secret, here solemnly require them to
" make their defence, if they be innocent: as
" men of honour, they owe this step to those,
" whose esteem they have gained by their agree-
" able intercourse; they owe it even to the empe-
" ror, who has sufficient magnanimity perhaps to
" make reparation for the consequences of a pre-
" cipitate act, if some villains have deceived
" him †."

[*Here follow the signatures of the friends and relations.*]

---

* Poor Russians! how they are obliged to lie.

† It is said, that the empress attempted to speak in favour of the younger Masson; but the emperor ordered her to be silent on the subject, threatening to punish her if she did not. Some time after he ordered her to be put under arrest for interceding on another occasion. Going his usual round about his palace of Pavlofsky, he caught a sentry asleep near his wife's pavilion. The unfortunate soldier was ordered the bastinado on the spot. At his cries the empress went to the window, and interceded for his pardon. " What!" exclaimed Paul, " dare you interrupt me in an " act of military duty? Do you forget, madam, that I am

To form a proper estimation of their courage, notwithstanding the caution employed in this citation, the circumstance of place, and the character of Paul must be fully known.

Another muscovitism of the magnanimous Paul likewise excited the public indignation. The french and swiss protestants have a church at Petersburg, in which they permitted the Germans also to perform divine service in their language: but as the original funds of the church were furnished by the French, they retained the property in it. The Germans pretended that they had a common right, and commenced a lawsuit, which they lost. On this they entreated the protection of Paul, who ordered the senate to revise the sentence; and the senate confirmed its former decree. The Germans made a fresh appeal, and Paul ordered sentence to be given in their favour. Mannsbændel of Mulhouse was the french pastor, and count Gollofkin, a captain in the navy, was one of the elders of the church *. These took

---

" your emperor also? I will make you remember it, how-
" ever." At these words, he ordered his aide-de-camp to put the empress under arrest. The aide-de-camp hesitating, Paul threatened to reduce him to the ranks: accordingly the officer went to inform the empress that she was under arrest, and placed a guard at her door. This was the second time of her being so served.

* The family of the counts Gollofkin having been disgraced under the reign of Elizabeth, came into Holland,

the liberty of making some remarks on the emperor's partiality. Mannsbændel was thrown into a dungeon, whence he was at length liberated with injunctions to quit Russia: count Gollofkin received orders to leave Petersburg immediately; and then fresh orders to repair on board the ship he commanded, where on his arrival he was immediately turned before the mast.

On the news of the death of Lewis XVI. Catharine, seized with affright, took measures of safety against the French in Russia. They were enjoined to take the oath of allegiance to Lewis XVII. and to their holy religion; and swear hatred and execration to the principles professed in France. According to the lists printed by order of government, there were seven or eight hundred Frenchmen in Petersburg, and more in Mosco; all of whom were obliged verbally to pronounce imprecations against their country. A few only, who had been for some time preparing to return to France, where their property was, chose rather to depart within the space of a week, as the ukase enjoined in case of refusal. This ukase was as absurd and barbarous in its composition, as it was ridiculous and inconsistent in its execution. Not only the

and embraced the protestant religion. Being afterwards recalled to Russia, they retained their religion, and it is the only russian family that professes protestantism.

French were obliged to take the oath, but almost all foreigners who spoke french, or who had their passports written in that language; so that Brabanters, Piedmontese, Milanese, and natives of Liege, were obliged to take the oath of allegiance to the king of France. It seemed as if the russian police had foreseen the grand redintegration, that was shortly to take place, and resolved to sanction it beforehand. Several natives of the thirteen cantons, Montbeliard, Neufchatel, and Wirtemberg, found themselves under the same necessity. The grand-duke Paul exacted it from all foreigners in his suite indiscriminately; and several officiously anticipated his wishes and commands. A greater number, however, excused themselves, saying they were not born subjects of France; and prevailed on the police, not on Paul, to hearken to reason.

Paul, on becoming emperor, went much farther than his mother had done; by ordering all the foreigners in Russia to profess the religion in which they had been brought up. Thus the catholics were enjoined a strict observance of the rites of their sect and the commands of the romish church. An ukase in all the different languages was posted up, enjoining every one of them, under pain of being treated as rebels, to take the holy sacrament of penance, and to prepare themselves for receiving the body of Christ at Easter: at the same time the priests were ordered to give absolution only to such as should merit it. The catholic church, which had before been empty, was now crowded: and the priests belonging to it, French, Germans, Italians, and Poles, assumed their seats in their confessionals. Before every confessional a box was set up, into which the penitent was obliged to throw a card, containing his name, profession, and abode; which cards were every evening carried to the emperor. The person confessed then received a ticket of absolution, signed by the priest, which admitted him to the holy table. This ticket was likewise a warrant of security to him, which he produced, when requisite, before the police. Innkeepers and housekeepers were directed to see these orders carried into execution with respect to persons lodging in their houses, and to inform against such as did not frequent the churches, or who wore pantaloons, round hats, or lapelled waistcoats. The sick were charitably informed, that they might require the confessor to attend them at home; and the poor, that the host* should be carried to them gratis.

The reader may judge of the embarrassment of most of the French, who before this had lived in Russia as free as possible with regard to religious

---

* The bon dieu.

opinions, of which the government took no notice. Let him figure to himself particularly the indignation, the humiliation felt by all those who entertained any rational and liberal sentiments. No choice, however, but implicit submission: the *compella intrare* was enforced with the utmost rigour by the soldiers of the police. The emigrants, who were depicted to Paul as libertines, though they had taken arms for the throne and the altar, were obliged to go to mass in form, walking two by two, between a double row of russian soldiers.

Such catholics as were in easy circumstances soon found means of obtaining tickets of absolution, even without confessing. The priests sold them at first for fifty rubles (5*l*.) then twenty-five (2*l*. 10*s*.) and at last disposed of them for ten rubles (1*l*.) apiece, agreeing to throw the cards into the box themselves into the bargain.

A scene that passed near this catholic church deserves notice here. Paul caused a service to be celebrated in honour of the Duke of Wirtemberg, father of the empress, who had just died at Stutgard. As it was not in character for him, the autocrat and russo-greek orthodox patriarch, to be present at a schismatic mass, he resolved to place himself at the head of the grenadiers drawn up round the church, to maintain order and dignity. It was extremely cold; his horse, doubtless, a native of some warmer climate, could not remain motionless. Weary of bridling, wheeling, and making useless efforts to keep him still, he began to gallop through the street, passing and repassing before the troops, and a great crowd of people, whom the funeral ceremony and the emperor's horsemanship had attracted together. As often as Paul came galloping by on one side, the crowd took off their hats, and made their reverences. A group assembled on the green bridge, upwards of four hundred paces from the spot where the emperor was prancing, at length put on their hats, on account of the extreme frost and the distance at which they stood. Paul spied it, and ordered them immediately to be surrounded by the troops, and sent to the house of correction. There were fifty or sixty persons of various conditions: they who were not nobles were whipped three successive days, the nobles were degraded, and such as were officers were turned into the ranks as common soldiers. Among them was a Genevan named Martin, who bribed an officer of the police to allow him to write to some friends at court. In consequence he was set at liberty, but, not brooking the insult, he instantly left Russia*.

* We have seen what happened to a madame Likarof for not getting out of her carriage as Paul passed by. The wife of Demuth, the wealthy keeper of a hôtel, met with the

Some time after, Paul ordered the corpse of the unfortunate king of Poland to be interred in the same church. He came himself to examine the funeral decorations, and the preparations for the ceremony. An upholsterer, employed in putting up the hangings, was at the top of a ladder, dressed in a jacket and pantaloons to follow his work more commodiously. Paul, being informed that he was a Frenchman, named Leroux, ordered him to come down, and immediately commanded him to be bastinadoed in the midst of the church.

These are some of the vexations to which foreigners, Frenchmen in particular, are exposed in Russia. It is certain that their situation became still more deplorable after Paul declared war against France. What humiliations, what outrages were they not forced to undergo at the house of correction in Petersburg, as if it had been the slave prison of Constantinople!

But this is not the worst. Frenchmen, after they have suffered these evils, may in vain demand an asylum even in their own country. They will be driven from it like the bird, seeking shelter in the tempest-beaten oak, which is forced away by the agitated branches. Liberty herself is a cap-

---

same accident: but, as she was not noble, she was flogged for three days consecutively at the house of correction.

tive, and insulted in France: she is Bradamante fallen into the cave of Merlin.

Frenchmen coming from Russia are refused permission to re-enter France, under pretence, that they must have taken an oath by which they virtually renounce their country. Ah, Frenchmen! do you forget how many contradictory oaths you yourselves have taken within the space of five or six years? Are those, which have been forced upon your unfortunate countrymen in foreign lands, alone to be religiously kept, at the very moment when you make sport of violating those which you yourselves have taken by acclamation in the face of heaven and of France? At least recollect the moment when this oath was exacted. It was when the head of Lewis had just fallen, and every monarch trembled for his own; when Leopold died, as report said, by poison; and Gustavus, as was asserted, by your assassinating weapons*; when Marat and Robespierre bore sway. Judge of the dreadful alarm such news must have produced in Russia. The French at Petersburg shut themselves up in their houses, and were afraid of being all massacred. The least they expected was a general

* At the court of Russia it was asserted, that the jacobins had assassinated Gustavus, and poisoned Leopold. It would have been dangerous there to seem to doubt it.

proscription. I say now, as I thought then, Catharine, even at that juncture, displayed her greatness and moderation. By the oath she required she placed the French under the protection of the government, and saved them from the fury of the blinded nobles and people. None of the allied powers, though reputed less barbarous, adopted a measure so humane. At the moment when the unfortunate French were massacred at Vienna, at Naples, and at Rome, a brother of Marat appeared in security at the court of Catharine.

DESCRIPTION OF THE TAURIDAN PALACE,
and of the entertainment which Prince Potemkin gave there to Catharine II. *

THE Tauridan palace was the place made choice of by prince Potemkin for the splendid entertainment that he gave to his sovereign, and which was considered as a testimony of gratitude for the greatness to which she had raised him. After the death of this favourite, Catharine made it her autumnal residence.

The façade of this building is composed of an immense colonnade, supporting a cupola. It opens into a grand vestibule, communicating with the apartments to right and left; having at the farther end a portico, that leads to a second vestibule of prodigious size, receiving light from the top, and surrounded at a great height by a gallery, intended for an orchestra, and containing an organ. From this a double row of pillars leads to the principal saloon, designed for grand entertainments. It is impossible to describe the im-

---

* As this palace has been frequently mentioned in the work, we have thought proper to add the following description of it, and of the entertainment which Prince Potemkin gave there to his sovereign. It is taken from Storch's " Picture of Pe-
" tersburg."

pression made by this gigantic temple: being upwards of a hundred paces long, wide in proportion, and surrounded by a double row of colossal pillars, between which, at mid-height, are boxes ornamented with festoons elegantly sculptured, and furnished with silk drapery. From the vaulted roof are suspended globular lamps and large lustres of cut-glass, from which the light is infinitely reflected by great plates of looking-glass, placed at all the extremities of this vast hall. It has neither furniture nor ornaments, except two superb vases of Carrara marble, astonishing for their size and the beauty of their workmanship, placed one at each of the semicircular ends of the saloon. Adjoining to this saloon is the winter garden, separated from it only by the grand colonnade. The vault of this enormous edifice is supported by pillars in the form of palm-trees; within the walls are flues, to conduct heat round the building; and tubes of metal, filled with hot water, keep up an uniform temperature beneath this delightful parterre.

The eye wanders with rapture over plants and shrubs of every clime, rests with admiration on an antique bust, or views with astonishment the various fishes of all hues in crystal vases. A transparent obelisk reproduces to the eye, under a thousand different tints, these wonders of art and nature; and a grotto, hung with mirrors, reflects them in endless multiplication. The delicious temperature, the intoxicating odour of the flowers, and the voluptuous silence of this enchanting spot, plunge the mind into a pleasing reverie, and transport the imagination to the groves of Italy. The illusion continues, till destroyed by the aspect of all the rudeness and severity of winter, as the enchanted eye wanders through the windows, and beholds the frost and snow surrounding this magnificent garden. In the midst of this elysium rises the majestic statue of Catharine II. in parian marble.

On this theatre of his grandeur Potemkin arranged the preparations for the entertainment he gave his sovereign, before he departed for the southern provinces, where death lay in ambush for him. This favourite seemed to have a secret presentiment of his approaching end; and therefore resolved once more to display the plenitude of the magnificence he enjoyed by her favour.

The preparations for this entertainment were immense, like everything to which his imagination gave birth; artists of all kinds being employed in making them for several months: more than a hundred persons assembled daily, to prepare themselves for the parts he designed them to perform; and every rehearsal was a kind of festivity.

At length the appointed day arrived to gratify

the impatience of the whole capital. Besides the empress and the imperial family, prince Potemkin had invited all the court, the foreign ministers, the russian nobility, and many individuals of the first ranks in society.

At six in the evening the entertainment was opened with a masked ball. When the carriage of the empress approached, meat, drink, and clothes, of all kinds, were distributed in profusion among the assembled populace. The empress entered the vestibule to the dulcet sounds of sprightly music, executed by upwards of three hundred performers. Thence she repaired to the principal saloon, whither she was followed by the crowd; and ascended a platform, raised for her in the centre, surrounded by transparent decorations, with appropriate inscriptions. The company arranged themselves under the colonnade, and in the boxes; and then commenced the second act of this extraordinary spectacle.

The grand-dukes Alexander and Constantine, at the head of the flower of all the young persons about the court, performed a ballet. The dancers, male and female, were forty-eight in number, all dressed in white, with magnificent scarves, and covered with jewels, estimated to be worth above ten millions of rubles (a million sterling). The ballet was performed to select airs, suitable to the occasion, and interspersed with songs. The celebrated Lepicq concluded it with a *pas* of his own composing.

The company then removed to another saloon, adorned with the richest tapestry the Gobelins could produce. In the centre was an artificial elephant, covered with rubies and emeralds; and his cornac was a Persian richly clad. On his giving the signal, by striking on a bell, a curtain rose, and a magnificent stage appeared at the end of the apartment. On it were performed two ballets of a novel species, and a lively comedy, by which the company were much amused, concluded the spectacle. This was followed by choral songs, various dances, and an asiatic procession, remarkable for its diversity of dresses; all representing the different nations subject to the sceptre of the russian monarch.

Presently after, all the apartments, magnificently illuminated with variegated lamps, were thrown open to the eager curiosity of the crowd. The whole palace seemed in a blaze: the garden was covered with sparkling stones; crystal mirrors innumerable, in pyramidal and globular forms, reflected the magic spectacle in all directions. A table was spread with six hundred covers; and the rest of the guests were served standing. The table service was all of gold and silver; the most exquisite dainties were served in vessels of the greatest richness; antique cups overflowed with the most costly liquors; and the table was lighted by chandeliers of uncommon magnificence. Officers and domestics in great number, richly habited, were eager to anticipate the wishes of the guests.

The empress, contrary to her custom, remained till midnight: as if dreading that her departure might interrupt the felicity of her favourite. As she retired, numerous bands of singers, and harmonious music, made the vaulted roofs of the palace resound with a hymn to her praise. At this she was so moved, that she turned towards prince Potemkin to express her satisfaction: he, overpowered by the sentiment of what he owed his sovereign, fell at her feet reverently, took her hand, and watered it with tears. This was the last time he had an opportunity of testifying in this place his gratitude to the august author of his grandeur.

ADDITIONAL NOTE CONCERNING KORSAKOF.

ON occasion of the retreat of the Russians from Switzerland, the following anecdote, taken from M. de Castéra's Life of Catharine, appeared in the public papers:

"Korsakof, the empress's favourite, was of a handsome stature, and a very elegant figure; but, possessing neither understanding nor knowledge, he was as incapable as Zoritch of diminishing the influence of Potemkin. A single fact will display his character. On his obtaining the post of favourite, he conceived that a man like him ought of course to have a library. Accordingly he sent for the most celebrated bookseller in Petersburg without delay, and informed him, that he wanted books for his house lately belonging to Vasiltchikof, of which the empress had just made him a present. The bookseller asked what books he wanted. 'You understand that better than I,' answered the favourite; 'it is your business to know the proper assortments: but there must be great books at bottom, and little ones at top; as they are at the empress's."

We are far from disputing the truth of this anecdote, which has been confirmed to us by several credible persons to whom the bookseller related the story at the time: but we must inform our readers, that the newspapers, when they took the extract, confounded the favourite Korsakof with another of the same name, who commanded the russian army in Switzerland. General Korsakof is a man of sense, and by no means destitute of knowledge: he made the campaign in Flanders under prince Cobourg, and well knows what a library is.

THE END.

C. WHITTINGHAM, *Printer*,
Dean Street, Fetter Lane.

BOOKS

Printed for T. N. LONGMAN and O. REES,

No. 39, Paternoster Row.

1. VIEW OF THE RUSSIAN EMPIRE during the Reign of CATHARINE the SECOND, and to the Close of the Eighteenth Century, &c. &c. Containing an accurate Description of the Government, Manners, Customs, Religion, Extent, Boundaries, Soil, Climate, Produce, Revenue, Trade, Manufactures, &c. &c. of the several Nations that compose that extensive Empire. By WILLIAM TOOKE, F. R. S. Member of the Imperial Academy of Sciences; and of the Free Economical Society of St. Petersburg. In Three large Volumes 8vo. Price 1l. 7s. in boards.

† The Monthly Review is lavish in its commendations in regard to the importance of the subject; the authenticity of the sources from which it appears to be drawn, the ability which it displays in arranging a vast variety of matter, and the circumstances which united to particularly qualify the Author for undertaking and executing such a performance; and only lament that it is difficult to give, within the limits of a miscellaneous publication, an adequate idea of a work abounding with such interesting and various information.

† See also the commendations uniformly bestowed on the work by the other Reviews

2. A HISTORY OF RUSSIA, from the establishment of Monarchy under RURIK to the Accession of CATHARINE II. In Two Volumes Octavo. With 60 Portraits, engraved from a series of Medals. Price 18s. in boards.

3. THE LIFE OF CATHARINE II. EMPRESS OF RUSSIA. The fourth Edition, with considerable Improvements. In Three Volumes 8vo. Price 1l. 4s. boards. Embellished with Seven elegant Portraits, and a correct Map of Russia.

‡*‡ The Authors of the Monthly Review bestow great encomiums on this Work: in confirmation of which they give ample extracts, and conclude their account by saying: "Did our limited space permit, we could transcribe with pleasure many other extraordinary passages from this curious Work." The British Critic also, after bestowing an uniform commendation on this Work, through no fewer than eight pages, concludes with saying, "Upon an attentive perusal of these Volumes, we cannot do otherwise than acknowledge their merit, and recommend them as fully adequate to repay the time that may be bestowed upon them, by the entertainment and information which they afford."

Books *printed for* LONGMAN *and* REES.

4. TRAVELS IN AFRICA, EGYPT, and SYRIA, from the years 1792 to 1798. By W. G. BROWNE, 4to. Price 1l. 11s. 6d. boards.

"Such is the outline of this journey, which vies with any land-tour described either in ancient or modern times. The learning, the ability, and the singular opportunities of the Author, have severally contributed so much to enrich his pages with new discoveries, or new observations, that his work will ever bear a high rank among books of travels. Long and perilous journeys have often been performed by men incapable of scientific observation; but in this case, profound learning and undaunted enterprize combine to produce a work perhaps UNIQUE in its kind."
Critical Review, Aug. 1799.

5. GLEANINGS THROUGH WALES, HOLLAND, and WESTPHALIA; with Views of Peace and War at Home and Abroad. To which is added, HUMANITY; or, The Rights of Nature: A Poem. Revised and corrected. By Mr. PRATT. In Three Volumes. 8vo. Price One Guinea in boards. The Fifth Edition.

"We have found so many lively and pleasant exhibitions of manners, so many amusing and interesting anecdotes, and so many observations and reflections, gay and grave, sportive and sentimental, (all expressed in a gay and familiar style,) better suited to the purpose than sentences laboured with artificial exactness, that we cannot but recommend it to our readers as a highly amusing and interesting performance."
Analytical Review, Jan. 1796.

6. GLEANINGS IN ENGLAND; descriptive of the Countenance, Mind, and Character of the Country. By Mr. PRATT; 8vo. Price 8s. boards.

N. B. In the Press, a Second Volume of the above Work.

"The Author continues to merit the character he has long and deservedly maintained, of a sprightly and agreeable writer; of an intelligent and often a sagacious observer of human life and manners; and he is entertaining throughout." *British Critic,* Oct. 1799.

"The Author has here, in manifold instances, shown himself a faithful delineator of his countrymen, and a generous and manly defender of his country; to which his performance is a tribute no less valuable than well timed." *Gentleman's Mag.* Aug.

7. FAMILY SECRETS. By Mr. PRATT. Second Edition carefully corrected. In Five large Volumes 12mo. Price 1l. 5s. boards.

"The work abounds with a variety of characters, exceedingly well delineated; with many scenes and descriptions, happily imagined and successfully introduced, and will considerably add to the fame Mr. Pratt has already obtained." *Brit. Crit.* Nov. 1797.

Lightning Source UK Ltd.
Milton Keynes UK
UKHW030921220922
409267UK00007B/595